CAVES OF THE HIGHLAND RIM

Larry E. Matthews
Featuring Photographs by Bob Biddix

Cave Conservation

Caves are fragile and extremely easy to damage—including speleothems such as described in this book, mineral deposits, cave flora and fauna, plus archaeological, cultural, and historical artifacts. Breaking or removal of cave formations deprives others of this priceless heritage and is against many state laws.

The conservation ethic of the National Speleological Society—and other speleological associations worldwide—is to enjoy the natural beauty of speleothems and other cave assets in place, without disturbing them in any way. Remember that cave conservation is more a state of mind than a set of rules. Use your common sense and always remember to take the action that will cause the least damage to the cave.

Front Cover: Carol Lamers in the Main Passage of Hayes Cave, Wilson County, Tennessee. Photo by Bob Biddix, January 26, 2012.

Back Cover: Erica Sughrue admires a stunning helictite in Blowhole Cave, Cannon County, Tennessee. Photograph by Bob Biddix, December 1, 2013.

Copyright 2019 Larry E. Matthews
Published by:
National Speleological Society, Inc.
6001 Pulaski Pike NW
Huntsville, Alabama 35810, USA
Phone: (256) 851-1300
http://caves.org

ISBN13: 978-1-68044-012-6   ISBN 10: 1-68044-012-8
Printed in China.

CONTENTS

Keith Filson crawls in a low section of a Highland Rim Cave. Photo by Bob Biddix, late summer, 2004.

ACKNOWLEDGEMENTS

As always, **Thomas C. Barr Jr.'s** classic book, *Caves of Tennessee*, provided a logical starting point for information on many of the caves described in this book. Tom was an inspiration to all of us.

Caver and computer expert **Jody Bailey** provided expert technical assistance and converted many old photographs and slides into a digital format. He kept my computers and printers running! Thanks Jody!

Cave photographer **Bob Biddix** provided many of the beautiful photographs in this book.

Caver **Kristen Bobo** provided photos of John Fisher Cave, Neil Fisher Cave, Piper Cave, and Robinson Ridge Saltpeter Cave, along with information on bats, saltpeter mining, and prehistoric Indians in various caves.

Cavers **Brian Buchanan** and **Tiffany Buchanan** provided photographs for Hardins Cave and Junkyard Cave.

Caver **Joel Buckner** provided information on Cripps Mill Cave, Espey Cave, Haws Spring Cave, Henpeck Mill Cave, Indian Grave Point Cave, John Fisher Cave, Junkyard Cave, Neil Fisher Cave, and Pleasant Ridge Cave.

Caver **Dave Bunnell** provided excellent photographs of Blowhole and Haws Springs Caves, and optimized the photos for printing.

Caver **Donna Cobb** provided important information on Haws Spring Cave.

Cave Historian **Joseph C. Douglas** was a wonderful source of information on both prehistoric and historical uses of the caves in this book. He provided photographs and information on Godwin Cave, Haws Spring Cave, Junkyard Cave, Neil Fisher Cave, Robinson Ridge Saltpeter Cave, and Ruskin Cave.

Caver **Keith Filson** provided a map of Henpeck Mill Cave and assisted Bob Biddix with his photography.

Caver **Richard C. Finch** provided photos of Blowhole Cave.

Public Relations employee **Ashley Schaffner Fletcher** with the Brown-Forman Corporation arranged access to the Jack Daniel Distillery Property including access to Motlow Cave.

Caver **Marbry Hardin** provided information on several caves, including Espey Cave.

Caver **Jason Hardy** provided a map of Motlow Cave.

Caver **Bobby Higgins** provided information on Blowhole Cave and Pleasant Ridge Cave.

Caver **Mark Hobbs** assisted Bob Biddix with his photography.

Caver **Kirk Holland** provided information on Cummings Pit, Melton Hole, and Youngs Pit, and proofread several chapters.

Caver **David Irving** provided information on Junkyard Cave.

Cave model **Carol Lamers** is featured in a number of Bob Biddix's photographs in this book and assisted Bob with his photography.

Caver **Don Lance** provided information and maps on Blue Crystal Well, Espey Cave, Haws Spring Cave, John Hollins Cave, Prospect Hill Cave, and Robinson Ridge Saltpeter Cave.

Caver **Alan Lenk** provided a photograph from Blowhole Cave.

Caver **Ray Maslak** provided information on Cripps Mill Cave.

Caver **Dan McDowell** provided information on DePriest Branch Cave.

Caver **Mark Mitckes** provided information on DePriest Branch Cave.

Caver **Gerald Moni** is the custodian for the Tennessee Cave Survey's files and is a remarkable repository of information on the caves of Tennessee. Gerald has been incredibly helpful in supplying information for this book.

Caver **Tom Moss** provided information and photographs on Haws Spring Cave.

Caver **Annette Oeser** provided excellent photographs of Jewel Cave and Ruskin Cave.

Caver **Ken Oeser** provided important information, maps, and photographs on Godwin Cave, Gregory Hollow Cave, Jewel Cave, Neil Fisher Cave, Mason Cave, and Ruskin Cave.

Caver **Bill Overton** provided information on Junkyard Cave.

Super Cave Surveyor **David Parr** provided information and maps for Devil's Hole, Fox Cave, Hardin's Cave, Henpeck Mill Cave, Indian Grave Point Cave, Junkyard Cave, and Pleasant Ridge Cave.

Cave historian **Doug Plemons** provided fascinating historical information on Godwin Cave and Neil Fisher Cave.

Caver **Jay Reeves** provided critical information on Haws Spring Cave.

Caver **James Reyome** provided most of the information on DePriest Branch Cave.

Caver and graphic artist **Elizabeth Rousseau** provided design and layout for this book.

Caver **Jeff Sims** provided information on Hardin's Cave.

Caver **Kelly Smallwood** provided information and excellent photographs of Blowhole Cave, DePriest Branch Cave, Jack Daniel Cave, and Motlow Cave.

Cave historian **Marion O. Smith** provided historical information on Godwin Cave.

Caver **John Smyre** provided an excellent map of Cripps Mill Cave.

Show Cave expert **Gary K. Soule** provided wonderful information on Jack Daniel Cave, Jewel Cave, Motlow Cave, and Ruskin Cave.

David Stang, with the Brown-Forman Corporation, provided information about Jack Daniel Cave and Motlow Cave.

Cave model **Erica Sughrue** is featured in many of Bob Biddix's photographs and assisted Bob with the photography.

Cave photographer **Chuck Sutherland** submitted excellent photographs for this book, including Blowhole Cave, Cripps Mill Cave, and Indian Grave Point Cave.

Caver and photographer **Edward M. Yarbrough** provided excellent photographs and information on several caves in this book, including Blowhole Cave, John Fisher Cave, and Reynolds Pit.

Caver **Dave Wascher** provided information on Junkyard Cave and Mason Cave.

INTRODUCTION

The city of Nashville sits in a geographic basin. Any direction that you go away from Nashville, you reach the "rim" of this basin. To geologists, this is known as the Highland Rim. The Central Basin would actually be a lake, if the Cumberland River had not cut an outlet on the Rim's northwest edge. For a variety of geological reasons, the Highland Rim is especially rich in large and interesting caves. Hence, the subject of this book is the Caves of the Highland Rim.

When I began exploring caves here in Tennessee back in the early 1960s, the Interstate Highway system was just being built and many rural counties had predominantly gravel roads. From my home in Nashville, the first really large caves available to me and my high school companions were the caves of the Highland Rim. We especially loved Cripps Mill Cave, Espey Cave, and Indian Grave Point Cave. We spent many wonderful days in these caves learning much about cave exploration and ourselves.

This book is the tenth in a series of books, starting with Cumberland Caverns in 1989, that has chronicled the history of exceptionally large caves (Big Bone Cave, Blue Spring Cave, Cumberland Caverns, Dunbar Cave, and Snail Shell Cave) or exceptional cave areas (Caves of Chattanooga, Caves of Grassy Cove, Caves of Fall Creek Falls, and Caves of Knoxville).

Wherever possible, the stories of the caves in this book are told in the words of the original explorers and surveyors. Enjoy.

Erica Sughrue in a stream passage in a Highland Rim Cave. Photo by Bob Biddix, January 13, 2019.

Section 1: West, North, and Northeast Section: Davidson, Dickson, Smith, and Sumner Counties

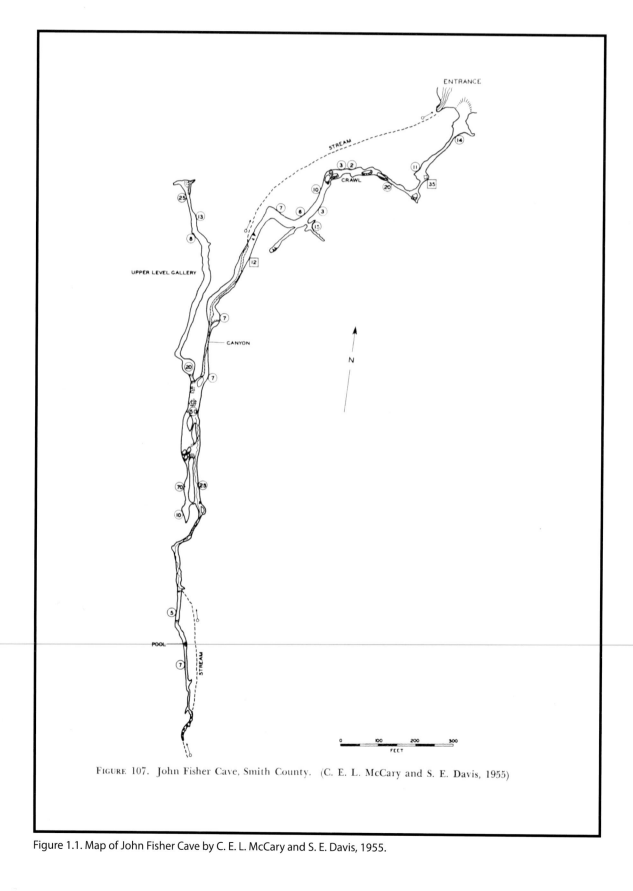

FIGURE 107. John Fisher Cave, Smith County. (C. E. L. McCary and S. E. Davis, 1955)

Figure 1.1. Map of John Fisher Cave by C. E. L. McCary and S. E. Davis, 1955.

CHAPTER 1
John Fisher Cave

John Fisher Cave is located in Smith County, Tennessee. At one time, it was one of the most popular caves in Tennessee due do its large, interesting passages and beautiful formations. This was one of Tom Barr's favorite caves.

A 1917 Visit to John Fisher Cave

Thomas L. Bailey's classic report, *Report on the Caves of the Eastern Highland Rim and Cumberland Mountains* (1918), gives the earliest known description of the cave:

> No. 71. FISHER CAVE
> Location.---Three miles southwest of Lancaster on the land of John B. Fisher in the west bluff of Smith Fork, about 100 yards northwest of the creek and 300 yards south of Fisher's house. The mouth is 150 yards from the Temperance Hall Road and 2 ½ miles from the Tennessee Central Railroad. It is in Ordovician limestone about 60 feet below the Ft. Payne.
>
> This cave has two mouths about 40 feet apart. The main cave is over a mile long and has a fork extending southeastward for 300 yards that is much wider than the main fork. The average width of the cave is 15 feet, but it varies very greatly at different points. The height is 25 feet. There is no stream in the southeast fork and none in the southwest, or main fork, for more than half a mile, but the earth is damp. Boulders and rocks practically block the passage in the main fork in places. The loose earth is about 5 feet deep. There are a few stalactites near the mouth of the cave and about half a mile from the mouth there are several large stalagmites, but these formations are for the most part lacking. A strong breeze blows through the cave and makes it quite cold in summer.[1]

Bailey conducted his field work from July 15 to September 15, 1917, so this visit occurred sometime during that time period.

1 Thomas L. Bailey, *Report on the Caves of the Eastern Highland Rim and Cumberland Mountains*, TN State Geological Survey, The Resources of Tennessee, Vol. 8 (1918), No. 2, p. 130.

Figure 1.2. Kristen Bobo at the lower entrance to John Fisher Cave. Photo by Kristen Bobo, 2015.

A Description of the Cave

John Fisher Cave is also described by Thomas C. Barr, Jr. in his book, *Caves of Tennessee* (1961):

> The John Fisher Cave is a large and well-known cavern, which derives its name from a former owner, John B. Fisher. The cave has two mouths, 8 feet apart, beneath a rock shelter-type opening at the base of a limestone bluff. The lower, or wet, mouth is 20 feet wide and 6 feet high, and the upper, or dry, mouth is 20 feet wide and 8 feet high. The cave extends southeast for nearly half a mile beneath Tater Knob.
>
> The wet mouth may be penetrated for only a short distance, to a point where large boulders block the way. The dry mouth opens into a passage which

Figure 1.3. Beautiful flowstone in John Fisher Cave. Photo by Edward M. Yarbrough, November, 1961.

rejoins the stream 750 feet from the mouth, and it is possible to reach the other side of the fallen blocks by going downstream from this point.

The cave runs 275 feet southwest, then makes a right-angle bend northwest for 165 feet and continues southwest or south for the remainder of its length. For 450 feet the dry cave is a breakdown passage 20 feet high and 8 feet wide. After a 300-foot crawl it rejoins the stream. From about 750 feet to 1,050 feet the stream flows along through a canyon 10 feet deep and 4 feet wide, but down into the floor of the upper passage. At 1,050 feet is a large room 50 feet high, 40 feet wide, and 150 feet long, from which two high galleries lead off. One gallery parallels the stream for 300 feet, and the other runs northward for 550 feet, averaging 15 feet wide and 10 feet high. Large and beautiful flowstone formations and many stalactites and stalagmites may be seen in both of these upper galleries. The large room appears to have been formed by the intersection of the main cave passage and the passage of which these galleries are a part, and it has been considerably enlarged by vertical solution through domepit formation. Since the original juncture of the upper galleries and the stream passage, the stream appears to have cut downward considerably. The cutting of the deep trench between the large room and the entrance was presumably the cave stream's response to the more rapid degradation of Smith Fork, into which it empties.

On the floor of the large room is a remarkable and attractive series of rimstone pools. A colony of bats sometimes frequents this part of the cave.

The main passage continues beyond the large room, with a graveled stream bed floor, and average 20 feet high and 12 feet wide. At 1,620 feet is a huge, sparkling drapery formation 10 feet long and 6 feet wide, above a mound-like stalagmite. A short lead to the left of this formation is 120 feet long. The cave continues as a large stream passage for 600 feet, at which point it becomes necessary to drop through a small hole in a flowstone curtain in order to proceed farther. The last 225 feet is a wet crawlway. The cave continues in a southeasterly direction and is 2

Figure 1.4. Mike Kish next to a large stalagmite in John Fisher Cave. Photo by Edward M. Yarbrough, November, 1961.

Figure 1.5. Beautiful flowstone grotto in John Fisher Cave. Photo by Edward M. Yarbrough, November, 1961.

feet high and 8 feet wide, with 8 inches of water in the stream.[2]

There is an excellent map of the cave that accompanies this description (Figure 1.1). There are also three (3) very nice photos with this description. The man in coveralls in these photos is apparently the owner of the cave back in the 1950s.

My First Visit to the Cave

I first visited this cave in 1964. This was a very popular cave because the entrance is next to the road and the cave is large and well-decorated. The owner's house was directly across the road from the entrance. I'm certainly glad I got to visit this cave before it was closed.

The Survey of John Fisher Cave

The surveyed length of John Fisher Cave is 10,000 feet (1.9 miles) and the vertical extent is 125 feet. At least, that is what the Tennessee Cave Survey's files say. This would appear to be based on the map in Barr's *Caves of Tennessee* (1961) by C. E. L. McCary and S. E. Davis, dated 1955 (Figure 1.1). Unfortunately, early

cave surveyors did not list the surveyed length on their maps, so 10,000 feet is just an estimate.

Shield Formations

In March, 1970 George Benedict, Paul Cragan, Marietta Matthews, and I visited John Fisher Cave. While we were in the Upper Level, where most of the cave's formations are concentrated, we noticed a very attractive shield formation. At the time, shield formations were considered to be very rare, but as time has gone on, we have noticed them in quite a few formation caves.[3] A photo of this formation is shown as Figure 1.15.

The Stream Passage Extension

Caver Joel Buckner reports that sometime during the 70s that the stream crawl described by Barr was pushed by Larry Johnson, Rodger Ling and himself. The stream crawl opened up into thousands of feet of stream trunk passages with white formations and two dome complexes.[4] Apparently this addition has never been mapped.

2 Thomas C. Barr, Jr., *Caves of Tennessee*, TN Division of Geology, Bulletin 64 (1961), pp 418-423.

3 Larry E. Matthews, "More Tennessee Caves With Shields," *Speleonews*, Vol. 14 (1970), No. 1, pp 13-14.

4 Joel Buckner, Personal communication, May 8, 2018.

Figure 1.6. Joe Douglas (left) and Alfred Crabtree (right) at the entrance to Neil Fisher Cave. Photo by Kristen Bobo, March 18, 2011.

Neil Fisher Cave

Neil Fisher Cave is also located in Smith County. It is also a large and very interesting cave.

A 1917 Visit to Neil Fisher Cave

Thomas L. Bailey's classic report, *Report on the Caves of the Eastern Highland Rim and Cumberland Mountains* (1918), gives the earliest known description of the cave:

No. 69. RIP VAN WINKLE CAVE

Location.—One and a half miles north of Sebowisha, near the top of the bluff on the opposite side of Caney Fork from Sebowisha Club House, on the land of W. M. Bellar.

The mouth is only about a mile from the Tennessee Central Railroad and is on the Caney Fork River, which is navigable up to this point. It is in Ordovician limestone, 30 feet below the Ft. Payne chert.

The bluff in which the cave is located is almost perpendicular and is wooded below the mouth of the cave. Above the mouth is an overhanging limestone bluff 30 feet high. When it was first discovered on February 1, 1916, by Harry Fisher, the mouth was very small and low, but it has since been enlarged so that entrance is easy.

The cave is very large and has two main forks. The southeast, or Dry Fork, is about a third of a mile long, while the northwest, or Wet Fork, is over half a mile long. There are also several smaller forks, especially on the Dry Fork, and at places there are other passages above the main ones. The average width is 40 feet and the height 75 or 100 feet. In the Wet Fork several bridges and flights of stairs have been built and many improvements made to accommodate tourists to whom the cave is open at certain times. Near the back of the Wet Fork is a small stream and the earth, which is heaped up in banks is wet. The earth in the Dry fork is peculiarly dry and contains a great abundance of transparent crystals of gypsum. These gypsum crystals, some of large size, cover the walls and the stalactites and

Figure 1.7. Joe Douglas (left) and Alfred Crabtree (right) in Neil Fisher Cave. Photo by Kristen Bobo, March 18, 2011.

Figure 1.8. Old stone steps in Neil Fisher Cave. Photo by Kristen Bobo, March 18, 2011.

stalagmites with a coat of sparkling gems. The depth of the earth could not be determined accurately but it averages probably over 6 feet, and in places is as much as 20 feet deep.

This cave is the most beautiful of the 109 caves visited, even somewhat surpassing Wonder Cave near Monteagle. It does not contain as many stalactites, stalagmites and natural columns as Wonder Cave, but they are much larger and more varied than those of Wonder Cave. The roof is also very much higher and more fantastic. The limestone formations are abundant in both forks, but probably the most interesting are in the Wet Fork. There is one especially beautiful group of stalactites called the Wedding Bells that is 60-feet long and 25-feet in diameter at the center. These stalactites are of all sizes and when struck, give forth musical sounds resembling a pipe organ and ranging from the highest treble to the deepest bass. Most of them seem to be hollow. There are other stalactites and columns that are even longer and larger than the Wedding Bells.

Near the end of the Dry Fork there are many shallow basins separated from each other by very thin, wavy partitions of limestone about 10-inches high that have been built up by the water with which they are filled in winter. In the bottoms of these basins was a deposit of loose crystals resembling salt 3 or 4 inches deep. The odd basin-like formations are not peculiar to this cave but the knife-edge partitions here are unusually high. In most caves in which these basins are found they are filled with such clear water that they appear to be empty. There are in this cave, also, many beautiful dome-shaped and waterfall-shaped stalagmites, some of dazzling whiteness.[5]

Clearly Thomas L. Bailey was very, very impressed with this cave. Forty-four (44) years later, Barr gives the following description for the cave:

Neil Fisher Cave formerly was developed commercially by the late W. M. Bellar and was occasionally shown to resort visitors at Sebowisha.

5 Bailey, op. cit., pp 128-129.

Figure 1.9. Joe Douglas in a large passage in Neil Fisher Cave. Photo by Kristen Bobo, March 18, 2011.

Figure 1.10. Alfred Crabtree in a well-decorated passage in Neil Fisher Cave. Photo by Kristen Bobo, March 18, 2011.

At that time it was called "Rip Van Winkle Cave." A number of steps were dug, and at least one bridge, now rotten, was built for the accommodation of visitors to the cave.

The mouth is 4 feet high and 5 feet wide, and the entrance passage, which averages 6 feet high and 3 feet wide, runs S. 50° E. for 135 feet, where it intersects the main cave. The main cave is a high gallery, which averages 30 feet high and 8 feet wide, but where the fill has been removed from below, it is 60 feet high. To the right the cave extends 400 feet S. 25° E., ending in a crawlway. There are two side passages in this section, each about 85 feet long and each trending northwest. To the left of the entrance passage the cave runs northeast for 150 feet to a pool, around which are large draperies and flowstone. At this point it is possible to scale the left wall of the cave, progress along a high, narrow ledge, and drop down through a slit into a continuation of the passage. Here, there is a colorful, massive, and beautiful drapery and flowstone formation fully 30 feet high. This branch continues northwestward

for about 150 feet. The total length of the cave is approximately 1,000 feet.[6]

The 1981 Discovery

Doug Plemons along with Mark Miller, Joel Buckner, Joe Douglas, and Don Tebbet went caving in Smith County on Sunday, December 20, 1981. Their first destination was Piper Cave, but the owner told them it was closed. Their next destination was Neil Fisher Cave. Here is their story:

> Joel Buckner said: "We'll go to Neil Fisher Cave. It's pretty big… ex-tourist cave from the early 1900s. Some going passages, big borehole. How about it gentlemen?" Doug Plemons replied: "How is the landowner?" "No worry, he is friendly," reassured Joel. "Let's go!" echoed the backseat trio in chorus.
>
> After at least ten false cave entrances and one going cave in Club Springs, TN, we reached the landowner's house. We surveyed the chicken-yards and hog pens and hoped for the best. Over to the left of one of the chicken yards there was a large metal

6 Barr, op. cit., pp 423-424.

Figure 1.11. Alfred Crabtree in a crawlway in Neil Fisher Cave. Photo by Joe Douglas, March 19, 2011.

sign that read: "Get Right With God." It was being used for a drinking trough for the thirsty chickens. I felt better already.

The owner was long accustomed to mud lovers, like us and we quickly secured his permission to cave and ridgewalk in the area. With the December air urging us on we surveyed hundreds of feet of bluffs along the Caney Fork River, in sight of I-40. It was grand. Somewhere under that huge pile of limestone was a very large cave.

Joel was the first to sight the 5-foot X 5-foot entrance which stood 50 feet above our footpath, in the bluff. We hiked up the ice-covered slope.

While the others were busy taking pictures and clowning for Mark's camera, cavorting under the overhanging, icicle-encrusted bluff face, I was busily investigating the entrance passage, a narrow canyon winding its way into the hill. In a side passage I labored to crawl to a spot where I found signs of the cave's ancient past, some very old rusted tin cans and a hobo mess kit.

By now everyone was ready. We trudged up the sloping tunnel and soon reached a large borehole, perpendicular to the entrance passage. There were basically two ways to go – left or right. We chose right and all noticed the change in the temperature (from 15° to 58°) and humidity. Mark said it felt so good he felt like abandoning his cave clothes and proceeding clad only in his boots, hard hat, and camera. He never did, much to the writer's amazement.

The well packed clay floor, lined with primitive rock benches for the tourist's comfort, led up and down a series of steeply sloped clay fills for 600 feet or so and led us nearly to the top of the sometimes 40-foot high ceiling where a clay fill looked impenetrable. Joe was the first to spot a tiny slit at the very top of the fill and slammed his body into the chest compressing crawlway. He went 30 feet and popped out at the ceiling level of yet another huge room, looking straight down a slippery pile of breakdown. He had discovered a completely virgin room, bristling with speleothems, huge dams, helictites, some 15-inch long soda straws, and large totem poles.

Figure 1.12. Alfred Crabtree in Neil Fisher Cave. Photo by Joe Douglas, March 19, 2011.

Figure 1.13. Julie Henry in a tight spot in Neil Fisher Cave. Photo by Joe Douglas, March 11, 2012.

He hollered back for me to follow but I was already pushing on, my nose in the stinking clay. We descended the breakdown into a 35-foot high, 30-foot wide, and 100-foot long chamber with a rubble slope on the far side offering the possibility of further passage beyond. Joe and I sat down on a rock and celebrated in the proper way.

Soon the others were plowing through the low slot and marveling at Joe's discovery, tentatively dubbed "the Born-Again Room" due to the womb like nature of the intimate crawlway.

Joe ascended the far slope and found himself in a low room that smelt vaguely of rat droppings; soon he had rousted out at least two Chihuahua puppy-sized rats and uncovered at least six cave rat nests. He knew he was nearing an entrance, at least a rat-sized one. He found some pine branches and straw, obviously materials for more nest. He felt a gush of cold outside air, but the passage was impenetrable, and we left the room via our grim tunnel.

In the left-hand passage was 200 feet of profusely decorated flowstone formations, some huge draperies and one free climbable stalagmite

hugging one wall. The flowstone had draped around it forming a huge tower nearly 30 feet high. Joel climbed up the tower, over another one above and beside it, and slid cautiously out along a narrow ledge before reaching a spot on the other side of an immense flowstone plug where he could climb down into a continuation of the borehole towards another virgin crawlway. The others followed while I stayed behind to examine the large room we were in. I laid down at the top of the slope, my head resting on my pack and was soon almost asleep. I was awakened by the other rowdy caver's approach via the questionable ledge. They said it may be worth another trip. Neil Fisher Cave may extend parallel to the face of the bluff for an undetermined distance.

Back at the entrance we stepped out into a startlingly clear and close night, one of those nights where the absence of clouds and pollution created an optical illusion whereby the stars look much brighter, larger, and much closer to Earth. One could stare into the depths and get dizzy. Joel pointed out constellations, red giant stars, and blue white dwarf stars, as well as a supernova, all billions and billions of miles away, yet still close as neighbors. The path back to the car was frozen and rutted.

Nature had blessed us with a clear day, some nice virgin cave, some good leads, and a fresh Arctic night to change clothes in. The twinkling stars seemed to beckon us as they echoed Mother Nature's call to us, "Thank you for coming. This show took a long time to put together!"

We piled into the car and drove off into the night. We'd all be back soon, on the road again to the secret and unknown depths of Tennessee, in the heart of TAG country, "Where the Big Ones Are!"[7]

It is interesting to note that they had visited a well-known, often visited, ex-commercial cave and STILL found a nice amount of virgin cave. Never assume in any large cave that there is nothing left to discover.

The Survey of Neil Fisher Cave

Here is the story of the survey of Neil Fisher Cave as told by Ken Oeser:

On July 16, 2005, Gerald Moni, Robert Van Fleet, and Rebecca Dettorre joined me, and we drove to Smith County and obtained permission to hike to the cave. After searching many obvious and not-so-obvious holes in the bluffs on the Caney Fork River, we finally located the inconspicuous entrance at the top of a steep ravine, at the base of a bluff.

The entrance passage is a narrow walking passage that winds 150 feet upslope and junctions into a large gallery. We surveyed left down the "wet" branch to some steps cut into the mud that led to a large formation blocking the 60-foot high passage. Some old wood at the base of the formation are likely remains of ladders used in the commercial days. Looking through a small hole showed that the cave continued on the other side, so we coerced Rebecca into squeezing through the hole. I tried in vain to fit through while she checked out the passage, then Robert climbed up onto a flowstone ledge and found a high route to get around the flowstone. We surveyed through some pretty formation areas and continued 200 feet to the end. Back at the main junction, we then surveyed the "dry" passage, a 20-foot wide, 30 to 50-foot high gallery 200 feet to

a junction. Some stone steps are found on a slope in this passage. On the left side of this section is a short side passage with some colorful rimstone dams 6 inches high. We surveyed upslope from the junction, then over some breakdown and through a tight crawl into a nice room over 100 feet long, 20-feet wide, and 10-20 feet high with several formations on the walls and floor.

On August 6 Robert, Joe Douglas, and I returned to do some more mapping. Joe explained that the room at the end of the main passage had been dug into on a trip he attended in 1981, so we decided to call it the 1981 Room. He also brought a copy of a newspaper article written in 1916 from a person who had taken the commercial tour of the cave, at that time known as Rip Van Winkle Cave, with descriptions and names of several passages and formations. We decided to use as many of these names as possible on the map, some of which are Capitol Dome, Wedding Bells, Bridal Veil, Fat Man's Misery, Hall of Fame, Bridge of Sighs, and Crystallized Cataract. That day we surveyed the right-hand passage off the main "dry" branch and surveyed a loop with a climb-down that Gerald had called a pit on the first trip. Of note in this loop is a smoked "Roy Davis '54" on one of the lower walls. Having finished all the leads, Robert decided to check out a small hole that I had talked Rebecca out of entering on the previous trip. This is a very small horizontal hole that immediately goes vertical 6 feet into a crawlway, and there are no footholds. Robert made it through and estimated about 300 feet of cave, which branched and ended in three directions. Joe and I were not going to fit, so we had to plan a return trip to this Periscope Extension.

I recruited Morris Sullivan and Heather Levy to join Robert for a final survey trip on September 3, 2005. Matt Gillard and his son Gabriel joined us for the hike and a short trip into the cave. After the small crew squeezed through the Periscope, I waited about an hour before I heard noise indicating their successful return with about 200 feet of surveyed passage. A full photo tour of the cave was then had by all. Total length of the cave was surveyed at 2,132 feet, over double the previous 1,000 feet in the TCS files. This cave turned out to be well worth the wait,

7 Doug Plemons, "Gonzo Cavers Invade Smith County," *Speleonews*, v. 26 (1982), no. 2, pp 26-30.

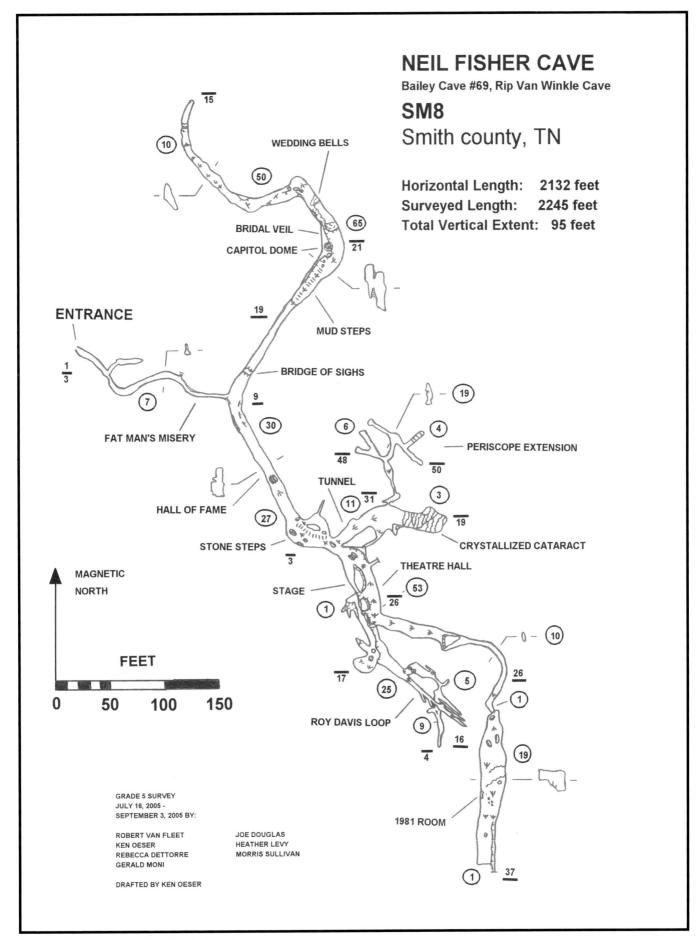

Figure 1.14. Map of Neil Fisher Cave by Ken Oeser, 2005.

with large, decorated passages, and some small holes and alcoves to explore.[8]

They surveyed 2,245 feet of cave (0.43 mile) which has a horizontal length of 2,132 feet and a total vertical extent of 95 feet. One large room is called Theatre Hall and is complete with a stage. (See Figure 1.14)

Cave Access

John Fisher Cave is CLOSED. The entrance has been bulldozed SHUT. The owner does not allow anyone to visit this cave. It is on private property. PLEASE respect his wishes.

Neil Fisher Cave is also located on private property. If you wish to visit this cave please be sure that you have the owner's permission.

---

8 Ken Oeser, "Neil Fisher Cave," *Tennessee Caver*, Fall 2005, pp 22-25.

Figure 1.15. Tommy Hutchison stands beneath a large shield formation in John Fisher Cave. Photo by Edward M. Yarbrough, November, 1961.

CHAPTER 2
Junkyard Cave

Junkyard Cave is located in Davidson County, Tennessee. It has a surveyed length of 2.9 miles, making it the longest known cave in Davidson County. At one time, it was the most popular cave in the Nashville area due to its large size, but it has been closed to explorers for several years.

Prehistoric Exploration of Junkyard Cave

There is evidence of Native American exploration of the main cave passage in Junkyard Cave. Historian Joseph Douglas observed stoke marks from cane torches on the cave walls in the Junkyard side of the cave. Later, on a biological assessment trip, Kristen Bobo found charcoal from American Indian cane torches in a large breakdown area closer to the Hardin section of the cave. These early Indian explorers could have come in the Junkyard Entrance, but there may also have been a spring entrance, now partially blocked, on the bank of the Cumberland River. There is no chronological date available yet on when the Native Americans explored the cave.[1]

The Discovery of Junkyard Cave

The earliest mention of Junkyard Cave in the caving literature is an article by David Irving from the East Tennessee Grotto. David was in Nashville for the SERA Winter Business Meeting and visited the cave after the meeting. Here is his description of that trip:

> On February 27, 1966, following the SERA Winter Meeting, twelve members of the East Tennessee, Nashville, and Smoky Mountain Grottoes visited what I shall call for lack of a better name Junkyard Cave. It is located half a mile up the hollow behind Southeastern Supply Company on Tenn. State Route 12, several miles from Nashville toward Ashland City. The entrance is a crawlway at the bottom of a small sink.

The main passage is a single stream passage extending about one kilometer to a point where it becomes a low crawlway. It is relatively uniform in dimensions, averaging about 7 meters wide and 6 meters high, although it is generally narrower near the entrance. There are almost no side passages. A few leads were seen close to the entrance but were not entered. Roughly two-thirds of the way in, the small stream, which had been meandering across the floor of the passage, bears off to the left and it may be possible to crawl alongside the stream for some distance. Several separate stretches of upper level passage were found. This upper level appears to roughly parallel the lower level with some meandering back and forth above it. The largest upper level stretch was followed for at least 100 meters back towards the entrance from a 10-meter-high dome that opens on the right about three quarters of the way down the main passage. The dome may be climbed without special equipment, although not without difficulty.

The main passage contains practically no formations whatever. The upper level passages contain a great deal of what appears to be gypsum which has been partially immersed and dissolved. Near the entrance there are signs of a phreatic origin to the cave, but the rest of the cave is apparently just a stream passage. The present stream was only a trickle when we were there despite the season and the drizzly weather on the surface. Leaves and other debris appearing in plentiful supply on the walls and ceiling are signs that the cave is completely flooded at times.

Quite a few bats were seen in the cave (at least it seemed like quite a few to those of us from East Tennessee where we can't find a cave with as many as fifty bats in it). There were no large groups, but about 200 bats were nesting individually. They were mostly *Myotis grisescens* and *Myotis pipistrelles* (probably, although I am no expert on bat identification) and a few bats from other species. Most of the bats were

---

1 This information was provided by Joseph Douglas, Personal communication, June 20, 2018.

Figure 2.1. Tiffany Buchanan at the entrance to Junkyard Cave. Photo by Brian Buchanan, September, 2018.

hibernating although a few had obviously recently come in from the wet weather outside. Two bats were observed in copulation and a picture of them was taken. The observation of bats mating is apparently a rare occasion and several Oak Ridge ecologists are eagerly awaiting the developments of the pictures.[2]

It is not clear from the above report who actually located the cave, but this is the first written report on Junkyard Cave. The entrance to Junkyard Cave appears on the topographic map as the point where the surface stream disappears underground. This stream reappears as a spring on the bank of the Cumberland River just below the entrance to Hardins Cave.

    The earliest mention of Hardins Cave in the caving literature is the following Trip Report by Larry E. Matthews:

      Louis Hardin and I set out one afternoon recently to go see Junkyard Cave. While we were driving out

Figure 2.2. Tiffany Buchanan at the gate in Junkyard Cave. Photo by Brian Buchanan, September, 2018.

there I remembered seeing a cave entrance along the Ashland City Highway last fall, so Louis and I drove on past the Junkyard to check this cave out first. The entrance turned out to be only ¾ mile past the

[2] David Irving, "Junkyard Cave," *Speleonews*, v. 10 (1966), no. 3, p. 31.

Figure 2.3. Erica Sughrue (front) and Brandi Cotten (rear) in the main passage of Junkyard Cave. Photo by Bob Biddix, November 15, 2008.

Junkyard and at the base of a bluff overlooking the Cumberland River. The entrance was rather small, and therefore we only grabbed our lamps and hard hats out of the car.

The entrance to this cave is 3 feet high and 3 feet wide. The passage goes back into the hill for 30 feet and by this time we had come to at least three side passages. By following the larger of the several possible routes, we found ourselves in a series of passages averaging five feet high and 2 feet wide. A small pile of bat guano at one point indicated the presence of a small colony of bats in the summer. We halted our exploration about 30 minutes before dark so that we could find Junkyard Cave before it got dark. However, we left many leads unchecked in leaving this cave. One particularly promising lead had a strong breeze blowing out of it. The entire cave was dry and dusty.

On the way back to the entrance, Louis spotted an animal claw. The curved claw spans 3.2 cm and probably belonged to some type of carnivore. The length of the outer edge measured along the curve is 4.7 cm.

I found a small bone fragment nearby, but nothing can be deduced from it. Much to Louis' chagrin, I am naming this cave Hardins Cave. Hardins Cave is located west of Scottsboro in Davidson County on Tennessee Highway 12, 1.4 miles east of the Cheatham County line. After leaving Hardins Cave, we hurried to Junkyard Cave, which we were able to find with the last glow of daylight. After exploring there for a while we returned home.[3]

The next year, on a return trip to Hardins Cave, a second entrance to the cave was located. Here is the story of that trip:

On Sunday, November 10, 1967, Marietta Waldrum, Bob Cook, and I visited Hardins Cave here in

---

3 Larry E. Matthews, "Hardins Cave," *Speleonews*, v. 11 (1967), no. 2, pp 30-31.

Davidson County. I showed Marietta and Bob most of the several hundred feet that Louis Hardin and I had explored when we first found the cave. To my surprise, the cave was actually damp in places due to the recent heavy rains. Since Louis and I had not made a very thorough exploration of the cave, we next proceeded to check out some unexplored leads. Most of the ones we tried pinched out as impenetrable crawls or became blocked by dirt fill, but Marietta found one squeeze which led through into another section of maze passages. One of these was a walking passage which led to a new entrance. Due to the fact that we all had to go our respective ways for dinner, we left a number of new leads in this new section unchecked, not to mention unchecked leads in the old section.

This new entrance to Hardins Cave is only 30 feet east of the old entrance, but it is about 8 feet above the road. It is 2 feet high and 3 feet wide and slopes down into a modest-sized walking passage. This new entrance is not visible from the road due to its position, small size, and vegetation growing in front of it.

Although Hardins Cave now contains several hundred feet of passage, it is generally of small dimensions throughout. Due to the maze-like character of its passages, the next logical step in exploration would be to start mapping it and systematically checking out each lead. Despite its small size, Hardins Cave makes an enjoyable afternoon trip.[4]

A Description of the Cave

Junkyard Cave is described by Larry E. Matthews in his book, *Descriptions of Tennessee Caves* (1971). However, in 1971 Hardins Cave had not yet been connected to Junkyard Cave, so there are two descriptions:

Hardins Cave has an entrance 3 feet high and 3 feet wide. It consists of at least 500 feet of joint-controlled stoopways and crawlways. The joints are oriented northeast and northwest. The passages are dry and dusty, and two of the crawlways blow large amounts of air.

4 Larry E. Matthews, "New Entrance to Hardins Cave," *Speleonews*, v. 12 (1968), no. 1, p. 6.

The entrance to Junkyard Cave is 2 feet high and 6 feet wide. The passage averages 3 feet high and 8 feet wide for 35 feet, but past this the main passage is of walking dimension for the next 3,220 feet with only two short stretches that require stooping. The main passage continues roughly southwest, with many large meanders, for a surveyed distance of 3,255 feet to a breakdown chamber past which it continues for an undetermined distance as a bedding-plane crawl.

A wet-weather stream flows into the entrance of Junkyard Cave and follows the main passage for 356 feet. This part of the cave averages 10 feet high and 10 feet wide. At this point the stream enters a low, bedding-plane crawlway which parallels the main passage and in places connects with it. The main passage continues 10 feet above the point where the stream splits off. The main passage averages 5 feet high and 8 feet wide for 214 feet, then enters a large meandering avenue which is 2,634 feet long and averages 20 feet wide and 15 feet high. This passage contains several interesting domes, occasional breakdown, and a number of side passages. This avenue ends abruptly at a breakdown which may be followed upward for 20 feet into a breakdown room 35 feet in diameter. A low, bedding-plane crawlway continues from this room in the direction of Hardins Cave, which is only 250 feet from this last breakdown chamber. It seems highly probable that the two caves connect, but the breakdown may prevent human passage.

The first map of the cave, dated 1968, accompanies this description. (See: Figure 2.6.)

The Hardins Cave-Junkyard Cave Connection

Since my 1968 survey of Junkyard Cave showed it to be within 250 feet of Hardins Cave, or closer, considering that the crawlway at the end of the cave where I had quit mapping continued on in that direction, and since Hardins Cave blew a lot of air, it was obvious that the two caves were connected.

In 1970 Paul Cragan and I began enlarging a fissure in Hardins Cave that could be seen to drop into a lower passage and which blew large amounts of air. We were using chisels and a sledge hammer in an attempt to enlarge the fissure to the point where we could get

Figure 2.4. Erica Sughrue stands on breakdown in Junkyard Cave. Photo by Bob Biddix, November 15, 2008. (Above.)

Figure 2.5. Erica Sughrue beneath a ceiling dome in Junkyard Cave. Photo by Bob Biddix, November 15, 2008. (Below.)

through. At some point, we gave up, deciding that it was too big a project for us.[5]

Years passed, and other Nashville Grotto cavers took up the challenge. Finally, David Parr and John Hoffelt succeeded at making the connection:

> On August 21st (1979) Hardins Cave called John Hoffelt and myself for another night of senseless pounding and digging in the legendary Hardins Crack. Just about everyone seemed to think we would never make it through and we were half believing it, but we went anyway. The sky was looking stormy as we arrived at Mr. Rice's house to park, so we hurried to the cave.
>
> The entrance was blowing strong as we crawled in and it kept getting stronger as we progressed. When I got to the crack I slipped on down without hesitation and started to dig.

5 Larry E. Matthews, "Bones from Hardins Cave," *Speleonews*, v. 14 (1970), no. 2, p. 18.

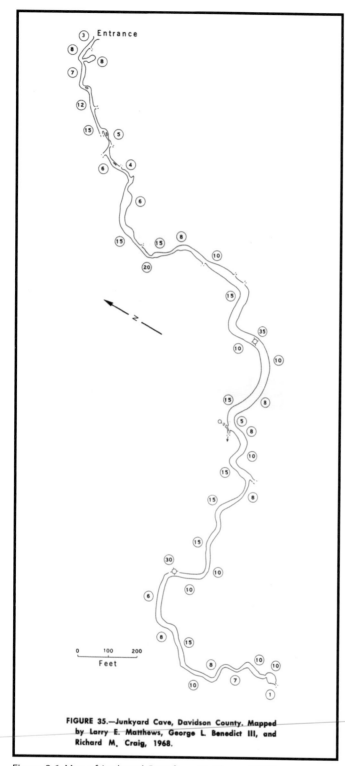

FIGURE 35.—Junkyard Cave, Davidson County. Mapped by Larry E. Matthews, George L. Benedict III, and Richard M. Craig, 1968.

Figure 2.6. Map of Junkyard Cave from Matthews (1971).

Figure 2.7. Tiffany Buchanan in the entrance to Hardins Cave. Photo by Brian Buchanan, September, 2018.

rocks and a mound of dirt aside and pushed on to a "C" bend around a breakdown block.

On the other side of this obstruction the passage was somewhat less confining. After a short crawl it got low again and looked very grim but upon trying it I found I had an inch to spare. Soon I saw a short stretch of virgin passage between me and a set of scuff marks. I laid there until John caught up and then we crawled out of the so-called terminal end of the Windy City Crawl into Junkyard Cave. When we got to the end of the main passage we sat dumbfounded on a mud bank thinking how worthwhile it all had been. Due to time and the lack of light and water we left the cave through our new route only to emerge in a very hard rain.

In order to make the connection we had to enlarge a 5-inch vertical crack through about 6 feet of solid rock with the "toothpick" (a 5-foot-long crowbar) and a sledgehammer, then remove 2 feet of large slab breakdown and 3 feet of dirt, small rocks, and mud. The project took about 10 trips ranging from 2 to 4 hours. Now, thanks to Joel Buckner, John Cauthen, Richard Greer, Steve Haynes, Phillip

The Hardins trip before had opened a small crawl 13 feet below the top of the crack but it was too small to do anything but look into. After filling the bucket about 10 times I was ready to try it. I laid on my stomach with my feet about 3 feet above my head, did a backbend and slid in about 3 feet. After calling for John to come on down I pushed some

Figure 2.8. The gate in Hardins Cave. The crack leading down into Junkyard Cave is visible, just past the gate. Photo by Brian Buchanan, September, 2018.

Hart, John Hoffelt, myself, Jeff Sims, Tim Whitty, and Larry Matthews (for bringing the idea to our attention) we have an entrance to the largest cave in Davidson County on State of Tennessee property.

At present the new route is very small and it is not known how well it will hold up to flood waters. The wet weather stream at the end of Hardins might plug it with dirt and small rocks, but it can always be reopened. Also the stream from Hardins-Junkyard Cave has to flow through a pile of rocks under the highway. During heavy rains this can cause almost the entire lower part of the cave to back up with water. Eventually this will probably cause major highway repairs to be undertaken.

A new survey of this cave will begin soon. With the present 913 feet of Grade 5 survey in Hardins Cave and what is known in Junkyard Cave I believe we will get almost 2 miles of surveyed passage in Hardins-Junkyard Cave. Quite a feat for a Davidson County cave![6]

6 David Parr, "The Hardins-Junkyard Connection," *Speleonews*, v. 23 (1979), no. 6, pp 133-134.

A trip through Hardins Crack is not a lot of fun. On one trip David Stidham dislocated his shoulder trying to get through. But, now that access through the Junkyard Entrance is no longer available, it is wonderful to have this route into the cave.

The Survey of Junkyard Cave

Like many caves, this cave has been surveyed several times. The first known survey of Junkyard Cave was made by Larry E. Matthews, George L. Benedict III, and Richard M. Craig in 1968. This map only shows the main passage and shows 3,255 feet of surveyed cave. (See Figure 2.6)

The first survey of Hardins Cave was made by Joel Buckner, Steve Haynes, and Jeff Sims on June 16 & 23, 1977. It shows a surveyed length of 913 feet. (See Figure 2.9) Jeff Sims describes the survey project:

Yes, it's true. Hardins Cave has been surveyed. It does not connect with Junkyard Cave. It does not go forever. It has a start and a finish, several entrances, and many ending passages. It has mazes, a few blowing crawlways, and a couple exhibits of graffiti. But enough about the facts, let's talk about the glory and fantasy of the actual survey. It all began when….

I was at a Nashville Grotto meeting. A mere suggestion about surveying caves in Davidson County aroused the interest of Joel Buckner, Nashville Grotto's most ambitious new surveyor. A date was set and the survey of Hardins Cave was on.

The main reason for surveying Hardins Cave was the fact that it was really close to Junkyard Cave. For many years spelunkers thought a connection was possible – as did Joel and me.

On a weekday night, June 16, 1977, Joel and I found ourselves standing on the highway in front of the Hardins Cave entrance. Five hours later we had surveyed 684 feet yet had not finished the cave. Approximately 11 feet of virgin passage was explored.

The next trip occurred one week later on June 23, 1977. Steve Haynes, a friend of Joel, joined us for a wrap-up survey trip. A short 3-hour trip netted 229 feet. The last hour of the trip was spent bashing and chiseling on a blowing crack near the back of the cave. This blowing air is probably related to Junkyard Cave, which also has a blowing crawl at the end of the main passage. The only way to make

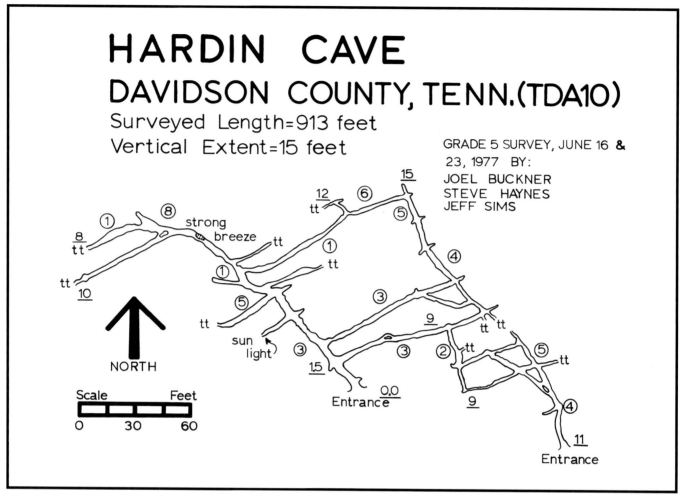

Figure 2.9. Map of Hardins Cave by Joel Buckner, Steve Haynes, and Jeff Sims, 1977.

a connection would be with explosives. It seems that the possible connection passage is clogged with breakdown. This, of course, is only speculation. But if one plots the passage in Junkyard Cave (see Matthews' book, *Descriptions of Tennessee Caves*) on a topo map and also plots the Hardins Cave passages, they come very close to each other.

After the second survey trip all passages had been surveyed. Approximately 913 feet of passages was surveyed. About 50 feet was virgin, the rest was pretty well traveled.

Even though the cave is mapped, the blowing crack still exists. A major project would be required to enlarge it. So, gung-ho cavers, go get it.[7]

And, of course, some of the Nashville cavers began mapping Junkyard Cave soon after the connection was made. The survey was finished on October 31, 1981, a little over two (2) years after the connection was made. The map was drafted by David Parr and sixteen (16)

different cavers participated in the survey. The final length was 15,424 feet (2.92 miles) of True Horizontal Cave with a vertical extent of 122 feet. (See Figure 2.11)

Joseph Douglas was on the first trip to start the resurvey of the cave by Parr and Hoffelt after the connection. However, the two only dug it open enough for themselves and he did not fit and was unable to enter. The connection crawl was later enlarged somewhat. However, it needs periodic re-opening as the cave back-floods from the lower spring for hundreds of feet (hence the silt and mud deposits in the lower trunk) in high water events. Once during a flood, cavers went into the connection crawl and found water beginning to slowly rise (at a rate of about an inch per 15 minutes) into the crawl.[8]

The Gating of Junkyard Cave

As the longest and biggest Cave in Davidson County, Junkyard Cave became the favorite of Nashville spelunkers. This resulted in several rescues and quite a

7 Jeff Sims, "The First and Last Survey of Hardins Cave," *Speleonews*, v. 22 (1978), no. 1, pp 12-13.

8 Joseph Douglas, Personal communication, June 20, 2018.

bit of vandalism to the cave. Nashville Grotto member William Overton gives a detailed history of the events leading up to the gating of the cave:

> Junkyard Cave is the longest cave in Davidson County at just over three miles. Junkyard Cave was placed on the Tennessee Superfund cleanup in the early nineties.
>
> The former owner of the property had allowed the storage of hundreds of 55-gallon drums on the property. The state demanded a cleanup be performed before the land could have any improvements or even be sold. The Tennessee Department of Transportation constructed a new highway through the middle of the old junkyard site and divided the cave entrance from the area where the drums were stored, helping keep the cave safe from any contaminants. The site was cleaned and finally removed from the Superfund list and placed for sale. Thanks largely to the devoted efforts of a few of the Nashville Grotto members, Hardins Cave is the only Tennessee Superfund site to ever be cleaned and removed from the Superfund list. The quality of the air and water in the cave today is well within the tolerances established by the Environmental Protection Agency making this a truly unique cave location.
>
> When Nashville businessman Barry Walker heard of the property being for sale, he purchased it for a development he planned to build, and another friendship was formed. Barry Walker has developed several unique sites in and around Nashville including the revamping of an old automobile factory, the Marathon Motorcar Company.
>
> Barry was approached by members of the Nashville Grotto and was asked what he planned to do with the cave on his property. At this point he didn't even know about the existence of the cave and wanted to see his newly purchased cave. On his first trip to the cave several members of the Nashville Grotto and Barry found a pair of bats tied together with a piece of string and left to die. Barry was shocked at the sight of this act of cruelty and almost immediately agreed to lease the cave with the provisions this kind of act would never happen again in his cave. He also requested the word "Junkyard" be dropped from the name. Once again the wheels were in motion and another cave would soon become the property of the Southeastern Cave Conservancy, Inc. and the Nashville Grotto would become the managers. A contract was drawn and, after both parties had agreed, a signing ceremony was held at the February 1999 Winter Business Meeting of the Southeastern Cave Conservancy. During the process of working out the details, the Nashville Grotto as an act of good faith and as a vote of confidence, engineered and constructed the gate on the Junkyard Entrance of Hardins Cave.
>
> This gate would prove to offer a completely different set of concerns and problems. Junkyard Cave is the longest cave in Davidson County and at over three miles is not a small cave by anyone's standards. The cave is also well known by locals and has always had a large number of visitors yearly. With such a well-known cave and party location, vandalism was our largest concern. And if that wasn't enough after the new highway was built the cave entrance is only 150 feet from the road and in plain sight of the traffic on Highway 12.
>
> The area near the entrance has been used as a dumpsite by people and had a wide collection of debris ranging from a water collection tank to used tires and everything in between. In all, seven truckloads of trash were removed just to get the entrance area cleaned. The cave itself has had numerous cleanup trips to remove the bulk of the trash, with trips still being held today. The cave, though not completely clean, is much better than when the Conservancy and the Nashville Grotto took control on February 13, 1999.
>
> Publicity wasn't a problem as Junkyard Cave has been on the local news several times. With three rescues performed at Junkyard Cave in the 1990s, the local papers and television stations are very familiar with the cave. The local newspaper and one of the local television stations came the day of the gating for an interview. Both ran favorable stories about the gating activities of the Nashville Grotto and how it would make the cave a safer place for everyone involved. The power of positive publicity can never be underestimated.
>
> The construction of the Junkyard Cave gate was held on December 5, 1998, a rainy day that produced a fast-flowing creek into the normally dry entrance crawl. Again Bill Overton was contacted to design

and engineer the gate. The gate was constructed about 60 feet inside the entrance of the cave. This was the first usable location in the cave for a sturdy gate. With the fear that locals might try to use force to remove any gate built, we felt the distance would assist in keeping the gate from harm. The gate was built in a narrow section of the cave approximately six feet wide and ten feet tall.

The team of volunteers consisted of members of three Tennessee Grottos, Nashville Grotto, Cumberland Valley Grotto, and Central Basin Grotto. Volunteers had come from as far as Alpine, Tennessee, about 180 miles away. A work site was set up, steel unloaded, and the gate was started. Placement of the base of the gate was done and a framework of steel rose from the six-inch angle iron. Three-foot pins were driven into the floor of the cave below the threshold of the gate. Later 1,100 pounds of concrete would be poured, and six drain holes would be placed. The work went steadily for ten hours and the Hardins Cave gate was built in one day. The door of the gate was built off site due to concerns of security for this cave.

The door was built at a steel fabrication facility owned by one of the oldest and largest locksmiths in Nashville. West End Lock Company donated time, materials, and years of knowledge to assist the Grotto in producing one of the most secure and solid gate doors I have ever seen. With such a well-known cave and one that has been actively used for so many years, closing off this cave could prove to be difficult if not down-right impossible. That is why the services of the West End Lock Company were enlisted.[9] (See Figure 2.2)

The details of the gate and locking mechanism that were listed in the above referenced article are not repeated here, for security reasons.

The Bats of Junkyard Cave

Being both the largest cave in Davidson County and securely gated, it was hoped that Junkyard Cave would provide a secure refuge for bats. The following is a long excerpt from an e-mail dated February 2, 2015 from Joseph Douglas to Cory Holliday of the Tennessee

9 William Overton, "The Management of Logsdon, Hardin, and Swirl Canyon Caves—A Cooperative Effort Between the Nashville Grotto and the Southeastern Cave Conservancy, Inc.," 1999 National Cave and Karst Management Symposium, pp 138-142.

Figure 2.10. Mike Craig next to the "Golden Fleece." Photo by George L. Benedict, III, August 13, 1968.

Nature Conservancy (TNC) concerning bat counts and research in Junkyard Cave:

The first bat count in the cave of which I am aware was in winter 1997 by Bill Overton. This was before either entrance was gated. There were only 18 bats observed, undifferentiated by species. The main (Junkyard) gate was installed subsequent to this first count in 1998. There were yearly counts by Overton in the winters of 1998, 1999, and 2000. I was verbally told that the number of bats grew significantly over those three years, but I never received the data, although I asked for it. In winter 2000-2001, Overton's count was 482 bats, undifferentiated by species.

Around January 2001 I visited the cave and looked carefully at bats. I observed at least four historic Gray bat (*Myotis grisescens*) roosts with ceiling stains and guano piles of varying age in the main passage beyond the "Narrows," plus one small roost just outside the gate. Gray bats are a federally endangered species. I saw two different species of bats in the cave. Most were Eastern Pipistrelles, now called Tri-colored bats (*Perimyotis subflavus*)

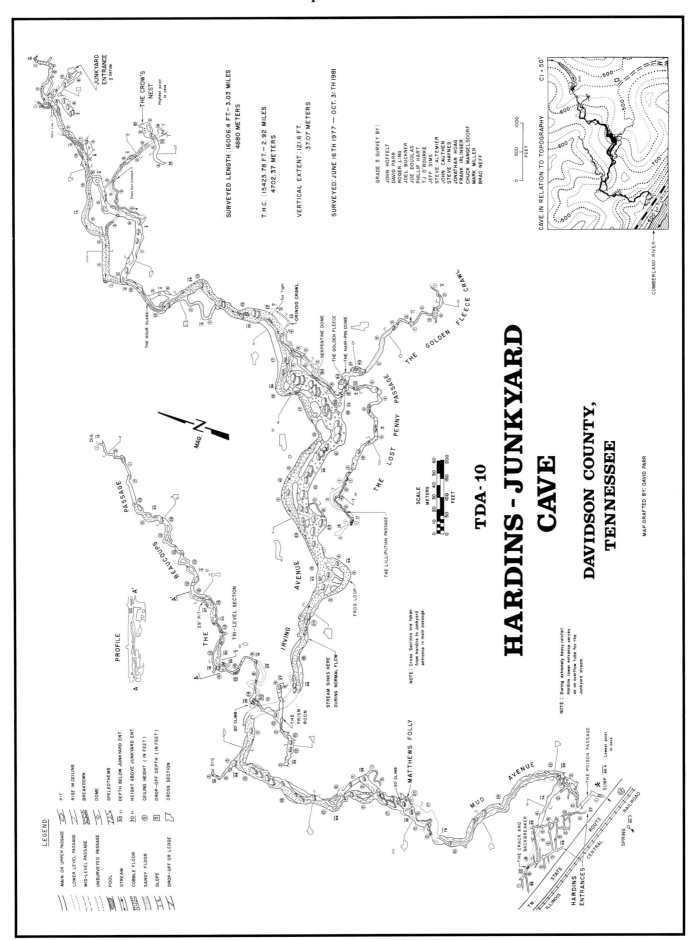

Figure 2.11. Final map of Hardins-Junkyard Cave by David Parr, October 31, 1981.

but there was another bat displaying semi-colonial behavior and splayed on the walls, mostly in the Golden Fleece area. I thought they might be Gray bats (which was incorrect). I thought this might be significant, as I was unaware of any Gray bat populations in Davidson County. Caver Chris Kerr visited the cave a few weeks later and also mentioned the large number of bats. I contacted Heather Garland of TNC, and on February 3, 2001, Heather, Chris Roberts (TNC), and I drove out to Hardins Cave. For a while we helped a large group of people put a gate on the key crawl in the Hardins Entrance. But then I took Garland and Roberts on a brief tour of the main passage via the Junkyard entrance, so they could see the "many dozens" of bats and identify them by species. We identified three species: Tri-colored bats (most), a few northern Long-eared bats (*Myotis septentrionalis*), and Little Brown bats (*Myotis lucifugus*) showing semi-colonial behavior, these were the ones I previously mistook for possible Grays.

Heather and Chris agreed that the historic roosts in the main passage (we saw six or more, some quite large) were likely from Gray bats and suggested I ask if anyone had seen colonial bats in the cave in the summer and then revisit the site. I did. Bill Overton said he had seen colonial bats roosting somewhere in the Golden Fleece area. I visited the cave in August 2001 but was unable to get up above the Golden Fleece, so I saw no bats. I returned to the cave September 6, 2001 with Kristen Bobo and we rigged a hand-line to get up. We found a small colony of clustered bats, which Kristen identified as Gray bats, although we did not have one in hand. It was clearly a 4th species of bat from the cave. The cluster was tightly packed and measured about 2 feet high by 2 feet wide. I returned to the cave once more on September 23, 2001 and observed that the number of Gray bats in the roost was only half of that in early September, which suggested they had started their staging activity.

On March 14, 2002, I counted bats in the cave, along with John Hickman of the SCCi and Nashville Grotto member Iris Bradley. According to Hickman, Bill Overton had not counted bats that year, and there had also been a break-in event at the cave. This count was in the early evening late in the winter season, so some bats were probably outside (we saw a few flying outside). Anyway, we checked the main passage back to the Beaucoups Passage and a bit beyond, and the Golden Fleece area. We counted a total of 433 bats. Based on what Heather had shown me previously, I observed 227 Tri-colored bats, 79 Little Brown bats, and 123 unidentified bats. Most of the unidentified bats were surely Tri-colored, but any bat too high on the ceiling for me to tell for sure I simply called unidentified. I did not see any I was sure were Northern Long-Eared. 75 of the Little Brown bats were in the wet domes below the Golden Fleece area. I also looked above the Golden Fleece at the Gray bat roost and none were there in March, as expected.[10]

Being both the longest cave in Davidson County and securely gated, Junkyard Cave could be an important refuge for bats. However, as long as the cave remains in private ownership, its security is questionable.

Cave Access

The Junkyard Entrance is CLOSED. The owner does not allow anyone to visit this cave at the present time. It is on private property. PLEASE respect his wishes. The Hardin's Cave entrance is on the State Highway right of way.

---

10 Joseph Douglas, Personal communication, June 20, 2018.

CHAPTER 3

Mason Cave

Mason Cave is located in Sumner County, Tennessee. It is the longest known cave in Sumner County, with a surveyed length of 1.6 miles. It is located near the main highway and is well known locally. Ken Oeser noted several old names and dates in the cave, including:

H. C. Cook, J. D. Allen, 1847

T. Boyers, August 1847

James Pike, 1851

T. B. Harris, 1856

Mr. C. Harris, 1896

J. H. Peyton, M. E. Barry, 1896

These names and dates are located on the 2009 map (See Figure 3.8).

A Description of the Cave

Mason Cave is described by Thomas C. Barr, Jr. in his book, *Caves of Tennessee* (1961):

Mason Cave is the largest cave in Sumner County. It is locally well-known and often visited. The mouth is a transverse slit 2 feet high and 5 feet wide and is located in the third major outcrop of limestone on the west wall of Adams Hollow, just north of a small gully extending west from the Hollow. Immediately inside the mouth the cave expands to 5 feet high and 30 feet wide. The cave is 750 feet long and trends north-northeast. At 200 feet is a large room full of breakdown, 120 feet long, 50 feet wide, and 20 feet high. Two *domepits* are developed here. From 500 to 550 feet is a crawlway. The cave is damp throughout, and a number of small dripstone formations are present. A large amount of breakdown, especially on the southwest side of the passage, results in the cave's highly irregular shape.[1]

My First Trip to the Cave

I first visited this cave in 1967 while I was a student at Vanderbilt University. It soon became a favorite with me and other members of the Nashville Grotto because it was a short drive from Nashville and we were finding lots of virgin cave. Here is a report of that first trip:

Recently Marietta Waldrum, Kirk Holland, Eddy Reasoner, and I went to explore a new cave which Eddy had located on the Turner's Station Quadrangle. The cave turned out to be quite large with about 2,000 feet of passage, formations, gypsum, and two entrances. Needless to say, we were all quite enthusiastic since this was almost three times as large as the largest cave that Barr had reported from Sumner County. Later, while plotting the latitude and longitude for this *new* cave, I found that it was the same as Barr's Mason Cave and that the description of the cave matched the first 750 feet which we had seen. Barr's description for this first section is generally correct, however: (1) the height varies from 5 to 20 feet rather than just 5 feet throughout as Barr implies, and (2) the largest room has two domes, each about 20 feet high, and not *domepits* as Barr states.

The cave continues for the next 750 feet with more modest dimensions than the first section, consisting of small rooms and passages of stooping to standing dimensions with occasional crawlways. This section of the cave is rather dry, and gypsum can be found on the walls and in the dirt. The cave then intersects

Figure 3.1. Cavers at the main entrance to Mason Cave. Photo by Larry E. Matthews, March, 1974.

1 Thomas C. Barr, Jr., *Caves of Tennessee*, TN Division of Geology, Bulletin 64 (1961), pp 442-443.

Figure 3.2. Dave Wascher in the Long Crawl in Mason Cave. Photo by Ken Oeser, September 2, 2018.

Figure 3.3. Gypsum lips in Mason Cave. Photo by Larry E. Matthews, March, 1974.

a stream canyon about 8 feet wide and 30 feet deep. There are several easy ways to climb down into this canyon. The passage is rather muddy and there are several low spots. It is about 400 feet long and ends in a mud sump at one end and a siphon at the other. The middle and first section of the cave contain a number of loop passages which add considerable length to the cave. Climbing up into a small room about 250 feet from the entrance and up through a narrow passage puts one at the bottom of a small semi-vertical entrance about 20 feet deep and 20 feet wide at the surface level. This entrance is located about 200 feet up the hill from the main entrance and about 30 feet higher. It is easily climbed.

Although we were all disappointed that we had not found a new cave, we did enjoy our trip. Mason Cave is interesting, easy, and would be particularly suited to beginners. We were also pleased to find that Sumner County does have something more than just small caves. This cave and the others which we recently explored in the same area indicated that Sumner County deserves more attention than it has been getting speleologically.[2]

The Survey of Mason Cave

The surveyed length of Mason Cave is 8,291 feet (1.6 miles) and the vertical extent is 90 feet. This map was drafted by Nashville Grotto member Ken Oeser and is dated March 8 - August 8, 2009. Eleven other cavers are listed as having participated in the survey. (See Figure 3.8)

2 Larry E. Matthews, "Mason Cave, Sumner County," *Speleonews*, v. 11 (1967), no. 6, p. 103.

Interestingly, there is a much earlier map of the cave, dated 1977, that was prepared by the Bethel Research Association. It was drafted by Angelo George, a well-known caver living in Louisville, KY. This map shows approximately half of the passages shown on the 2009 map.

The map by Oeser (2009) shows that the cave generally trends north and just slightly east from the Main Entrance. The Spring Entrance is located at the far north end of the cave. For much of the length of the cave there is a larger Left Fork(west) passage and a smaller Right Fork(east) passage. Near the end of the Left Fork is a room noted on the map as the Shale Room. This room extends up into the Chattanooga Shale and there is a shale breakdown slope at this point.

Ken Oeser shares with us his exploration and survey of Mason Cave:

In 1987 Mason Cave was one of the first caves I explored after discovering Barr's book *Caves of Tennessee*. I soon discovered the Nashville Grotto, caving friends, and even more information on Tennessee caves. I found a copy of a map of Mason Cave in an old Kentucky Speleofest Guidebook, but it only covered the first 2,000 feet to the Junction Room and a little beyond plus a couple of side branches. I knew the cave kept going from my own explorations but didn't know anything about mapping.

Once I had learned how to map caves and had a dependable crew, I decided it was time to map Mason Cave. On March 8, 2009 Robert Van Fleet, Ted Burch, Joe Douglas, Sherri and Zion Person, and I began the official survey of the cave. We mapped

Figure 3.4. Dave Wascher in the Shale Room of Mason Cave. Photo by Ken Oeser, September 2, 2018.

the Main Passage through the Double Dome Room and breakdown, and along the easy stream passage to the Junction Room. Here we opted to map the Gypsum Branch and reached the end after 600 feet. We tried pushing through some breakdown at the right side at the end, to no avail. Some names and dates we recoded on this trip were Mr. C. Harris 1896 halfway down the Main Passage, J. H. Peyton and M. E. Barry 1896, and James Pike 1851 in the Junction Room, and T. B. Harris 1856, H. D. Cook 1847, J. D. Allen, and T. Boyers Aug. 1847 in the Gypsum Branch.

On March 28 I led a trip of friends and coworkers into the cave to visit the Gypsum Branch. Troy Fox and daughter Noel, wife Shelly Allen, Heidi Kocalis and daughter Naomi, Jennifer Rojas, my children Alexandra and Braxton Oeser, and two other families were those in attendance. On the way out of the cave, Robert and I mapped a few hundred feet to a loop in the Main Passage past the Junction Room.

Robert and I were joined by Julie Henry on April 5 and picked up mapping the Main Passage. As we mapped past a low crawl called The Eye of the Needle, we heard cavers coming from the back of the cave, and I casually asked if they had been down the pit. They replied that they had been through a long crawl to a large room rather than going down the pit and indicated the passage to the pit off to their left. I had no idea that the long crawl existed, so we were excited to map that direction. After mapping 300 feet of belly crawl passage, we came to a drop-off into the Shale Room, 100 feet in diameter and 20 feet high. To the left was some large breakdown

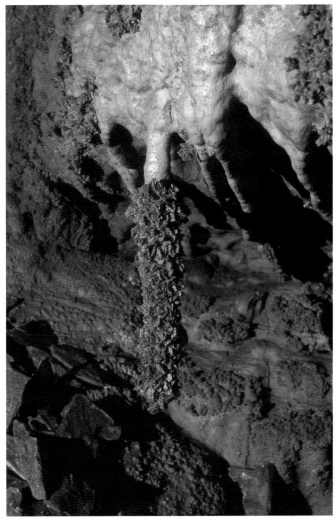

Figure 3.5. Crystal-coated stalactite in Mason Cave. Photo by Larry E. Matthews, March, 1974.

and just across our corner of the room was a sloping passage going up into an upper passage. This led to the Shale Room, a very steep 28-foot tall room with loose pieces of shale on the floor. The ceiling here is the highest point in the cave. We mapped across the Shale Room and stopped in continuing passage since our lights were dying, while our extra batteries were on the other side of the 300-foot crawl. Once back at our packs, we decided to map the passage to the top of the pit before stopping for the day.

Robert, Julie, and I returned April 19, joined by Joe Douglas, Gerald Moni, and a coworker of mine from Japan, Jun Ogino. We first descended the rope down the pit, then mapped the stream passage several hundred feet to the terminal rooms and the end of this passage. We were then eager to revisit the long crawl to the Shale Room, it's many formations, and more importantly the going passage that was totally unknown to me. Some large stalactites and

Figure 3.6. Dave Wascher admires flowstone in the Shale Room in Mason Cave. Photo by Ken Oeser, September 2, 2018. (Above.)

Figure 3.7. Bacon draperies in the Shale Room in Mason Cave. Photo by Ken Oeser, September 2, 2018. (Below.)

stalagmites are in this area along with a variety of other speleothems, and the whole area is quite pristine due to the filtering nature of the long belly crawl. After 200 feet we encountered a down-climb to a small stream, then climbed back up into the large passage, only to find it ended after less than 100 feet. Robert explored the stream passage and came back to tell us that it led to another entrance. With the option of mapping out 100 feet of low stream passage to an exit, or going back through the Long Crawl, it was an easy decision: we mapped out. The stream exits into a small pool that the owner uses as a water supply for a house next to this entrance. Due to this, the owner of this property does not want cavers using it without prior permission.

A week later on April 26, Robert and I returned and mapped a small, right-hand passage out of the Double Dome Room near the entrance. We only mapped a couple hundred feet before stopping at a belly crawl over a pool of water. We then decided to map out the passage leading to the entrance at the bottom of a sinkhole just uphill from the main entrance.

Robert and I returned on May 20 and pushed the right-hand passage through the water crawl, two other very tight belly crawls, past some very nice gypsum corn flakes, and to a tight spot leading into a small room. We tried digging into it, but everything was rock, so Robert finally removed his coveralls and was able to squeeze into the room. We

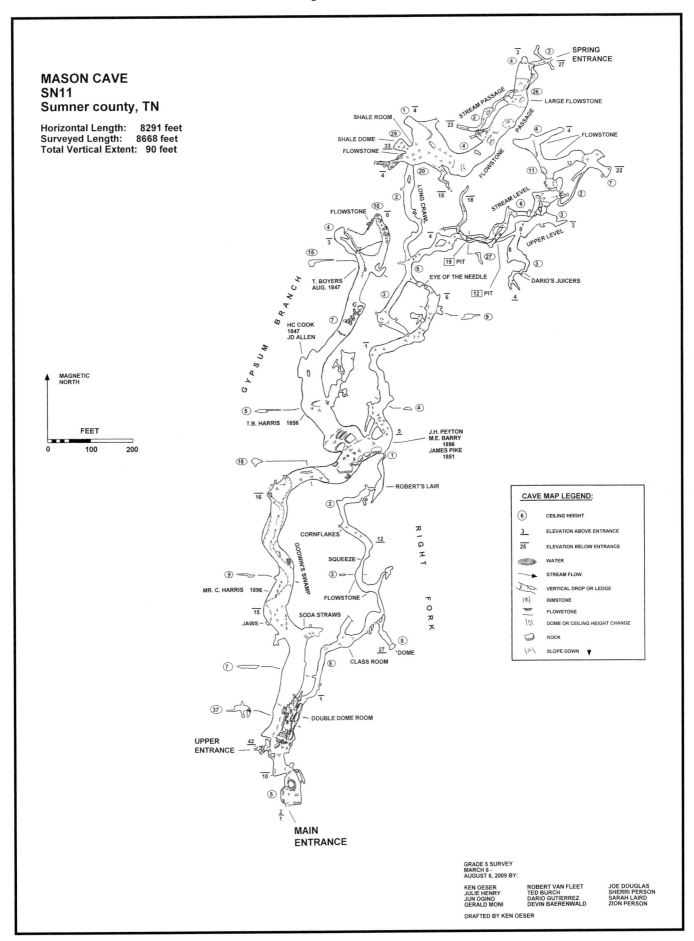

Figure 3.8. Map of Mason Cave by Ken Oeser, 2009.

Figure 3.9. Crystal "cornflakes" in Mason Cave. Photo by Ken Oeser, September 2, 2018. (Above.)

Figure 3.10. Dave Wascher near the Chattanooga Shale ceiling of the Shale Room in Mason Cave. Photo by Ken Oeser, September 2, 2018. (Below.)

decided to name it Roberts Lair, which is 50 feet long and has some formations.

(On) May 31, I took two of my coworkers from Vanderbilt, Dario Gutierrez and Devin Baerenwald, to explore and map some obscure leads. We pushed and mapped the breakdown on the left edge of the Shale Room. Although this is only 150 feet from the end of the Gypsum Passage, we were only able to push through about 50 feet of breakdown, and primarily west rather than south to the other passage. We also mapped upstream from the bottom of the pit/rope climbdown, and then another couple of leads.

Robert and I returned June 6 and finished mapping an upstream passage and a couple of other leads at the back of the cave near the Shale Room and Spring Entrance.

After mapping Gregory Hollow Cave and finding that it runs just under a part of Mason Cave, Robert and I returned to Mason Cave June 10 and 20, even blowing a whistle in hopes of a sound connection,

but with no luck. That afternoon the owner of Mason Cave had the cave mappers up to his cabin for a cookout.

On August 8, Robert, Dario, Sarah Laird, and I returned with a plan. Robert and Dario would attempt a through trip of the right-hand branch, through Roberts Lair, and out to the Junction Room, while Sarah and I went to the Junction Room and waited. I took Sarah for a quick tour of the Gypsum Passage, and as we went I discovered what looked like an alcove was actually a low passage unmapped and perhaps virgin. We returned to the Junction Room, and were able to make voice connection with Robert, but Dario had not been able to squeeze into

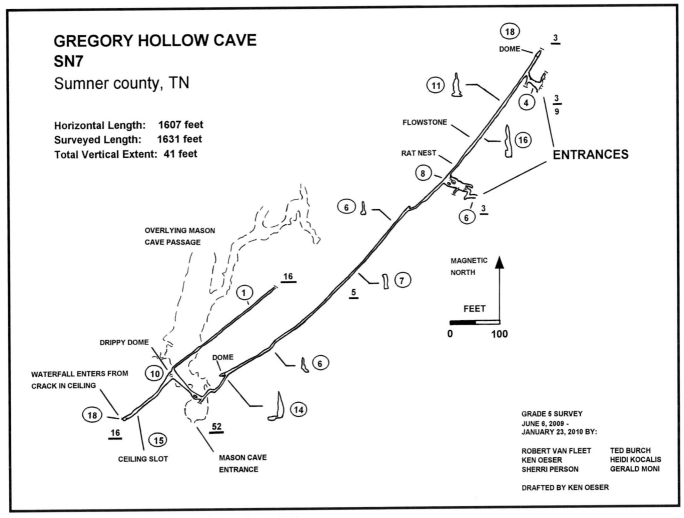

Figure 3.11. Map of Gregory Hollow Cave by Ken Oeser, 2010.

the room. They then headed back and around to where we waited. We then mapped almost 200 feet of new passage with gypsum ceiling.

Thus ended the official survey of Mason Cave, but Robert and Devin returned with me on August 22, November 11, and finally November 17, when Devin and I were able to finish the dig into Roberts Lair from the Junction Room. Heidi helped me map from the entrance of Mason Cave to the entrance of Gregory Hollow Cave, so that I was able to determine that passage near the end of Gregory Hollow Cave goes directly under Mason Cave between the entrance and the Double Dome Room. Robert and I were not able to make any kind of connection, sound or light.[3]

Since Gregory Hollow Cave passes directly beneath Mason Cave, we will discuss it next.

Gregory Hollow Cave

As Ken Oeser noted, the two entrances to Gregory Hollow Cave are located 650- and 800-feet northeast of the entrance to Mason Cave. Gregory Hollow Cave is described by Larry E. Matthews in his book, *Descriptions of Tennessee Caves* (1971):

The southwest (lower) entrance to Gregory Hollow Cave is 2 feet high and 2 feet wide. A crawl extends straight into the hill for 10 feet, turns right for 5 feet, then turns left into a room 40 feet long, 20 feet wide, and 8 feet high. A passage to the southwest was left unchecked. A passage to the northeast is developed along a joint. It ranges in height from 3 to 10 feet and is 3 feet wide. After 250 feet a crawlway leads for 25 feet to the northeast (upper) entrance, which is 7 feet high and 8 feet wide. The main passage continues northeast for 50 feet to a small dome-pit. The passage appears to continue on the other side

3 Ken Oeser, Personal communication, September 23, 2018.

of the dome-pit but was not explored farther. The domepit is only 10 feet deep and 10 feet high.[4]

The Survey of Gregory Hollow Cave

Ken Oeser describes the exploration and survey of Gregory Hollow Cave:

After mapping out a third entrance of Mason Cave in April 2009, and talking to the owner of that entrance, he informed us that he owned another cave, Gregory Hollow Cave. I had looked for this cave in the past but couldn't find anyone who knew where it was located. As it turned out it is in a bluff visible from the highway, although the entrance cannot be seen. With the two entrances to Gregory Hollow Cave in between the Mason Cave entrances, I asked for and was given permission to map the cave.

After finishing some passages in Mason Cave near the Spring Entrance, Robert Van Fleet and I began mapping Gregory Hollow Cave on June 6, 2009. We mapped from one entrance to the other, each entering a passage about 50 feet long that intersects a passage parallel to the bluff. This passage is a narrow canyon 6-8 feet high and 3-4 feet wide for 1,900 feet. We only mapped a few hundred feet of this passage on the first day.

Robert and I returned on June 20 and mapped to a 14-foot dome in the main passage 1,000 feet southwest of the southern entrance. A low, tight crawl 100 feet past this dome was too tight for me to fit through, so Robert continued and dug on another low spot at the end. I went up the hill to Mason Cave and worked my way a short distance into the cave to the Double Dome Room and attempted to make a sound connection with Robert using a whistle. Talking with Robert at a cookout on top of the hill by the thankful owner of Mason Cave, we confirmed that neither of us had heard a sound from the other. We returned again on July 22 and checked all leads in the floor of the main entrance area, Double Dome Room, and right-hand branch of Mason Cave for any leads, but only tiny holes were found that went down, only big enough for a cave rat to fit.

Heidi Kocalis and I mapped from the Mason Cave entrance to the southern Gregory Hollow Cave entrance on August 22, which then allowed me to do an overlay of the cave passages. Finding that the tight spot where I had to stop was under the back of the entrance room, and that the continuing passage that Robert had pushed headed under more Mason Cave passage, we decided to find some way to map the rest of the cave. By January I was able to coax a friend of mine, Ted Burch, importantly slimmer than me, into joining Robert for a mapping trip. The trip was on January 23, 2010 and while I waited in the entrance room, they mapped a passage 100 feet to a drippy dome at a junction with a parallel passage to the main passage. This was mapped northeast 250 feet as a 1-foot high crawl until it became too tight. They were able to continue the other way, under the 10-foot tall dome and map 150 feet southwest to a small waterfall coming from a crack in the ceiling. The mapping was done, with no pushable passage at either end, thereby ending hopes of a connection to Mason Cave. The small waterfall seems to be under the streambed east of the Mason Cave entrance, while the northeast end of the parallel passage heads toward the right-hand fork in Mason Cave. This parallel passage is also shown to be about 16 feet below some holes in the floor of the Mason Cave passage just before the Double Dome Room, so it is very likely that there is a hydrological connection between the caves even if it is too small for human passage.[5]

As you can see from the accompanying map, the passage to the southwest which I did not follow led to most of the cave! (See Figure 3.11)

Cave Access

Mason Cave is located on private property. At the time this book was being written, the current owner of Mason Cave, Mr. Johnnie Godwin, does allow access to his cave, but he requires that you contact him for permission before going to his cave. His email address is johnnieg71@gmail.com. The respect and courtesy that you show to this owner will help in insure this cave stays open for future visitors. Gregory Hollow Cave is also located on private property. Please be sure you have the owner's permission before you enter this cave.

4 Larry E. Matthews, *Descriptions of Tennessee Caves*, TN Division of Geology, Bulletin 69 (1971), pp 93-94.

5 Ken Oeser, Personal communication, September 25, 2018.

CHAPTER 4
Piper Cave

Piper Cave is located in Smith County, Tennessee. It is well-known locally and has been visited by thousands of people over the years.

A 1917 Description of Piper Cave

Thomas L. Bailey's classic report, *Report on the Caves of the Eastern Highland Rim and Cumberland Mountains* (1918), gives the earliest known description of the cave:

No. 3. PIPER CAVE
Location.---A mile west of Monoville on the farm of Jim Phillips, 100 yards south of Phillips' house. The mouth is about a half mile from a public road and easily accessible to the Tennessee Central Railroad at Carthage and the Cumberland River which is only about 2 miles from the cave at places. It occurs in Ordovician limestone about 50 feet above the Cumberland River.

The mouth of the cave is 6 feet high and 8 feet wide and is near the bottom of a small depression in a pasture. There is a rude wooden gate in the mouth.

A little water drips from the roof and forms pools but there is no regular stream in the cave. This cave is very large. It has two large and several smaller forks. The cave forks a quarter mile from the mouth. The northwest fork is the longest. It is definitely known to extend for 2 miles when it narrows to a small hole through which it is necessary to crawl in order to penetrate farther. This fork is said to extend another mile to the bluff of the Cumberland River. The south fork is a mile long and is damper than the northwest fork. In both forks there are numerous old hoppers that were used for making niter during the Civil War times. These are still in a fair state of preservation. Considerable quantities of saltpeter were mined by Jos. Piper who used to live near the entrance of the cave. However, a large amount of earth containing niter apparently still remains and clear crystals of niter can be found between rocks on the floor of the cave. The average thickness of loose earth is 5 or 6 feet though in many places it is as much as 10

Figure 4.1. The entrance to Piper Cave. Photo by Larry E. Matthews, February 22, 1975.

feet. This appears to be one of the best prospects in the State for niter caves. The width of the cave is 35 feet and height 20 feet. There are a few large and beautiful stalagmites in it, but stalactites are rare.[1]

Bailey conducted his field work from July 15 to September 15, 1917, so this visit occurred sometime during that time period. It is interesting to note that he states that the cave was mined during the Civil War.

A 1961 Description of the Cave

Piper Cave is also described by Thomas C. Barr, Jr. in his book, *Caves of Tennessee* (1961):

Piper Cave, well-known to residents of Smith County, received its name from Joseph Piper, who in years past owned the property on which the cave is located and mined saltpeter in the cave. It is a typical Allegheny-pattern cave of rather large dimensions. Many remains of saltpeter hoppers are to be seen in the cave. They are poorly preserved, most of the wood having rotted away because of the high humidity. Most of the vats are V-shaped troughs, although some were apparently barrel-shaped. Speleothems are few, although a beautiful flowstone is developed on the west wall of the north branch, and an interesting series of rimstone pools

1 Thomas L. Bailey, *Report on the Caves of the Eastern Highland Rim and Cumberland Mountains*, TN State Geological Survey, *The Resources of Tennessee*, Vol. 8 (1918), No. 2, pp 124-125.

Figure 4.2. Round saltpeter vats in Piper Cave. Photo by Larry E. Matthews, February 22, 1975.

may be seen at the end of the south branch. These rimstone formations are dry in summer but fill with water during the winter and spring. The cave is notable for the relative ease with which it is possible to negotiate its 2,600 feet of large passages, and there is a well-trodden path throughout.

The entrance, in a collapse sink 100 feet in diameter, is 6 feet high and 12 feet wide. Across the sink, in the south wall, is the mouth of an extension of the cave, described below. Piper Cave averages 25 feet wide and 12 feet high. From the entrance it trends westward for 400 feet to a fork; on the right is a short, muddy crawlway into which surface water pours when it enters the mouth of the cave in wet weather. The main cave makes a sharp bend to the left and continues S. 55° W. for 220 feet to a second fork. The right branch extends northward for 700 feet to a ceiling collapse; a small hole over the breakdown leads into a room 120 feet long. The left branch is 1,200 feet in length, and its direction varies from S. 25° W. to S. 40° W., with a mean azimuth of about S. 35° W. The ceiling of this branch is remarkably smooth and level, and the floor varies

in height according to the amount of broken rock and dirt which covers it.

Piper Cave is inhabited by a variety of animal life. A large colony of bats, predominantly *Myotis griescens*, inhabits the cave during the summer months. The cave is the type locality for a species of blind beetle, *Pseudanophthalmus cumberlandus* Valentine. Across the sink from the main entrance is an extension of the cave (New Piper Cave). The mouth of this section is 4 feet high and 15 feet wide and opens into the side of a large passage which extends east for 300 feet and west for 220 feet. The west branch is comparatively dry, but the east branch contains a wet-weather stream which flows into the mouth of the cave in winter and spring. This stream has trenched a small canyon into the thick silt and gravel fill of the east branch. The cave has rather large cross-sectional dimensions and in places is 35 feet wide and 10 feet high. Isopods, amphipods, spiders, springtails, and millipedes are abundant, most of them deriving their nourishment from the extensive deposits of bat guano.[2]

2 Thomas C. Barr, Jr., *Caves of Tennessee*, TN Division of Geology, Bulletin 64 (1961), pp 424-426.

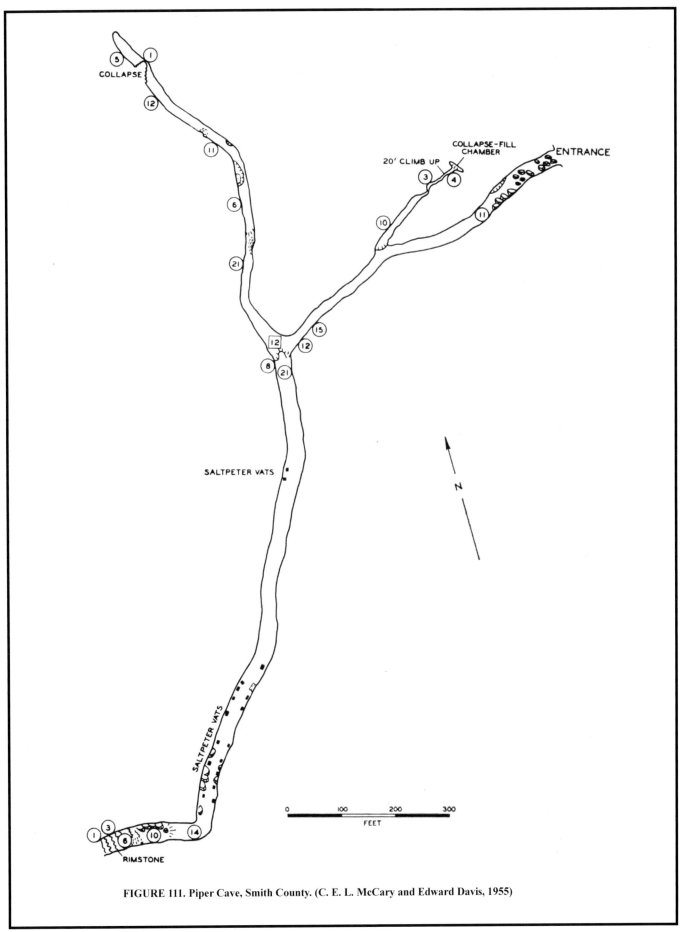

FIGURE 111. Piper Cave, Smith County. (C. E. L. McCary and Edward Davis, 1955)

Figure 4.3. Map of Piper Cave by C. E. L. McCary and Edward Davis, 1955.

Figure 4.4. A double V-shaped saltpeter vat in Piper Cave. Photo by Larry E. Matthews, February 22, 1975.

My First Visit to Piper Cave

My first visit to this cave was on August 12, 1968. I didn't visit this cave again until February 22, 1975. This was a large and well-attended Nashville Grotto Field Trip. By this time I had a camera and took some photographs of the large, bore-hole passages and the saltpeter vats. Several of the photos from that trip are included in this chapter.

The Survey of Piper Cave

Barr's *Caves of Tennessee* (1961) has an excellent map of Piper Cave on page 425. This map was prepared by C. E. L. McCary and Edward Davis in 1955. Like most maps of that era, it does not give the surveyed length of the cave. But a reasonable estimate, based on this map, would be that the cave is approximately 3,000 feet long. (See Figure 4.3.)

Saltpeter Mining in Piper Cave

Piper Cave had one of the largest saltpeter mining operations in Tennessee. Bailey (1918) states that the cave was mined during the Civil War, but it is possible that the cave was also mined during the War of 1812.

The inscription "James Piper Worked this prong in 1863" is written on the wall in black pigment. (See Figure 4.6.)

The map by McCary and Davis (1955) shows the location of sixteen (16) saltpeter vats. It is unknown if these are only the V-shaped saltpeter vats shown on the map. It would require a field visit to make this determination. Two (2) of the vats shown on the map are half way from the entrance to the end of the cave and the other fourteen (14) are located near the southwestern end of the cave. Figure 9 on page 8 of *Descriptions of Tennessee Caves* (1971) has a photograph of two (2) round, barrel-shaped saltpeter vats in Piper Cave with a person in the photo for scale. On the preceding page of this book is the following description:

The remains of round vats have been reported from only one cave. Figure 9 shows the casts of two round vats in Piper Cave, Smith County. It seems likely that these round vats were made by using available barrels. The round vats are all small and would have had the disadvantages of being difficult to build and not holding much cave dirt. The conventional

Figure 4.5. John Andrews next to casts of saltpeter vats. Note the impressions of the wooden boards left on the dirt casts. Photo by Larry E. Matthews, February 22, 1975.

Figure 4.6. "James Piper Worked this prong in 1863" written on the wall of Piper Cave. Photo by Kristen Bobo, January 29, 2012.

Figure 4.7. John Andrews by a large flowstone formation and pool in Piper Cave. Photo by Larry E. Matthews, February 22, 1975.

Figure 4.8. A large trunk passage in Piper Cave. Note the casts of saltpeter vats along the right wall. Photo by Larry E. Matthews, February 22, 1975.

Figure 4.9. John Andrews next to rimstone dams in Piper Cave.Photo by Larry E. Matthews, February 22, 1975.

Figure 4.10. Walker Howell in front of the entrance to New Piper Cave. Photo by Larry E. Matthews, February 22, 1975.

V-shaped vats in the cave probably were built after all the barrels in the vicinity had been used.[3]

It would have been a worthwhile project for someone to re-visit this cave and carefully locate each saltpeter vat, both round and V-shaped, on a map and take photographs of this saltpeter operation. However, as you will read below, this is no longer possible.

Destruction of the Piper Cave Saltpeter Mine

When Kristen Bobo and Cory Holliday went to Piper Cave in 2012 and 2013 to conduct a bat count for the Nature Conservancy, they found that the owner had used a bulldozer to flatten the floor of the cave and in the process had destroyed most, if not all of the saltpeter vats. One photo taken by Kristen Bobo showed dirt pushed to the side of the passage with brown pieces of wood from the former saltpeter vats sticking out. She

Figure 4.11. Old names and dates on the wall of Piper Cave. Photo by Kristen Bobo, January 29, 2012.

believes that all of the Civil War saltpeter vats have now been destroyed.[4]

One has to wonder if the owner of the cave even realized what these relics were and how old they were? If he did, he clearly did not care. Another part of our Civil War heritage has been wantonly destroyed.

3 Larry E. Matthews, *Descriptions of Tennessee Caves*, TN Division of Geology, Bulletin 69 (1971), p. 8.

4 Kristen Bobo, Personal communication, October 3, 2018.

Figure 4.12. Erica Sughrue rappels into the entrance of Reynolds Pit. Photo by Bob Biddix, June 11, 2018.

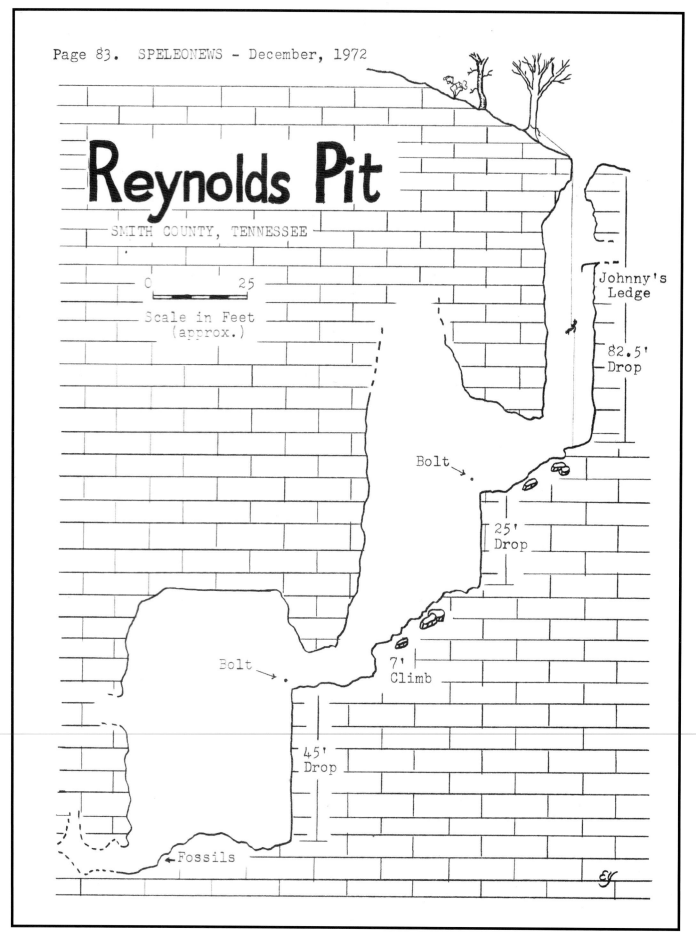

Page 83. SPELEONEWS - December, 1972

Reynolds Pit

SMITH COUNTY, TENNESSEE

0   25

Scale in Feet
(approx.)

Johnny's Ledge

82.5' Drop

Bolt →

25' Drop

Bolt →

7' Climb

45' Drop

← Fossils

Figure 4.13. Profile drawing of Reynolds Pit by Ed Yarbrough, 1972.

Figure 4.14. Keith Filson on rope in Reynolds Pit. Photo by Bob Biddix, June 7, 2018.

Figure 4.15. Erica Sughrue by formations and pool in Lancaster Cave #2. Photo by Bob Biddix, January 3, 2015.

Reynolds Pit

Reynolds Pit is a deep, interesting pit also located close to Carthage in Smith County. It was first explored by Ed Yarbrough in 1972. Ed gives the following report of that trip:

"Twas the day after Christmas when Alan Lenk and I returned to Nashville from a trip to Cumberland Caverns, the pit in Ben White Cave, and other delights. As I walked in the door Judy told me that Jimmy Hiett, an old friend from high school days, had called about a "three-hundred-foot pit at Carthage." Hmmm.

This may be the age of miracles, but I was still a bit skeptical as Jimmy told me about the hole his brother Johnny and their family had found during a Yuletide hike in Carthage, Tennessee. He reported that Johnny had descended thirty feet to a ledge and saw no bottom. Rocks seemed to bounce down the shaft for a long time, hence the modest 300-foot estimate. Next day Jimmy, Alan, and I were on I-40 with rope in the trunk and gleams in our eyes.

The pit was on the property of Ed Reynolds, actually within the corporate limits of Carthage. The opening was about four feet by six feet and did indeed go "straight down." Still the incurable skeptic, I only put 150 feet of rope in the hole and started down. I passed the ledge Jimmy had mentioned and found the floor 82.5 feet below the surface. But there was a slope.

Loose breakdown and bones formed the steep slope that led to a twenty-five foot drop some fifteen feet below the bottom of the first pitch. I remained on the rope and did this drop only to find another slope and short drop beyond. By then I was running short of rope, so I got off and called for Alan. He soon joined me on the slopes and stayed on rappel to do the seven foot (climbable) drop beyond me.

Figure 4.16. Erica Sughrue by draperies and a large stalagmite in Lancaster Cave #2. Photo by Bob Biddix, January 8, 2015.

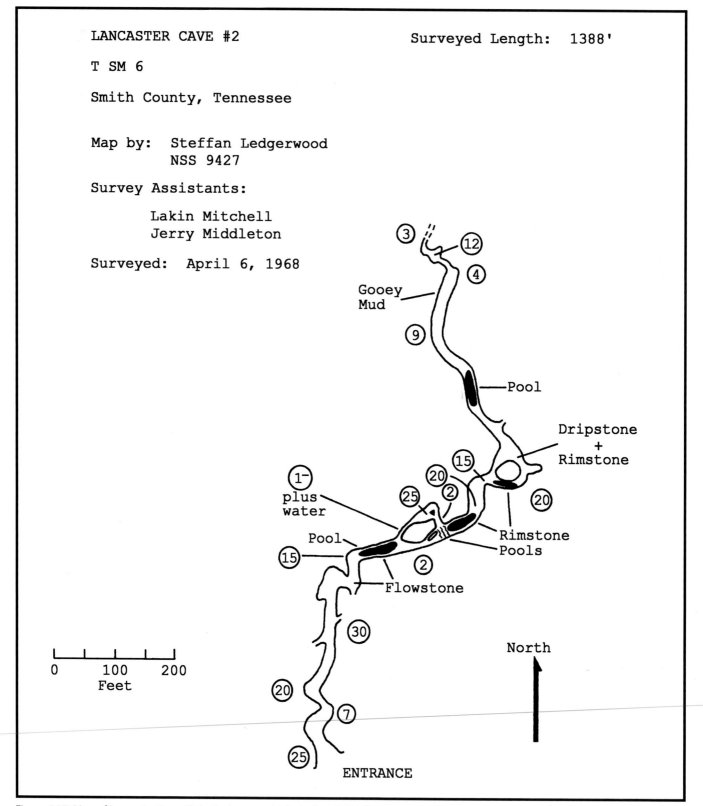

LANCASTER CAVE #2   Surveyed Length: 1388'

T SM 6

Smith County, Tennessee

Map by: Steffan Ledgerwood
         NSS 9427

Survey Assistants:

     Lakin Mitchell
     Jerry Middleton

Surveyed: April 6, 1968

Gooey Mud

Pool

Dripstone + Rimstone

1- plus water

Pool

Rimstone Pools

Flowstone

North

0   100   200
     Feet

ENTRANCE

Figure 4.17. Map of Lancaster Cave #2, by Ledgerwood, Mitchell and Middleton, 1968.

As I was going down the climb he went ahead and found another drop.

This is where those of little faith had to go back up and re-tie the rope. I clipped on the Jumars and climbed out of the pit, amid some grumbling.

("Smith County pits aren't *supposed* to require more than 150 feet of rope.") Jimmy was elated to hear that we were still going down. He had built a nice fire and waited patiently as I again disappeared over the rim of the pit.

Figure 4.18. Mark Hobbs in a well-decorated passage in Lancaster Cave #2. Photo by Bob Biddix, April 14, 2015.

The final drop proved to be 45 feet deep and somewhat wet. We explored a short passage at the bottom and then began the ascent. The total depth of the cave was put at about 200 feet, something of a record for Carthage!

Three days later I returned to the pit with Harry White, Buzz Rackley, and David Stidham (who lives only a quarter mile away from it). We installed bolts above the 25- and 45-foot drops and measured them with tape. No new leads were found. Reynolds Pit is located on a prominent hill northeast of the SmithCounty Courthouse at an elevation of 860 feet.[5]

Reynold's Pit is a nice find that is still enjoyed by cavers today.

The Lancaster Caves

Also located in Smith County, near the community of Buffalo Valley, are four (4) interesting caves known as the Lancaster Caves. The entrances are located alongside the road. These caves are described in Larry E. Matthews' 1971 book *Descriptions of Tennessee Caves:*[6]

Lancaster Cave #1

The entrance is 6 feet high and 4 feet wide. The cave averages 20 feet high and 1 to 3 feet wide for about 100 feet. At this point a larger passage is intersected, which extends both left and right. To the right the cave averages 8 feet wide and 15 feet high for 200 feet and ends in a flowstone block. Several attractive formations were noted. There are several short loop passages in this branch. To the left, the cave averages 8 feet wide and 25 feet high for 150 feet and ends in a flowstone block. Several attractive formations also were noted in this section.

Lancaster Cave #2

The entrance is 10 feet high and 15 feet wide. The cave consists primarily of a single passage 800 feet long,

5 Ed Yarbrough, "Reynolds Pit," *Speleonews*, v. 16 (1972), no. 6, pp 82-83.

6 Larry E. Matthews, *Descriptions of Tennessee Caves*, TN Division of Geology, Bulletin 69 (1971), pp 85, 87-91.

Figure 4.19. Erica Sughrue (front) and Mark Hobbs (rear) in a passage in Lancaster Cave #2 Photo by Bob Biddix, January 4, 2015.

which averages 15 feet wide and 15 feet high. Although there is no cave stream, there are several deep pools of water which must be crossed, and areas with deep mud on the floor. Several large and massive formations were observed. A shield formation almost 4 feet in diameter was noted, but vandals had broken off many of the draperies that once hung from it.

Lancaster Cave #3

The front of this cave is a rock shelter 10 feet high, 30 feet wide, and 15 feet deep. From the back of the rock shelter a crawlway extends into the hill for 30 feet before ending.

Lancaster Cave #4

The entrance is at the back of a rock shelter 10 feet high and 20 feet wide. It is 4 feet wide and 5 feet high. The passage slopes steeply downward for 25 feet into an entrance room 40 feet high, 20 feet wide, and 100 feet long. The cave continues for 100 feet past the entrance room, and gradually lowers until it ends in mud fill. One side passage 65 feet long was noted.

As can be seen from the accompanying photographs by Bob Biddix, these caves contain some very attractive formations. Since you can park on the side of the road at the entrances to these caves, they make an interesting and easy group of caves to visit.

Cave Access

Access to these caves varies from year-to-year. Sometimes they are open and sometimes they are closed. Before you go into these caves be sure that they are open and that you have the owner's permission.

CHAPTER 5
Ruskin Cave

Ruskin Cave is located in Dickson County, Tennessee. It is well-known locally and has a long and fascinating history. It has a mapped length of 1.3 miles. It has also been known as the Great Cave of Yellow Creek.

Early History

With its huge mouth, Ruskin Cave must have been known to the prehistoric inhabitants of the area. The large, inviting entrance was probably used as a campsite, especially in very hot or very cold weather. When Caucasian settlers moved into the area in the late 1700s, they too would have been drawn to such a conspicuous and useful site. The stream flowing from the cave entrance was used to power a large mill.

The Ruskin Colony

The Ruskin Colony was located in Tennessee City from 1894 to 1896. It was a utopian socialist colony that was named for John Ruskin, an English socialist writer. There was a fee of $500 to become a member of the Colony. In 1896 they purchased the Ruskin Cave property which included over 800 acres of land, including the settlement of Cave Mills, Ruskin Cave, Pickett Cave, and the Stalactite Cave.

A huge three-story central building called the Commonwealth House was built to house "The Coming Nation" newspaper which was produced by the Colony. The first floor of this building housed the print shop, press room, stock room, and offices. The second floor housed the mailing rooms, editorial rooms, a barber shop, living quarters, a great room, and a library. The third floor housed the Auditorium and the Dining Hall for the Colony's 700 members.

There was already a grist mill on the property (Cave Mills) when it was purchased by the Colony. They built a steam plant next to the central building to provide heat. A water reservoir was built on the hillside above the cave to provide gravity fed water to each home in the Colony.

Like many such ventures into utopian living, they had a variety of enterprises to produce income, including a

Figure 5.1. Photo of a large mill in front of the Ruskin Cave entrance. About 1894.

Figure 5.2. Ruskin Cave Cannery, 1896. Provided by Joseph C. Douglas.

chewing gum factory, a photo gallery, a steam laundry, a machine shop, a café, a bakery, a school, a sawmill, a cotton gin, a blacksmith shop, a wagon shop, a suspender and clothing factory, a plant to produce a cure-all medicine called "Ruskin Ready Remedy," a print shop, a coffee plant, and a canning plant which was set up inside the Ruskin Cave entrance.

The newspaper, "The Coming Nation," was owned and edited by Julius Augustus Wayland, the founder of the Colony. At one point this newspaper had over

60,000 subscribers. The newspaper was used both to promote the Editor's socialist philosophy, to raise money, and to advertise the products made and sold by the Colony. Apparently, the "magical" waters of Ruskin Cave spring were touted as the key ingredient of "Ruskin Ready Remedy," but most cure-alls of the day were high in opium and alcohol, and sometimes cocaine. Yes, you really did feel much better, really fast !!!

The "coffee" plant was also unusual. The product they manufactured and sold was known as Ruskin Cereal Coffee. It was made from toasted grain and contained no coffee at all.

Apparently the "religion" of the Ruskinites was their belief that socialism was the solution to all the world's problems. The colony had no church and only a few members attended the nearby Methodist church.

A website called "The History of The Ruskin" provides the following fascinating information:

> Despite all of its financial success, the end of the Ruskin Colony came swiftly. Heated disputes continued to occur over various issues until the group felt that it could no longer continue. Among the issues of dispute by the colonists were religion, education, the running of "The Coming Nation," the advocacy of "free love," feminism, and differing views on the nature of socialism. The end came in 1899 with remaining members moving to Ware County, Georgia. They merged with another group from Dayton, Ohio and renamed the combined colony the Ruskin Commonwealth.

It was a short-lived, but fascinating episode in the history of Ruskin Cave.

Ruskin Cave College

Open from 1904-1918, the full name was the Ruskin Cave College Preparatory School. The cave entrance provided the auditorium for the school. In those days, few students in rural areas attended school past what we today call elementary school. This "college preparatory school" would be somewhat equivalent to the modern high school.

The founder of the school was Reverend R. E. Smith. He limited the enrollment to 200 students and required military training. The school was coeducation, which was unusual in those days. The classes focused on musical education, both instrumental and vocal, and

RUSKIN CAVE
DICKSON, TENNESSEE
(615) 763-9141 OR (615) 383-2887

Figure 5.3. An old commercial cave brochure for Ruskin Cave from the collection of Gary K. Soule, circa 1960s.

there were also classes on literature and religion. Many of the faculty left during World War I to serve in the military and many of the students were drafted, which forced the school to close in 1918.

Figure 5.4. The entrance of Ruskin Cave. Chrys Hulbert is on the left and Annette Oeser is on the right. Gary and Misty Chambers are behind the rear of the car. Photo by Ken Oeser, October 30, 1999

The school reopened in September 1922 when Professor Luther A. Dickson and George Tubb Cooksey, Sr. purchased the property from Colonel R. J. Kelley for $10,000. The new school had all twelve (12) grades and students from Dickson, Houston, and Montgomery Counties were in attendance. Professor Dickson died on May 3, 1922, but the school remained open for two more years. After the closing of the school Mrs. Julia Dickson began operating the Ruskin property as a resort.

Mrs. Dickson died December 8, 1926, leaving her property to her daughter, Gladys, who was then a junior in college at Asbury in Wilmore, Kentucky. Gladys ran the property for twelve years. In 1932 Gladys married John O. Hunt, a former Ruskin Cave College student and six years later (1938); they sold the property to Lucy Meriwether of Clarksville, TN.

The Ruskin Cave Development Company, Inc. was formed by Mrs. Meriwether. They made numerous improvements to the property while operating it until 1941. Mrs. Meriwether moved dirt from in front of the cave and leveled the floor with concrete. She also built the swimming pool across from the cave, refurbished

the college building into a hotel, and installed a water wheel in front of the cave. A road was built to circle the outside of Ruskin near the rock wall bordering Yellow Creek to avoid having to drive directly past the college building. The Grand Opening of the Ruskin Resort was held on June 30, 1938 and lasted for four days. In all likelihood, Mrs. Meriwether was greatly influenced by the operation of Dunbar Cave in Clarksville, TN where she was from.

Ruskin Cave was advertised as the world's largest underground ballroom. There was a swimming pool, picnic areas, bowling, baseball, softball, tennis, croquet, badminton, shuffle board, and many other activities for the guests. The enterprise was never particularly successful, probably due to its remote location as much as anything else.

The property continued to be a resort for many years, changing hands frequently, until it was leased by the Jackson Foundation in 1999. Since that time, the cave and property have been closed to the public.[1]

1 Much of the above information is from a website about the history of Ruskin Cave.

Barr's Description of the Cave

Ruskin Cave is described by Thomas C. Barr, Jr., in his book, *Caves of Tennessee* (1961):

> Ruskin Cave has long been a landmark on Yellow Creek and for many years was the site of Ruskin Cave College. Since the closing of the college, the cave has been used from time to time as a recreational area. The entrance is floored in concrete, and behind the concrete is a large siphon pool 50 feet in diameter. Beyond the pool, which is more than 60 feet deep, no artificial improvement has been made.
>
> The entrance, which is 60 feet wide and 30 feet high, is at the base of an impressive limestone bluff more than 100 feet high. The cave runs north for 510 feet, then northwest for 360 feet to a low crawlway which is usually filled with water. The crawlway reportedly is about 80 feet long, but beyond it the cave is said to be much larger and to extend for nearly half a mile. Although the cave is large at the entrance, a short distance inward it narrows to 4 or 5 feet high and about 15 feet wide.[2]

Perhaps the most prominent feature of Ruskin Cave is its large, scenic entrance.

My First Visit to Ruskin Cave

I first visited Ruskin Cave in the summer of 1968 on the same day that I took the commercial tour of nearby Jewel Cave. I was impressed by the many historical buildings and the fascinating history of the place but did not put much faith in the "rumors" that the cave extended past the flooded crawlway.

Ken Oeser's First Cave

Ruskin Cave was the first cave visited by veteran cave explorer Ken Oeser. He describes his family's trip to the cave:

> It was 1968, when I was only six years old. My family camped sometimes on weekends, and we happened to go to Ruskin Cave and campground that year. It was a nice place with plenty of things to do: searching for minnows, turtles, and crayfish in Yellow Creek, playing in the swimming pool, fishing for trout with my dad, and hanging around the huge

2 Thomas C. Barr, Jr., *Caves of Tennessee*, TN Division of Geology, Bulletin 64 (1961), p. 180.

Figure 5.5. Annette Oeser in the Dome Room of Ruskin Cave. Photo by Ken Oeser, October 30, 1999.

cave entrance at night when the stage in the cave was crowded with square dancers. I even did the Hokey Pokey once or twice myself. I remember some bats flying around over the bleachers and stage at night. I also remember the *bottomless* pool just beyond the stage, but the cave passage beyond was only a mystery. This was the first cave I had ever been in, and the darkness of the passage seemed scary to a small kid like me. The huge building that was the centerpiece of Ruskin Cave College and the Ruskin Colony was dominant on the grounds. Some historical pictures were in an exhibit close to the building.

We returned several times during 1969 and 1970. The cave was the center of activity, visible from practically anywhere in the campground, which stretched all over the field and along the stone wall beside the creek. Special events, highlighted by mule

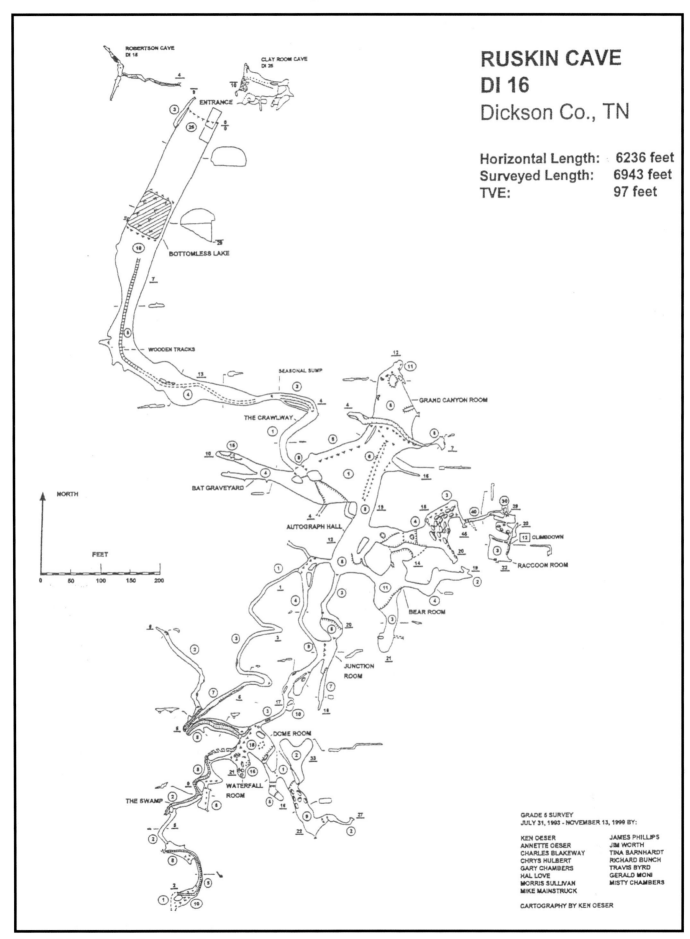

Figure 5.6. Map of Ruskin Cave by Ken Oeser, 1999.

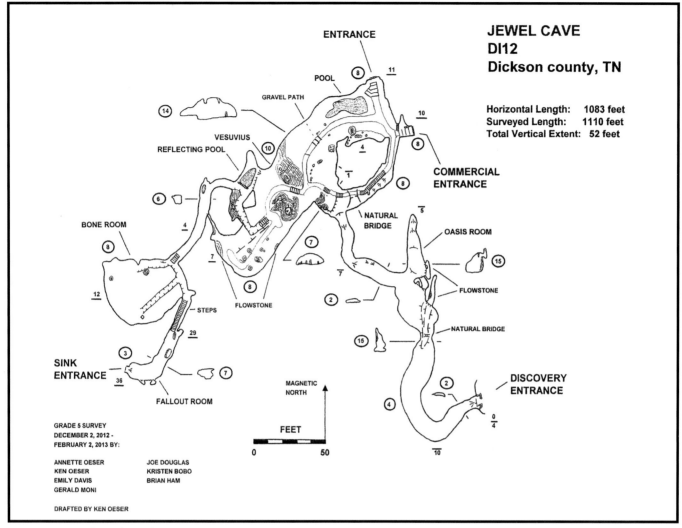

Figure 5.7. Map of Jewel Cave by Ken Oeser, 2013.

pulls, were held on holiday weekends, and square dances were held every weekend. Although I went in the cave several times, I was not interested in the cave or its unknown passages. My interest in caves began in 1986, and the next year I joined the Nashville Grotto. Ruskin Cave was just another part of my past.

This reminds me so much of my visits to Dunbar Cave in Clarksville, TN when I was Ken's age. Like Ruskin Cave, Dunbar Cave also had a swimming pool, fishing, music, and dancing. Ah, those are happy childhood memories.

The Reopening of Ruskin Cave and Jewel Cave

Caver Ken Oeser tells the following story of the reopening of Ruskin Cave and Jewel Cave to the public in 1993. This had been the first cave that Ken had ever visited, back in 1968 with his family.

In the spring of 1993, Ned Littell called and told me that some new people had bought the Ruskin Cave property and would like some cavers to come tour the grounds with them. This sparked my interest as images and memories of the cave came to mind. I volunteered to get a group together to meet the new owners and began to scour the Tennessee Cave Survey printout for all of the caves in the close vicinity of Ruskin Cave. John Donegan, Richard Bunch, Elyse Muench, Annette Oeser, and I met Tom Thacker, Jr. (son of the new owner) and a relative on the Ruskin property on April 24.

We made introductions, and then began to visit the caves on the property. First was Ruskin Cave because it was the largest. We went past the "bottomless" pool and followed the passage about 750 feet to a sumped crawlway. The passage gradually gets smaller from the 30 feet high by 60-foot-wide entrance area, but it is still a stoopway

Gift Shop and Entrance, Jewel Cave, Tenn.

Figure 5.8. A postcard from the collection of Gary K. Soule showing the Gift Shop and entrance to Jewel Cave.

Mr. Thomas Rodgers and his Daughter Fanny, Discoverers of Jewel Cave in Tennessee

Figure 5.9. A postcard from the collection of Gary K. Soule showing Mr. Thomas Rodgers and his Daughter Fanny, the discoverers of Jewel Cave, Tennessee.

and walkway all the way to the sump. The striking thing about this part of the cave is all of the historic signatures, many of them dating to the 1800s. We afterwards visited Robertson Cave and Clay Room Cave (immediately on each side of the Ruskin Cave entrance), Cooks Cave, Billy Goat Cave, formerly commercial Jewel Cave, and lastly Hunt Cave, which has about a 30-foot entrance pit. It was a busy day with many caves, but the most interesting feature was the sumped crawlway. I didn't even remember the Robertson or Clay Room Cave entrances on the side of Ruskin Cave. The owners were thankful for our visit and invited the Nashville Grotto to have a picnic on the Ruskin property that summer. We

Figure 5.10. A page from a Jewel Cave brochure in the collection of Gary K. Soule showing the Jewel Cave Ticket Office and a scene with steps inside the cave.

also volunteered to survey the caves starting that summer. This would give me the opportunity to fully explore my *first* cave.

That summer the owners began working on the property for commercialization. The grand opening for "The Great Caves" was on July 4th weekend, with the opening of the swimming pool, music in the cave, and the snack bar at the mouth of the cave was opened. The Jewel Cave building was refurbished and tours were led through the short, very decorated cave. T-shirts were sold advertising "The Great Caves," with a picture of the mouth of Ruskin Cave on the front. Camping was allowed on a level area at the front of the property. Square dances, musical competitions, and other activities were held on the stage inside Ruskin Cave on other weekends that summer. The property was beginning to resemble the times when I first visited the property in 1968.

During the grand opening weekend, Terry Barnes, a Nashville Grotto member with cave diving experience, donned scuba gear and dove with a friend into the unknown depths of the "bottomless" pool. Many stories had been told of the pool, such as an anvil dropped on a rope and never touching bottom, and other similar stories. Many curious onlookers were present when Terry dove, and all were amazed that the depth was only 25-30 feet deep. Terry found that the pool is only 3-4 feet deep on the west side, but slopes down steeply to a depth of 30 feet on the east side, just below the concrete walkway. He also went into an underwater passage at the southwest corner of the pool, finding that a slight current was coming from this passage into the pool. He saw about 75-100 feet of passage that continued, but the silt stirred from the bottom caused very limited vision, forcing him to turn around. Old rumors never seem to die, however. In 1996 when Terry helped survey the back of the cave, one of the overseers of the property stated that he had held the rope for the divers back in 1993, and that the divers went over 100 feet down and found a strong current at the bottom. He adamantly stated that he and the other overseer had struggled with the rope to help the divers back to the surface. Terry finally convinced him that he was the diver; the misconception was apparently from Terry venturing into the side passage with a small amount of current. Time and memory had worked together to bring back the other "facts" about the bottomless pool.[3]

Ken and other members of the Nashville Grotto would return soon to begin the survey of Ruskin Cave.

3 Ken Oeser, "My First Cave," *Tennessee Caver*, v. 2 (2001), no. 2, pp 4-12.

The Survey of Ruskin Cave

Ruskin Cave was surveyed from July 31, 1993 to November 13, 1999 by fifteen (15) different surveyors. The final map was drafted by Ken Oeser. The surveyed length of the cave is 6,943 feet or 1.3 miles with a total vertical extent of 97 feet. Ken Oeser describes these survey trips:

At the Nashville Grotto picnic that summer, we walked along the creek bank, were allowed access to the pool, and wandered the grounds. After lunch, we surveyed Ruskin Cave to the sumped crawlway. Newcomers to the cave were impressed with the size of the entrance and passage beyond. Hal Love led the survey team, with Lisa Cummings, Charles Blakeway, Mike Mainstruck, Chuck Mangelsdorf, Annette Oeser, and I assisting. The weather had been dry, but the crawlway was still totally sumped.

We returned in October to survey Robertson and Clay Room Caves, the two short caves on each side of the Ruskin entrance. After we finished, we walked to the end of Ruskin Cave to check the crawlway, finding it totally dry! I was first to crawl into the passage, eager to see where it went. After about 200 feet, mostly belly-crawl, the passage opened into a room where I could stand. I quickly looked around and found that passages went three or four directions, then turned and went back through the crawlway to let the others know about the cave beyond. We then proceeded to survey through the crawlway, and then headed home. I called the owner's son and let him know of the open crawlway. He wanted us to wait until he could visit from California and get his dad to meet us at the cave, and then all tour the cave together.

We returned on January 15, 1994 and met Tom Thacker Sr. (the owner) and his son Tom Jr. The high that day was a chilly 8° F, and the wind was blowing strongly out of the crawlway. The tightness of the crawlway was intimidating to the Thackers, and they were glad to see that the cave opened back up after 200 feet. We explored much of the back part of the cave. Highlights were the Grand Canyon Room (named for the 4-foot-deep and 6-foot-wide trench that crosses the room), Autograph Hall with many old names and dates on the ceiling (roots hanging down the middle of one), a water passage

leading off in one direction, and a breakdown passage lead on the other side. The owners were impressed with the back portion of the cave but did not enjoy the crawlway on the way out of the cave. We had another survey trip in the back part of Ruskin that month but found the crawlway sumped when we returned on my birthday (February 8). We therefore surveyed Cooks Cave at the front of the Ruskin property instead. The sump did not reopen that winter due to more rain. It was a productive winter, with 4 survey/exploration trips into the back of the cave.

In July of 1994, the Nashville Grotto again had a picnic on the grounds. Several new faces were at this picnic; about 20 Nashville Grotto members and family were present. The pool was open, and a free tour of Jewel Cave was offered for those interested. Annette visited Ruskin Cave on November 29 and found the crawlway open and dry. On December 8 we surveyed the Grand Canyon Room and some small side passages in the area, then surveyed to the first part of the water passage at the back of the cave. The water in this passage is 3-4 feet deep, with 6 inches of mud on the bottom, making travel interesting. One blind fish was noted on this trip through the water passage. A return trip on New Year's Eve found the crawlway sumped, so only one survey trip to the back was achieved in the winter season of 1994/1995.

In 1995 we began checking the sump in September, but it was full of water until early December. To fill time we wrote down names and dates from the 1800s and early 1900s in the passage before the sump. On December 16, two survey teams made it to the back of the cave, split up, and finished all but two passages at the end of the water passage, and the ends of the two upper breakdown passages. We returned on January 13, 1996 only to find the crawlway sumped again. Another disappointing winter with only one survey day, but it was a productive one.

We were on the watch for falling water again in the fall of 1996 and found the sump open on October 4. We hoped to finish mapping the cave that winter and began surveying at the end of the month. On one survey/name recording trip, we looked for eyeless cave beetles and Terry Barnes caught one

Hanging Drapery, Jewel Cave, Tenn.

Hanging Gardens of Babylon, Jewel Cave, Tenn.

Figure 5.11. A postcard from the collection of Gary K. Soule showing a woman standing next to the Hanging Drapery in Jewel Cave.

Figure 5.12. A postcard from the collection of Gary K. Soule showing the Hanging Gardens of Babylon in Jewel Cave.

on some rocks in the Waterfall Room. We passed the one-mile mark of surveyed cave passage in November. We also began writing down names and dates from the back part of the cave. Many names were traced to the commune days of the late 1800s, but most were from the Ruskin Cave College days from 1904-1918. Some large claw marks were found on one mud wall; probably bear claw marks due to the size and similarity to those in other caves. A lead was found by Gary Chambers at the end of the first breakdown passage. A small hole opened to a low room with many raccoon tracks, and a climb-down led to three joint passages. Annette and I returned on December 7 to survey these passages and one last dead-end passage just off the main route, only to find the crawlway sumped! Instead we wrote down more names and dates from the front passage, then surveyed from the Ruskin Cave entrance to the large bluffs along Yellow Creek about 750 feet to the southeast. The cave plot showed that the new lead and rooms were headed directly for these bluffs, only about 200 feet away. The sump never reopened that winter, but we had passed the milestone and gathered many names, dates, and photographs from the back of the cave. Gathering historical data from the cave had come at the cost of not finishing the survey that winter. We had three successful trips to the back of the cave that winter, which was more than the last two winters, combined.

In the fall of 1997, Annette and I checked the crawlway a couple of times, but there was only about 3 inches of airspace at the end of October.

Mt. Vesuvius, Formed in Onyx, Jewel Cave, Tenn.

Figure 5.13. A postcard from the collection of Gary K. Soule showing "Mt. Vesuvius Formed in Onyx" in Jewel Cave.

The property sold that November, and heavy rains set in for November and December. We knew from previous years and rain patterns not to bother checking the sump again that year.

In 1998 Annette headed out to the Ruskin property armed with our incomplete map to see if she could find the new owners, show them our map, and gain access to finish our survey of the cave. She found that there was a large gate and tall, sturdy fence guarding the property. The area was now an exotic animal viewing farm, with camels, musk ox, llamas, African cattle, exotic goats, and many trout in the cave pool for a pay fishing operation. The caretaker was impressed with the map and gave permission for us to visit the cave. There was another problem; however, it was rainy in November

and December. Annette checked the crawlway a couple of times, and the caretakers were watching the sump also, but it never opened that winter. This was now two years in a row that the crawlway had remained sumped.

In October 1999 Annette visited the Ruskin property and found that it was soon to be leased by the Jackson Foundation, a group of people running the Renaissance Center in Dickson. She talked to Doug Jackson, the president of the Jackson Foundation, and got permission for us to finish mapping the cave when the water level went down. On October 27, a weeknight, Annette visited the property and found the crawlway open, so she went through and checked the upstream portion of the water passage (based on my hunch) and found the water continuing in that direction. To avoid another one trip winter, we organized a survey trip for that weekend. On October 30 Chrys Hulbert, Gerald Moni, Gary and Misty Chambers, Annette, and I finished surveying Gary's Chamber and a dry passage in the back of the cave. In the dry passage I found a roll of film I had lost on the last trip of 1996, when I had first discovered the passage. The upstream passage was explored to a room, but not surveyed due to time limitations. Only 298 feet were surveyed, but now we were down to only one lead left that would require wetsuits.

Morris Sullivan, Annette, and I returned two weeks later on November 13. Doug Jackson decided to meet us at the cave and go to the back with us, being interested in the history of the cave. Morris had to give Doug a push to get him through the last part of the crawl, and he was glad to get to the larger passages in the back. While Doug checked the passages with a metal detector, Morris, Annette, and I surveyed up the water passage. I couldn't believe we missed this stoopway lead years before. After the initial standing room, the passage soon became a low swamp, with slick mud sloping down into the water. Gravity pulled us toward the deep water, but we were determined not to drown. An upper crawl was found bypassing a sump. This was followed to a continuation of the stream passage, which was stooping to walking height for a couple of hundred feet to a low mud crawl. This crawl is too low for passage but could possibly be dug for

Figure 5.14. W.E. Lawson, Ed Yarbrough, and Bob Laird in Jewel Cave. Photo by Standiford R. (Tank) Gorin, 1960.

further exploration. A possible bypass was checked but connected into the too low stream passage about 20 feet past the other low spot. The survey was finally complete, with another 477 feet added. On the way out, we found Doug stuck in the first part of the crawlway (the tightest spot). He couldn't move because the mud was so slick he couldn't get any traction. Morris slid into the crawl and pushed on his boots to get him started, and he made it the rest of the way with no problem. Doug said he had been there for a while; he had decided to crawl out and wait for us rather than waiting for us inside the cave.

Annette and I returned with Troy Fox on December 4, to check for names in the back portion of the cave one last time, and to take more photos of the names. We found several new names, some carved on blocks of mud. These were dated from the colony and the college days. Some mud figures were also found in Autograph Hall with college names under them; these figures had been seen several times before, but we had never noticed the names,

thinking they were recent. Annette and I returned on January 2, 2000 and finished the name survey of the cave, checking the rest of the back of the cave for names, photographing most of them.

Since Doug was leasing the Hunt property next to Ruskin, we obtained permission to survey Hunt Cave also. On December 31, 1999, Brian Wilson, Troy Fox, and I surveyed a large loop in Hunt Cave, and noted several names from the late 1800s to the present. Also noted were several names from the Ruskin Cave College days (1904-1918) seen in Ruskin Cave. Near the back we also found a small group of names including Gladys Dickson, dated September 5, 1918. She later married Mr. Hunt, who became the owner of the Ruskin, Hunt, and Jewel Cave properties. I returned with Brian and Jason Moore on June 25, 2000 to finish surveying the cave. A couple of loop passages were found and mapped, and then we recorded and photographed many of the names found in the cave.

We obtained permission from Doug Jackson to visit re-commercialized Jewel Cave. On January 22,

Figure 5.15. Gerald Moni next to attractive flowstone formations in Jewel Cave. Photo by Ken Oeser, December, 2012.

2000, Annette, Alexandra, and I explored Discovery Pass in Jewel Cave to the second, original entrance. We discovered some small, gray fish that look similar to blind cave fish in a small pool in this passage. Tom Barr had mentioned them in Jewel Cave in his book *Caves of Tennessee*. There were no names in the Discovery Passage, but there were many in the tourist section of the cave. Most are now too faded to read, but some could be made out with dates as old as the Ruskin Cave College days.

Over 7 winters, we had 26 people involved in 14 trips mapping and recording historic names in Ruskin, Cooks, Robertson, Clay Room, and Hunt Caves. Jewel Cave is the only cave left on the property to be mapped and will have to wait until a dry summer or fall for the Discovery Passage to dry out. The Ruskin crawlway sump was the big factor in the project. It didn't dry out for two consecutive winters and was open only a month during two other years. The earliest month the sump was found open was October (3 out of 7 years), as early as October

4 in 1996, while the latest the sump was found to open was December 9, 1995. The sump closed by December 7 in 1996, and as late as by February 8 in 1994. The longest the sump was open was about 3 months from late October 1993 until early February 1994. That year gave us false confidence that the crawlway remained open for a few months every winter, which we found was wrong over the next six years. It was a neat experience exploring the cave I had first entered 25 years before as a child, finding the many old names and dates in the caves on the property, surveying the cave, finding virgin passages, blind fish, a blind beetle, bear claw marks, and gaining experience cave mapping over 7 years.[4]

Thanks to Ken Oeser and his crew, we have a wonderful map of Ruskin Cave and an inventory of the historical names and dates in the cave.

---

4 Ibid.

Figure 5.16. Gerald Moni standing under the Natural Bridge in Jewel Cave. Photo by Ken Oeser, December, 2012.

Jewel Cave

The entrance to Jewel Cave is located one mile north of Ruskin Cave on Yellow Creek Road. Barr gives the following description of the cave:

> Jewel Cave, "The Stalactite Cave," is the smallest, yet in many respects one of the most beautiful, of Tennessee's commercial caves. It consists mainly of two rooms connected by a short artificial tunnel. The cave was discovered in 1885 by the daughters of Thomas Rogers, who crawled up through a spring into the part of the cave now known as Discovery Pass.
>
> Two artificial entrances have been developed. The whole cave is electrically lighted and has gravel walks throughout. The larger of the two rooms is profusely decorated with stalactites, stalagmites, columns, flowstone, and terrace formations. Much of the dripstone is pure white, but most has been delicately tinted by mineral matter in the overburden to pastel shades of light tan, orange, blue, and red.

This room is 100 feet long, 15 to 20 feet wide, and 8 to 15 feet high.

> The second room was discovered in 1930, and the tunnel was dug to permit access from the first room. In excavation of the pathways a number of late Pleistocene mammal bones were discovered, among them peccary (*Platygonus*), bear (*Euarctos*), and wolf (*Canis*). This room is 50 feet in diameter and 7 feet high. The general trend of the cave is northwest.[5]

There is a very nice photograph of this cave that accompanies Barr's description. It shows a woman standing next to "stalactites and stalagmites on the Natural Bridge."

According to a Jewel Cave brochure in the Gary K. Soule Collection, Jewel Cave was discovered in 1895. This differs from Barr's date of 1885 given above. This brochure also states that the cave was first opened to the public in 1924.

---

5 Barr, op. cit., p. 177-179.

Figure 5.17. Emily Davis (top) and Braxton Oeser (bottom) in the Connector Room of Jewel Cave. Photo by Ken Oeser, December, 2012.

Figure 5.18. Emily Davis (left), Braxton Oeser (middle), and Annette Oeser (right) in the Vesuvius Room of Jewel Cave. Photo by Ken Oeser, December, 2012.

The Underground Weather Station

The February, 1954 NSS News had the following information in the "Commercial Caves Column:"

> The Nashville Grotto, together with Jewel Cave, Dickson, Tenn., is currently operating what may be the nation's only underground weather station. Since September a constant record of temperature fluctuations in the second room of the cave has been kept by a thermograph on loan to the Society from the Office of Naval Research. The splendid cooperation of Mr. W.E. Lawson, owner and operator of the cave, is truly amazing. Mr. Lawson services the instrument weekly, keeps it in running shape, and reports any abnormal fluctuations, as, for example, when parties are taken through the cave. This is a fine example of a scientific project which the Society alone could not readily carry out and pioneers a new field of joint undertakings with our commercial cave affiliates and institutional members.[6]

There is an excellent photograph of Mr. W.E. Lawson adjusting one of the Thermographs in Jewel Cave on the Front Cover of the April, 1955 NSS News. The caption for the photo says that there were two thermographs and a barograph in the cave.

It would be interesting to know if those records from this project still survive.

My First Visit to Jewel Cave

I first visited Jewel Cave during the summer of 1968. At that time it was still open as a commercial cave and I took the guided tour. I visited Jewel Cave again in the summer of 1993 when it had re-opened as a commercial cave. I was amazed to find original postcards on sale in the Ticket Office left over from the 1950s! I again took the short, but interesting tour.

---

6 Anonymous, "Commercial Caves Column," NSS News, v. 12 (1954), no. 2, p. 6.

The Surveys of Jewel Cave

A map of Jewel Cave appears in the August, 1962 Nashville Grotto *Speleonews*. The surveyed length is not listed on this map, but it would appear to show approximately 1,000 feet of passages. The map is labeled: "Draftsman: Sally M. Child" and "Original Drawing: W.E. Lawson," so it is not clear if this is an actual survey or merely a sketch map.[7]

The next survey of Jewel Cave was done by Ken Oeser, Annette Oeser, Emily Davis, Gerald Moni, Joe Douglas, Kristen Bobo, and Brian Ham. The survey lasted from December 2, 2012 until February 2, 2013. The total surveyed length was 1,110 feet with 1,083 feet of horizontal cave and 52 feet of total vertical extent.

Cave Fish in Jewel Cave

Barr (1961) describes *Chologaster agassizi* from Jewel Cave and states that it is known elsewhere from springs and wells. According to Barr, it has small eyes and is pale brown to gray in color. These fish were noted by Ken, Annette, and Alexandra Oeser on January 22, 2000 in the Discovery Passage which leads to the original, spring entrance.

Cave Access

These caves are located on private property. Do not enter these caves, or any other caves, without the owner's permission.

WARNING:

The crawlway to the back of Ruskin Cave sometimes stays sumped shut for months, or even a year, at a time. Never go through this crawlway when rain is in the forecast.

Suggested Reading

William E. Anchors, Jr. wrote a booklet titled "Ruskin and Jewel Caves: A Brief History" that was published March, 1989. It is 71 pages long, has several interesting historical photographs and goes much more deeply into the history of Ruskin Cave. There is a very good Bibliography in the back.

Joseph C. Douglas wrote a paper titled "Dancing in the Cool of a Cave: Historical Social Use of the American Underground." It was published in the Journal of Spelean History, v. 41, no. 1 (Issue 131), January—June 2007. Ruskin Cave is one of several caves discussed where dances and other social events were held.

---

7 Kenneth W. Bunting, "Jewel Cave – August 25, 1962," *Speleonews*, v. 6 (1962), no. 5, pp. 17-18.

Erica Sughrue in Riverside Pit, Cannon County. Photo by Bob Biddix, August 11, 2018.

Section 2: East Section: Cannon, Coffee, and De Kalb Counties

70

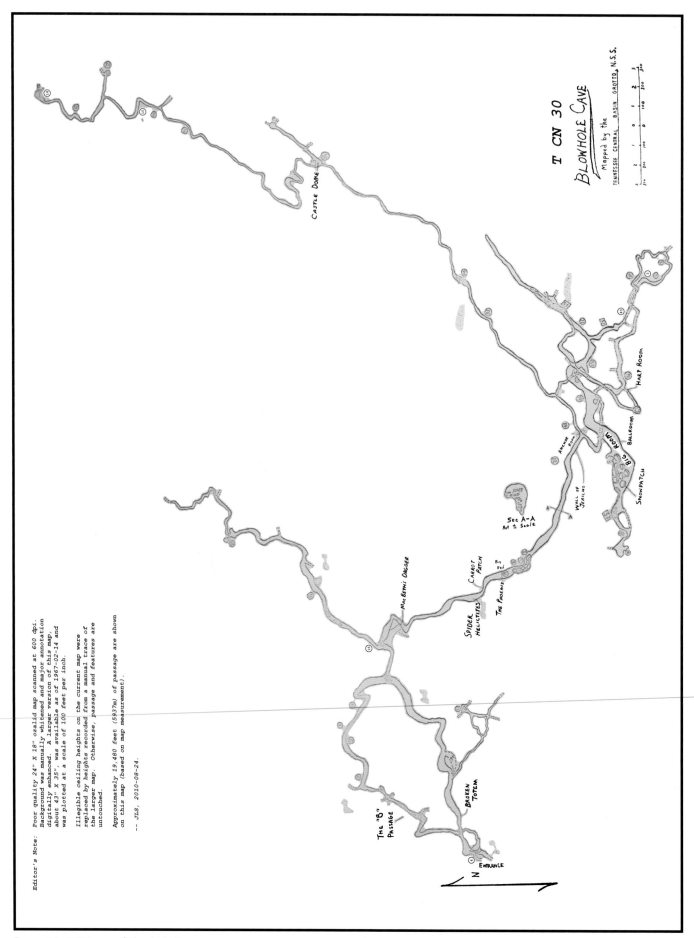

Figure 6.1. 1967 map of Blowhole Cave.

CHAPTER 6
Blowhole Cave

Blowhole Cave is located in Cannon County, Tennessee. The current surveyed length is 40,314.5 feet (7.64 miles) The first mention of Blowhole Cave in the caving literature is in the June, 1963 *NSS News*:

Martin L. DeLong, 41, of Highland, Illinois, was drowned while attempting to negotiate a siphon in Blow Hole Cave near Woodbury, Tennessee, on Easter Sunday. Blow Hole Cave has long been well known to residents of the county because of the strong blast of air that may be felt sometimes as far as 60 feet from the entrance. Until last summer the cave's known extent was a forty-foot crawl passage averaging about two feet in diameter. This ended where it met an underground stream which springs a few feet from the cave entrance. There is normally a clearance of several inches above the water and through this air pours with sufficient force to extinguish a carbide light.

DeLong learned of the cave from a one-time Cannon County resident, Martin Campbell, who now lives in Indiana. He first visited the cave last summer. Using the air space above the water he worked upstream and found that the ceiling rose to allow head space after about twenty feet. After a continued crawl of about 100 feet, the cave enlarges into walking passage. Campbell accompanied DeLong on the initial exploration and he reports that they traveled about half a mile, finding beautiful formations and rooms as large as 100 feet wide and 75 feet high. Last November DeLong again visited the cave, which he claimed to be the most beautiful of the many he had seen. Meanwhile this description of the cave had so fascinated some experienced local cavers that with the aid of diving equipment, they made at least two visits in the past year.

On Easter weekend, DeLong again returned to Tennessee with Campbell and six girls and boys of teen age who he wanted to show the cave. Martin Grizzle, owner of the home where DeLong spent the night, accompanied the party to the cave but did not intend to enter. They arrived at the cave about 9 am and DeLong was the first to enter, followed by the young people. Cameras and other effects were wrapped in plastic for protection against the water. DeLong tied a rope to his belt and entered the water. One rope end was left with the party, and his intention was to tie the other end to a rock on the far side and to indicate by a tug when the others were to follow, using the rope as a guide line.

When no signal had been received after waiting for about ten minutes, the party became concerned and they attempted to call DeLong. Campbell, who had been waiting at the entrance, then entered the crawl passage and pulled on the rope. He found that it gave sluggishly, was obviously not tied to a rock, and soon brought DeLong's body in view.

Figure 6.2. Erica Sughrue at the gated entrance to Blowhole Cave. Photo by Bob Biddix, December 31, 2013.

Figure 6.3. William Alan Camp by the Big Red column in Blowhole Cave. Photo by Dave Bunnell, July 11, 2014.

One of the boys, an Explorer Scout, gave mouth to mouth respiration for a few minutes in the cramped quarters. Grizzle then entered the cave and helped drag the body to the outside where continued efforts at resuscitation were in vain. An autopsy in Woodbury indicated death by drowning.

What actually went wrong? Several theories have been advanced. The blowing effect was not noticeable that day, although the temperature was in the seventies. This may indicate that the water level was higher than usual and the duck-under further than anticipated. In March, Cannon County experienced the worst flood in its history. Water pours from Blow Hole Cave in a torrent after a heavy rain; heavy flooding may have altered the inside of the cave in some way. Or perhaps the cold water caused a cramp or heart attack.

DeLong was not an NSS member, though he was reported to be the organizer of a cave exploring group in Highland. Even the most superficial cave safety code would have dictated against this

Figure 6.4. Erica Sughrue by the Chandelier formation in Blowhole Cave. Photo by Bob Biddix, March 24, 2014.

Figure 6.5. Richard Finch at the cave register in Blowhole Cave. Photo by Alan Lenk, January, 1966.

expedition. Experienced local cavers refused to enter without diving equipment, but DeLong intended talking a group of novices through the siphon and, according to Grizzle, there did not seem to be any doubt in his mind that the trip was other than routine. If there is no other lesson to be learned from this tragedy, it points up the need for the NSS to contact isolated caving groups with its message of personal safety practices.[1]

Clearly, from this article there were other, local cave divers who were aware of this cave, but unfortunately, this article does not identify who they were.

Caver Bobby Higgins lived nearby at the time he recalls the following story:

> I was six years old when DeLong drowned. We lived on Highway 53 at the foot of the hill that leads up to Pleasant Ridge Road (the head of Rock House Creek) and someone from DeLong's group stopped at our house wanting to use a phone. I always thought it was strange they traveled that far wanting

to use the phone, but this happened on Easter Sunday and I guess most folks were at church. My father didn't go to church that day and was home. Unfortunately, we didn't have a phone, but I doubt it would have made any difference.

> I did get to visit Blowhole once. I will never forget the sound the wind made when the door was first opened. Very impressive. I heard this was a most beautiful cave when first explored, but there was a lot of vandalism that occurred. I remember people showing us formations they had removed from the cave. Glad it got gated.[2]

The next mention of Blowhole Cave in the caving literature was in the Chattanooga Grotto's newsletter, *Limestone Ledger*:

> Blowhole Cave is located in Cannon County near Auburntown, Tenn. The owner, Buck Nichols, has constructed a small, wooden padlocked door over the entrance to keep children and animals from wandering into the cave and to keep out vandals.

> The entrance room of the cave is a low, wet, muddy crawl, but the next room encountered is a

---

1 Tank Gorin, "The Tennessee Cave Drowning," *NSS News*, Vol. 21 (1963), no. 6, pp 65, 71-72.

2 Bobby Higgins, Letter to Gerald Moni dated October, 24, 2014.

Figure 6.6. The MacBeth's Dagger stalactite in Blowhole Cave. Photo by Edward M. Yarbrough, August, 1963.

Figure 6.7. Erica Sughrue by the Hodtite formation in Blowhole Cave. Photo by Bob Biddix, December 1, 2013.

very large chamber where one of the many beautiful formations may be seen. The first prominent formation is a large white flowstone slide. The cave's height averages about thirty to forty feet high, and there is a stream flowing through most of it.

Soda straws are very abundant, and we also noted some large stalactites that were carrot-like in form and color. If you are planning to take a trip to Indian Grave Point Cave to see the "Red Apple" formation, plan to go to Blowhole and see about ten of them.

After a while of walking through the main part of the cave, we noticed that it narrows into a fluted stream canyon. In this section of the cave there are some tremendous domes, including one about 150 to 200 feet high and another about 130 feet high with a waterfall cascading out of it. We counted about twelve waterfalls throughout the cave.

The only torturous part of the cave is a rough crawlway about thirty feet long over breakdown.

In various parts of the cave you are able to see some fine helictite clusters and gypsum crystals.

Slab breakdown covers the floor in many parts.

The farthest point we penetrated before turning around was well over a mile from the entrance. At this point the ceiling was about two feet high, but as far as we know, the passage continued.

Blowhole is a very photogenic and totally unvandalized cave which is well worth a visit.[3]

An article two (2) years later in the *NSS News* does give more information:

A cave register has been placed in Blowhole Cave, Cannon County, Tennessee. (See Figure 6.5)

In an effort to curb name-writing on cave walls, the recent NSS-sponsored trend has been to provide more appropriate autograph space, in the form of registers (which serve double duty, providing also much information on cave traffic).

One drawback of this approach to the name-writing problem is that the registers are too often placed in caves whose walls are already evidencing

3 Leroy Presley, "Blow Hole Cave, Cannon County, Tenn.," *Limestone Ledger*, Vol. 2 (1964), No. 3, p. 30.

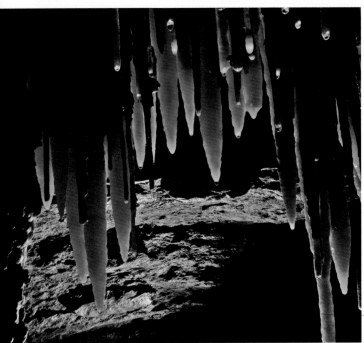

Figure 6.8. Kristen Bobo by soda straws and "carrots." Photo by Chuck Sutherland, December 8, 2013. (Above.)

Figure 6.9. The Carrot Patch, a group of orange stalactites in Blowhole Cave. Photo by Dave Bunnell, July 11, 2014. (Left.)

Figure 6.10. Orange soda straw stalactites in Blowhole Cave. Photo by Kelly Smallwood , January 1, 2014. (Next page.)

Central Basin Grotto have worked with the owner to keep the cave gated and protected.

With conditions thus so favorable for the cave's preservation, the validity of placing one of the now hard-to-come-by registers in this location might be questioned. We feel, on the contrary, that the opportunity to protect a cave from the very start is rare enough to warrant the full compliment of protective measures available. Mr. Nichols, the owner, was mighty pleased that yet a third group was this interested in his cave. We hope it works.[4]

the need for such an item. The Nashville Grotto is currently experimenting with the use of a cave register as "preventive medicine" to cave writing.

The unusual opportunity of having access to a significant cave -- both in size and beauty -- which has not yet suffered the vandal's ravages, is due to a combination of factors: the extent of Blowhole Cave has not been long known and since its opening by Don McFerrin of Woodbury, he and members of the

So, by 1966 the cave has an artificial entrance that has been gated and there appears to be excellent cooperation between the owner and the local Grottos.

A Description of the Cave

Blowhole Cave currently has a surveyed length of 40,314.5 feet (7.64 miles). The map indicates that the

4 Richard C. Finch, "Pre-Need Conservation Experiment," *NSS News*, Vol. 24 (1966), no. 4, p. 59.

Figure 6.11. Erica Sughrue by a large, white stalagmite in Blowhole Cave. Photo by Bob Biddix, April 14, 2018.

cave is basically developed along joints that are oriented northeast-southwest and northwest-southeast. The main stream passage is shown on the map as the "A" Passage. The "B" Passage splits off about 250 from the Entrance and rejoins the "A" Passage about 1,200 feet from the Entrance. About 250 feet further down the "A" Passage from this junction the "C" Passage splits off and heads generally northeast for over 1,500 feet. Looking at the survey, it would appear that the "B" Passage and the "C" passage were one continuous passage at some point in the past, until they intersected the "A" Passage and the stream flowing down the "C" Passage now joins the main stream in the "A" Passage.

The "D" Section is a small group of side passages that lead off from the "A" Passage approximately 500 feet from the Entrance. The "E" Section is also a small group of side passages that lead off from the "A" Passage approximately 2,000 feet from the Entrance.

Over the years, the owners of this cave have considered opening it to the public as a Show Cave. Although the cave is very beautiful, it is not close to a major highway or to any other tourist attractions. The likelihood of attracting a significant number of tourists seems unlikely.

My First Trip to the Cave

In April 1981 I visited Blowhole Cave to take photographs. I got some good shots, but looking back at them, I notice two photos with graffiti on the walls where one group had written their names with carbide lamps. Even though this cave had been gated since its initial discovery and exploration, it had been broken into several times and vandalized in places.

The Surveys of Blowhole Cave

According to the Derek Wolfe, the current surveyed length of Blowhole Cave (November 2017) is 40,325.4

Figure 6.12. Erica Sughrue admires a flowstone curtain in Blowhole Cave. Photo by Bob Biddix, December 31, 2013.

Figure 6.13. A group of cavers take a breakdown break. Blowhole Cave. Photo by Dave Bunnell, July 11, 2014. (Above.)

Figure 6.14. Red flowstone spirals to a red soda straw in Blowhole Cave. Photo by Chuck Sutherland, December 8, 2013. (Right.)

Figure 6.15. Kelly Smallwood by a large stalagmite in Blowhole Cave. Note long, white soda straws in the distance. Photo by Dave Bunnell, July 11, 2014. (Next page, above.)

Figure 6.16. 2017 map of Blowhole Cave. (Next page, below.)

BLOWHOLE CAVE

CANNON COUNTY, TENNESSEE

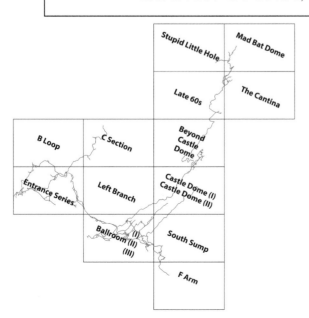

Total Surveyed Length: 40,314.5 Feet   12,287.9 Meters   **7.64 Miles**
Total Surveyed Depth: 172.3 Feet   52.5 Meters

Suuntos and Fiberglass Tape Survey
August 1981- January 1984

Surveyed By:

Larry Adams	Nick Littlepage
Steve Altemeier	Lawrence Loveless
Darlene Anthony	Sue Loveless
Joc Douglas	Mityi Marske
Drex Freeman	Gerald Moni
Jim Freeman	Jim Nichols
Philip Hart	David Parr
Jim Hodson	Jeff Sims
John Hoffelt	Don Teblet
Chris Kerr	Leah Vian
Roger Ling	Bill Walter
Sharon Littlepage	

Suuntos, Laser Disto, DistoX and Fiberglass Tape Survey
November 2013 - November 2017

Surveyed By:

T. Evan Anderson	Ryan Marsters
Joel Buckner	Bruce Robtoy
Bernie Eskesen	Andrew Szabados
John Hoffelt	Derek Wolfe
Cody James	Donna Wolfe
Ed LaRock	Jason Wyatt
Hal Love	

Cartography by
Derek A. Wolfe

Labels on index map: Stupid Little Hole, Mad Bat Dome, Late 60s, The Cantina, B Loop, C Section, Beyond Castle Dome, Entrance Series, Left Branch, Castle Dome (I), Castle Dome (II), Ballroom (I) (II) (III), South Sump, F Arm

Figure 6.17. Spider helictites in Blowhole Cave. Photo by Dave Bunnell, July 11, 2014.

feet (7.64 miles) and the cave has a vertical extent of 150 feet.

The first survey of Blowhole Cave was conducted by the Tennessee Central Basin Grotto and that map is dated February 14, 1967. It supposedly shows 19,480 feet (3.69 miles) of cave and was produced as blueprint copies.

The next survey of Blowhole Cave was conducted from August 1981 through June 1982 and is labeled "preliminary." It lists John Hoffelt as the person who compiled the data and David Parr as the person who drafted the map. It gives a length of 10,817.3 feet (2.05 miles) and a vertical extent of 96.2 feet. This "preliminary" map shows less than half of the passages shown on the 1967 map.

The current survey of Blowhole Cave is being conducted by Derek Wolfe. This map show much more detail than the previous two maps and is being prepared as a folio which currently consists of thirteen sheets.

Each sheet is 24 inches by 36 inches in size and shows the cave passages at a scale of 1-inch equals 40 feet.

Cave Access

Blowhole Cave is securely gated, and access is by permission only. Due to the fragile nature of this cave, access is severely limited.

Even a well-gated and well-managed cave like Blowhole Cave will still receive some deterioration. Accidents do happen, and some cavers are more careful than others. For example, some of the famous "Spider Helictites" on the ceiling at one point in the cave were broken off when one caver did not duck low enough when passing under them. Another caver crawled over the "Bear Tracks," even though there was a warning sign present. But the worst damage comes from the dedicated vandal who breaks into the cave. One such person broke off the famous "MacBeth's Dagger" and removed it from the cave.

Figure 6.18. Jerry Davis in the Harp Room in Blowhole Cave. Photo by Edward M. Yarbrough, 1963.

84

Figure 7.1. The entrance to Cripps Mill Cave. Photo by Larry E. Matthews, March, 1976.

CHAPTER 7
Cripps Mill Cave

Cripps Mill Cave is located in Dry Creek Valley in De Kalb County, Tennessee. It is a very large and interesting cave.

The earliest mention of Cripps Mill Cave in the caving literature is in an article in the *NSS News*, reporting the discovery of luminous worms in the Goat Cave section of the cave. It is clear that Goat Cave was not yet considered to be connected to Cripps Mill Cave from this article. The article is as follows:

Tiny segmented worms which dot the darkness with pinpoints of blue light have been discovered in Goat Cave, a half-mile-long joint caverns of the Cannon limestone just on the eastern border of Tennessee's Central Basin of Ordovician rocks. These minute animals belong to the Oligochaeta, the class of segmented worms of which the common earthworm is a member. They lack pigment and are covered with fine bristles; the posterior end of the body contains the luminescent organ.

The organisms were seen on June 2, 1949 by Tom Barr and Bert Denton on a preliminary exploration of the cave. A large colony of the Indiana bat (*Myotis soladis*) occupied a series of large, rock-strewn rooms at the end of the main passage, providing food for the worms. The glow-worms, unnoticed until the carbide lamps were extinguished for refilling were flourishing on moist, guano-coated flowstone.[1]

If Tom Barr and Bert Denton had not blown out their carbide lamps for refilling, the discovery would not have been made. Interestingly, only two (2) months later, Barr wrote another article stating that the "glow-worms" were not worms, at all, but were actually the larvae of a fungus gnat.

The luminous "worm" of Goat Cave, Tennessee, has been identified as a larva of a fungus gnat (fam. [Mycetophilidae]). The luminescence proceeds from bead-like organs in the head and tail.

The fungus gnat larvae live on fungal mycelia growing on the droppings of a bat (*Myotis sodalis*) colony. Similar insects have been reported from Germany on two occasions. Tests are being made to determine whether the constant, bluish glow is caused by luminous bacteria or is a product of the luciferin-luciferase reaction.[2]

More information about these organisms was given two (2) months later:

The luminous "worms" previously reported (*NSS News*, Oct., 1949) from Goat Cave, Tennessee, apparently are not, strictly speaking, especially adapted to "bioluminescence" in caves, but have been found in crevices and sheltered places around springs in North Carolina. The worms have been tentatively identified by Dr. C. S. Shoup, Department of Biology, Vanderbilt University, as *Platyura fultoni*, a fungus gnat. For the original description see Fisher, Elizabeth: New Mycetophilidae from North Carolina; Entom. News, Vol. 51 pp. 423-247, 1940. A description of the habits of the type specimens is given by Fulton, B. B.: a luminous fly larva with spider traits; Annals Amer. Entomological Soc., Vol. 34, pp. 289-302.[3]

Now that you know what they are, be sure to look for them when you are in the Goat Cave section of Cripps Mill Cave. They are well worth sitting in a dark for a few minutes to let your eyes adjust enough so that you can see them.

The first mention of the Cripps Mill Entrance appeared eight (8) months later:

On Thursday, June 22, a group of five spelunkers from Nashville made an extensive exploration of the isolated Cripps Mill Cave, and on the afternoon of the same day broke through a maze of dangerous crawlways and crossed a natural bridge to make the first connection between Cripps' Mill and nearby Goat Cave.

1 Thomas C. Barr, Jr., *NSS News*, Vol. 7 (1949), no. 8, p. 6.

2 Thomas C. Barr, Jr., *NSS News*, Vol. 7 (1949), no. 10, p. 3.

3 Thomas C. Barr, Jr., *NSS News*, Vol. 7 (1949), no. 12, p. 1.

Figure 7.2. Looking out the Cripps Mill entrance. Photo by Chuck Sutherland, November 25, 2016.

Cripps Mill Cave, known for over a hundred years, lays near one end of Dry Creek Valley, near Dowelltown, DeKalb County, Tennessee, and for decades the stream issuing from its mouth has served as a source of water power. A sluice gate is opened at one end of the dam in the entrance of the cave, and a stream of water is shot through the millrace around the base of the hill to the present mill, which is of the old-fashioned water wheel type. Wading is necessary if one is to reach the large room called "Grand Central," from which radiate the three other forks of the cave--Bat Avenue, the Calcite Boulevard, and the Waterfall Branch, which leads to the Hidden Room.

Goat Cave, previously reported in the (*NSS News)*, is the home of the luminous larva of the fungus gnat, *Platyura fisheri*. The entrance is on the side of the hill in which Cripps' Mill Cave is located and is about 50 feet higher. For the first 1,000 feet there is only one main passage, which terminates in the Bat Chamber, a large, boulder-strewn room. At certain seasons of the year a colony of the social bat, *Myotis sodalis*, coats the walls and ceiling of the cave. In winter, warm, humid air coming from the 5X5 entrance sheathes nearby trees in ice.

Emerging on the morning in question from the dry haven of a local hayloft, a party of three--Tom Barr, Frank Butler, and Don Maynard--entered Cripps' Mill at 8 o'clock. After wading through waist-deep water as far as "Grand Central," they promptly dubbed the wet passage, "the Grand Canal." All explored forks of the cave contained numerous dripstone formations in an excellent state of preservation. The re-deposition of broken formations in the Calcite Boulevard offers an opportunity for the study of rate of growth, if the approximate date of breakage can be determined. The groups called a halt at noon and made preparations to enter Goat Cave.

This time the exploration began at 2 o'clock, with four members to the party--Butler, Maynard, Jack May, and Carl Storey. Opening unobtrusively into the Bat Chamber is a narrow, sinuous passage which is easily overlooked. After some trepidation

Figure 7.3. Alison Harris at the Goat Cave entrance of Cripps Mill Cave. Photo by Chuck Sutherland, November 25, 2016.

Figure 7.4. Erica Sughrue (left), Carol Lamers (middle), and Mark Hobbs (right) in a large passage in Cripps Mill Cave. Photo by Bob Biddix, December 3, 2016.

Figure 7.5. Tina Mills by large flowstones in Cripps Mill Cave. Photo by Chuck Sutherland, November 25, 2016.

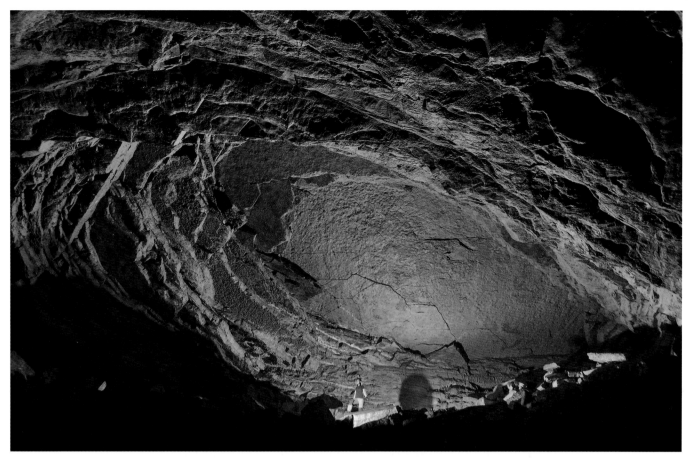

Figure 7.6. Erica Sughrue in a large breakdown dome in Cripps Mill Cave. Photo by Bob Biddix, December 3, 2016.

it was pronounced passable and after crawling and chimneying, the four reached a deep crevice which would be crossed on a natural bridge. Beyond the bridge Maynard and Butler suddenly announced to the other two that they were in the Hidden Room of Cripps Mill Cave. It was after 5 P. M. when they made the steep ascent from the level of the cave to the Goat Cave entrance.

The discovery explodes a century-old belief and makes the Cripps Mill-Goat Cave combination one of the largest caverns in Middle Tennessee. It is in line with previous explorations in the Dry Creek Valley area which are rapidly making Dowelltown the most important center of speleological work within a hundred miles of Nashville. It presents a sizable problem for work by Nashville spelunkers, and last, but not least, reduces Mr. Petrie's grand total by one.[4]

Mr. John S. Petrie was an NSS member who was compiling a grand list of all of the known caves in the United States. So, connecting two caves into one cave reduced his list by one!

4 Thomas C. Barr, Jr., *NSS News*, Vol. 8 (1950), no. 8, pp 5-6.

A Description of the Cave

Cripps Mill Cave is described by Thomas C. Barr, Jr. in his book, *Caves of Tennessee* (1961):

Cripps Mill Cave is one of the largest and most interesting caves in the area covered by this report. It has two mouths. The main entrance is 90 feet wide and 15 feet high, and there is a sizable pond behind the dam constructed across the mouth. The cave has been used for 150 years to operate Cripps Mill. The other entrance is known locally as "Goat Cave" and is situated on the hill, 100 yards above the mill. It is 5 feet in diameter and drops down at a steep angle into a very large entrance room.

The main stream channel runs north from the large, wet entrance for 900 feet, averaging 30 feet in width and 20 feet in height. It leads into a huge rockfall chamber ("Grand Central Station") 50 feet high, 75 feet wide and 150 feet long. Three branches of the cave and a stream crawlway radiate from this room.

One of these branches runs S. 40° E. for 960 feet, and is 25 feet wide and 10 feet high, lowering near the end. Some small columns, flowstone, and delicate bubbles of calcite are found at the end. The second branch, which is low and wide, continues north for 300 feet and ends in silt fill. The third branch, the largest, leads into "Goat Cave." It consists of two large rooms, connected by low crawlways on top of fill which nearly reaches the ceiling. At 450 feet west of the first large breakdown room (and 1,350 feet from the main entrance) a stone arch bridge spans a 20-foot pit which leads into the Bat Chamber, the "end" of Goat Cave. The stream passage beyond Grand Central is low and wide and may be followed for 235 feet, at which point the ceiling lowers. At 200 feet a right-hand fork, containing a tributary stream, is encountered. This passage averages 5 feet high and 10 feet wide for 700 feet, and then degenerates into a low, tortuous stream crawl which becomes impenetrable after another 150 feet.

From the Goat Cave entrance a spacious avenue extends north-northeast for 1,000 feet to the Bat Chamber. This passage averages 15 feet high and 25 feet wide but is rather irregular, and there are many short climbs and descents. Bat guano is abundant in this branch. Several small but attractive formations and a huge stalagmite, 40 feet in diameter and 15 feet high, may be seen. A small stream flows through the Goat Cave Branch and emerges at a spring beside the mill.

The fauna of Cripps Mill Cave is of exceptional interest. The most prominent feature is a large colony of gray bats (*Myotis grisescens*). Among the invertebrates are luminous larvae of fungus gnats, isopods, pseudoscorpions, centipedes, millipedes, spiders, springtails, and three species of cave beetles.[5]

This description still covers most of the known cave, as the accompanying map will attest.

Prehistoric Visitors to Cripps Mill Cave

Cave historian Joe Douglas reports evidence that Cripps Mill Cave was visited in prehistoric times by American Indians:

> Throughout most of the cave, cane charcoal deposits and stoke marks on walls, and rocks, from bundled cane torches can be found. A single radiocarbon sample of cane charcoal from the end of the Long Dry Passage revealed an age putting it in the Late Mississippian Period, between 1,400 to 1,420 years ago.[6]

There is no evidence of mining in the cave, so Joe suggests that these people visited the cave for either recreational or religious purposes.

My First Visit to the Cave

My first visit to Cripps Mill Cave was sometime in 1962. I was still too young to have a driver's license, so my mother drove me and a couple of my friends to the cave. I'm pretty sure my grandmother was along on this trip, too, so she and my mother waited in the car while we explored the cave. Nearby Indian Grave Point Cave had been our first BIG cave, and this may have been our second. Previously, we had been exploring the dinkies of Davidson County.

The Trout Farm

Within just a few years, the Cripps Mill property changed hands and the stream flowing from the Cripps Mill Entrance was used to supply water for a trout farm. Here are the details of that enterprise:

> On July 11th Charles Youman and I made a trip to Indian Grave Point Cave. After leaving this cave I decided to drive down to Cripps Mill Cave and find out about the rumors that I had head about a trout farm there. As I drove up I saw a group of cars and the millwheel was turning under water flowing through the sluiceway. Closer observation showed that it had been painted, too.
>
> By talking with Mr. Fletcher Hughes, manager, I learned that the cave had been bought by a group of five men: Messrs. Claude Comer, Frank Fuson, Huland Spicer, Louis Benford, and Dr. Donald LeGuire. The place is now called the Old Mill Trout Farm. The dam at the main entrance has been rebuilt to store water. Two additional dams have been built outside, across the stream flowing from the cave, creating two pools in which the trout are kept. These ponds were originally stocked with 20,000 trout. Anyone fishing there pays $1.28 a pound for the undressed fish he catches. No trout stamp is required but the receipt must be kept showing

---

5 Thomas C. Barr, Jr., *Caves of Tennessee*, TN Division of Geology, Bulletin 64 (1961), pp 159-161.

6 Ray Maslak, *Exploring This Blue Dot*, "Cripps Mill Cave."

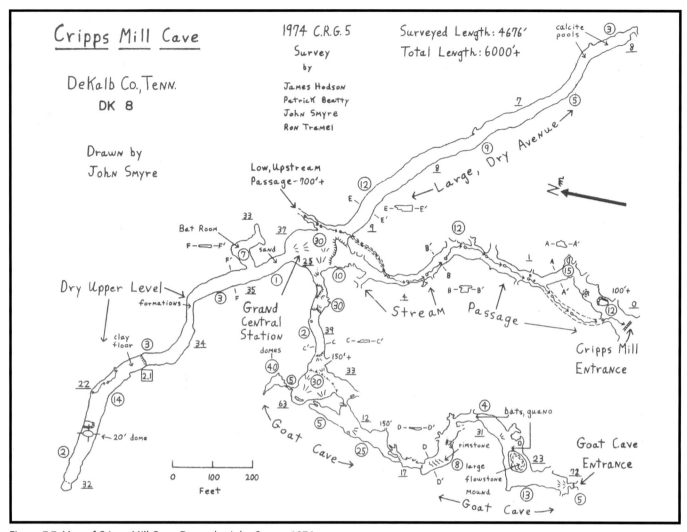

Figure 7.7. Map of Cripps Mill Cave. Drawn by John Smyre, 1974.

the origin of the fish. The fish are then dressed and packed in ice so that they will not spoil en route.

The cave is now posted, and a gate closed the Goat Cave entrance. However, it is constructed of cedar poles and the bats can easily pass through. The Manager explained that any carbide dumped into the stream would kill many valuable fish; therefore, there could be no exploring. He also said that the owners were going to look into the possibility of commercializing the cave as an added attraction. To date, they have not entered the cave.

The most interesting bit of information that I picked up came when we were discussing the water supply. Mr. Hughes said that they had the water traced to insure its constant supply and against pollution. It was traced to a sinking creek near Bluhmtown which he said was fed by several springs. By looking at the Gassaway Quadrangle, it could only be Bluhmtown Creek, which starts three

miles away from Cripps Mill Cave. It seems likely that it may sink about two miles or more away in dry weather and then flows underground for the remaining distance. Since many stream caves are observed to run parallel to surface streams, being wet-weather overflows and sometimes the only drainage in dry weather, it seems probable that this is the case here, and that the underground stream flows parallel to the Bluhmtown Creek. If this is the case, a hike along the Bluhmtown Creek might reveal another entrance into the system.[7]

Although the trout farm was well done, it was in a remote area and accessible only by a rough, gravel road. It only remained in business for a few years.

7 Larry E. Matthews, *Speleonews*, Vol. 9 (1965), no. 8, p. 102.

Figure 7.8. Tina Mills by a large stalagmite and large rimstone dams in Cripps Mill Cave. Photo by Chuck Sutherland, November 25, 2016.

The Survey of Cripps Mill Cave

The surveyed length of Cripps Mill Cave is 9,000 feet (1.7 miles) and the vertical extent is 100 feet. However, the only finished and drafted map shows only 4,676 feet of passages. This map was drawn by John Smyre in 1974. It shows all of the passages described above in the description of the cave. (See Figure 7.7)

Joel Buckner reports one major passage not shown on the map:

> The upstream passage in the Grand Central Station in Cripps Mill Cave was pushed sometime in the 80's by a group of us in wetsuits. Several low air spaces were passed and we found an estimated half mile or so of crawling passages without it opening back up. David Parr pushed it the farthest but stopped when he realized he was by himself with just a carbide lamp. No air flow was noted that day so the passage likely sumped somewhere ahead but might be worth another check during a severe drought.[8]

This would put the total length of the cave at well over 2 miles.

Fox Cave

The entrance to Fox Cave is located approximately 120 yards east of the entrance to Cripps Mill Cave. Barr gives the following description for the cave:

> From the mouth (8 feet wide and 3 feet high) a short crawlway leads into a passage 15 feet high and 10 feet wide. An incised meander trench some 8 feet deep has been formed in the middle of the passage, and its walls are sharply scalloped by the corrosive action of water. At 375 feet an avenue 15 feet wide and 8 feet high is intersected; the floor of the avenue

8 Joel Buckner, Personal communication, September 21, 2018.

is at the same level as the shelves on either side of the meander trench. This avenue was explored for 1,575 feet farther. It winds about considerably, but the main direction is southeast.

The main passage has two interesting adits. One is a domepit, 20 feet high and 8 feet in diameter, with large and beautiful dripstone formations on the walls. The other is a 50-foot-high recessional gorge. At many points along the passage are extensive banks of cave fill, which is a mixture of silt and gravel usually arranged in alternating layers, some of them cross bedded.[9]

Although Fox Cave is not as large at Cripps Mill Cave, it is still quite interesting.

---

9 Thomas C. Barr, Jr., *Caves of Tennessee*, TN Division of Geology, Bulletin 64 (1961), p. 162.

The Survey of Fox Cave

On December 14, 1980, Joel Buckner and David Parr began the survey of Fox Cave. Here is David's account of that survey project:

Trip # 1 - 12/14/80

It all started innocently enough, Joel Buckner and I were to survey the last remaining leads in the Schoolhouse Passage of Indian Grave Point Cave. After arriving at the parking place below the mouth of the cave we began to sort through our gear. It didn't take long for me to realize the shocking fact that my caving boots were still back in Nashville. Since Dingos don't provide adequate traction on treacherous mud walls we decided to survey a nice easy horizontal walking cave in DeKalb County.

A quick look in Barr's book and we were in route to Fox Cave. The cave description seemed to fit our needs perfectly, a walking passage with two short

side passages all of which totaled 1,900 feet. Taking into mind Barr's usual conservative estimates we figured on approximately one-half mile.

The entrance was a crawl 20 feet wide that led for 50 feet to a walking passage. To the left it ended at a low spot with daylight leaking through. To the right the passage took on the shape of an hour glass. We surveyed along the ceiling of this passage for 200 feet passing two side passages and then emerging in an elliptical tube 30 feet wide and 8 feet high. This was great we thought as we stretched the tape one shot after another through this obstruction-free walking tube. After 400 feet we came to a 50-foot-high recessional gorge which we briefly investigated. Returning to station A-11 we resumed the survey of the main passage.

Everything went quite well for the next 700 feet and then the passage made a radical change. The nice cobblestone floor we had been walking on earlier had given way to a sticky, gooey, boot-grabbing substance that extended from wall to wall. We soon came to a spot where the floor dropped into a perpendicular passage. After marking station

Figure 7.9. Erica Sughrue (left) and Carol Lamers (right) in a large passage in Cripps Mill Cave. Photo by Bob Biddix, December 3, 2016. (Above.)

Figure 7.10. Tina Mills by columns in Cripps Mill Cave. Photo by Chuck Sutherland, November 25, 2016. (Next page, above.)

Figure 7.11. Grand Central Station, the largest room in Cripps Mill Cave. Photo by Chuck Sutherland, November 25, 2016. (Next page, below.)

A-23 we decided to go to the right (the largest passage, of course).

The ceiling soon got lower and the mud got deeper as we slithered along the right wall of this rapidly degenerating mud river, trying desperately not to be sucked into its murky depths. After 400 feet of this we encountered a large shallow pool of water. We waded to the other side and were surprised to find that the passage opened back up into walking cave. We passed a really grim lead to the right and then proceeded a short distance to where the ceiling almost met the surface of another large pool. Being unequipped for such a wet encounter, we marked station A-33 and turned around to map the last lead we had passed by. We surveyed this mud lined

Figure 7.12. Kristen Bobo by bear claw marks in Cripps Mill Cave. Photo by Chuck Sutherland, November 25, 2016.

tube (2 feet high and 3 feet wide) for 180 feet before becoming grimed out by its constant low nature.

After emerging from this passage we hurried toward the entrance to survey the other side of the mud passage (later called Hunchback Hall). The mud soon turned to gravel as we mapped along the stooping/crawling passage and then the gravel became covered with water one to three feet in depth. After 450 feet we were stopped by a 6-inch air space in a 4-foot-high passage. We decided to call it a day, having surveyed 3,157.9 feet in 6 hours and 50 stations. It had now become apparent that this was not as small a cave as we had thought.

Trip # 2 - 12/27/80

Two weeks later Joel and I returned to do some more surveying in Fox Cave. We started at a small loop at the entrance and systematically surveyed leads going into the cave. We worked our way up to the recessional gorge. The ceiling was 50 feet high with several domes along its 175-foot length. A low virgin belly crawl was found near the gorge and was surveyed for 200 feet before it became too low to continue. At the head of this passage there was a strange little room that changed the tones of our voices to high ear-splitting sound. This unusual phenomenon was called the analog delay. The water crawl was the next lead on the list, so we returned to the car to put on our wet suits. Soon we were staring at the 6-inch air space that had stopped the trip before.

After 30 feet of nose-up passage the ceiling rose to 5 feet high and then went to another low air space of only 4 inches. On the other side we followed the passage to a 25-foot-high dome with a waterfall cascading from the ceiling. The crawl continued on the other side of the dome for several hundred feet passing some side passages and diminishing in size.

By this time the compass had become unreadable and the hour was growing late so we left the cave with 1,555 feet of passage added to the map in 41 stations.

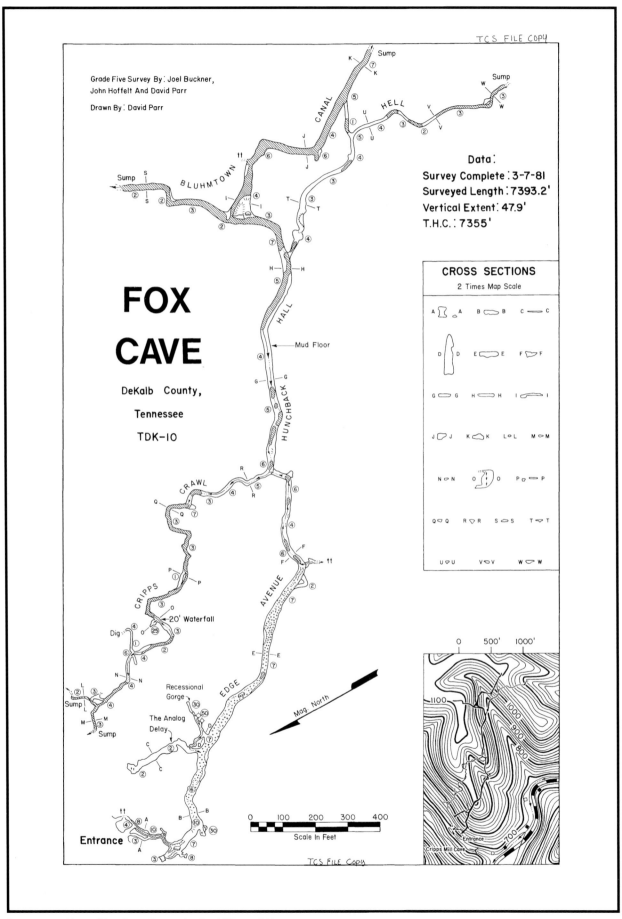

Figure 7.13. Map of Fox Cave. Drawn by David Parr, 1981.

Trip # 3 - 1/3/81

After plotting the crawl Joel and I had surveyed on the map I saw that it was heading directly towards Cripps Mill Cave, the second largest cave in DeKalb County. All it had to do was go under one hollow and the two caves would become one (sounds easy doesn't it).

It didn't take long to talk John Hoffelt into going on a Fox trip with me. After all he had never been there before and my story of a passage heading towards Cripps Mill Cave intrigued him. Soon we were crawling into the passage we were now calling Cripps Crawl with connection fever beckoning us on. Connection fever soon vanished as we slithered and squeezed through 460 feet of passages ending in hopeless sumps and mud walls.

With the completion of Cripps Crawl we head towards the end of the cave to check the other wet passage Joel and I had stopped at. As luck would have it the compass was drowned by the time we got there so all we could do was explore. Approximately 100 feet in the passage split – John went to the right and I went to the left. The passage I was in went 400 feet to a sump, the last 50 feet of which was very low. John's passage was the upstream end of the passage I was in. It was floored in deep water and still continued when he turned back. Now the cave was almost a mile long with at least 900 feet of unmapped passages to be surveyed.

Trip # 4 - 1/17/81

It was a cold January day when John and I returned to Fox Cave. One of John's boots was threatening to fall apart but a strip of duct tape wrapped around the boot saved the day. We were soon at station A-33 ready to extend the survey. After crawling into the water we realized just how cold it was. Our feet and hands quickly became numb as we surveyed in this icy cold-water crawl.

When we reached the junction we chose to survey the right-hand passage first. It started as a crawl in water 2 feet deep but soon enlarged to a walking passage in neck deep water. After surveying 420 feet in six stations our neoprene-less feet and hands could stand the cold no longer. I checked ahead for 100 feet and saw that the passage still continued

Figure 7.14. Linda Phelps by a column in Cripps Mill Cave. Photo by Larry E. Matthews, March, 1976.

with wall-to-wall water. During our retreat from this passage John's boot came apart in water 4 feet deep. His face turned every shade of the rainbow as he plunged into the frigid water trying desperately to retrieve that battered piece of leather.

After a lengthy boot repair we surveyed to the sump in the left branch and then left the cave. We had surveyed 925 feet and at least one more trip would be needed to finish the cave. Our newly found river passage (Bluhmtown Canal) could theoretically go all the way to the influx, 1.5 miles away.

Trip # 5 - 3/7/81

Almost two months passed before we got up the nerve to go back to Fox Cave. This time we actually had a three-man survey team - John, Joel, and I. We were equipped with neoprene booties this time and were determined to push Bluhmtown Canal to the bitter end.

The bitter end was only five stations from our last survey point. Bluhmtown Canal had abruptly ended

Figure 7.15. Linda Phelps by flowstone columns in Cripps Mill Cave. Photo by Larry E. Matthews, March, 1976.

at a large, water-filled sump. Having noticed a small side passage along the way we returned to map it.

The side passage looked too small at first but when I entered it I found that the floor was covered with 6 inches of soupy mud that gave way under the weight of my body. After 100 feet of this we found ourselves at a junction. We decided to go to the left since it seemed to be heading upstream. Again we were shown no mercy as its entire 550 feet was muddy belly crawls and near sumps. Joel kept saying couldn't we just sketch it in. Finally we reached a very welcome sump which ended this hellish passage.

Now all that was left to do in the cave was to survey the other end of the nightmare passage we had just finished. We suspected that it might connect to the belly crawl that Joel and I had wimped out in on the first trip. We were quite surprised when it actually did. After tying in to station B-4, we had successfully completed a 1,200-foot loop with a 0.5% error. This was quite good considering the extreme grimness of some of the passages.

After packing up our mud-covered survey gear we made the final trip out. When the footage was added up we found we had mapped 1,300 feet in 25 stations. This brought the surveyed length of Fox Cave up to 7,393.2 feet with the average shot being 52.5 feet. We had set 141 stations and spent 57-man hours in the cave.

It seems as if the only hope for finding more cave in Fox Cave would be to dive the sumps at either end of Bluhmtown Canal. The upstream sump might be followed for over a mile while the downstream sump could lead into Cripps Mill Cave 3,000 feet away. This connection could make a cave system well over 5 miles long.

How is it that a 1,900-foot-long cave became 7,400 feet long? The obvious answer is that many, if not most, Tennessee caves have been grossly underestimated in length. Exploration and surveying of the previously looked at caves will inevitably lead to substantial extensions and greater lengths. Although we probably would never have surveyed Fox Cave had we known that it is one of the muddiest caves in Tennessee, it is hard to

Figure 7.16. Two cavers entering a large breakdown chamber in Cripps Mill Cave. Photo by Bob Biddix, December 3, 2016.

regret any of our endeavors knowing that we have successfully solved on of the many riddles that await the explorers of the Tennessee underworld.[10]

The final (1981) surveyed length of Fox Cave is 7,393 feet (1.4 miles). There is always the chance that future explorers might connect Fox Cave to Cripps Mill Cave during an extreme drought.

Cave Access

Like most caves on private property, access to Cripps Mill Cave and Fox Cave varies from year to year. Always be sure you have permission from the owner before you enter these or any other caves. It is especially important that you do NOT enter the Goat Cave Section of Cripps Mill Cave when the bat colony is present.

Suggested Reading

Cave historian Joe Douglas published an article titled "The Prehistoric Exploration of Cripps Mill Cave, Tennessee" in the 2017 *Tennessee Caver* on pages 3-8. This article describes prehistoric visitation to Cripps Mill Cave as well as historic information about the cave. Stoke marks and cane charcoal deposits indicate that the cave was frequently visited, although the purpose of these visits remains unknown.

---

10 David Parr, "Five Tales of the Fox," *Speleonews*, v. 25 (1981), no. 4, pp 35-39.

CHAPTER 8
Espey Cave

Espey Cave, earlier known as Asby Cave and Jamison Cave, is located in Cannon County, Tennessee at the head of Cave Hollow. Cave Branch flows out of the entrance of the cave and down the hollow. Espey Cave is one of the most popular and most visited wild caves in Middle Tennessee.

Early Descriptions of the Cave

The earliest known description of the cave by modern cavers appeared in the December 1957 edition of the *Southeastern Caver*:

> Asby Cave located near Woodbury, Tennessee, about 50 miles southeast of Nashville, runs into one of the large hills which characterize the terrain surrounding the Highland Rim. The vadose aspect is immediately apparent as one approaches the 30 X 30-foot entrance at the head of a gulch, where a large stream tumbles into daylight. The cave is divided into two levels, the upper being only 15-30 feet above the lower level. After 150 yards, the stream seeps under the rock floor and reappears only as a siphon at the end of the cave.
>
> Forty yards along the 15-foot-high entrance canyon is the first major intersection, from which it is possible to go into the Left Branch via a small passage to a circular breakdown 50 feet in diameter and 40 feet high. After crossing a small stream, this branch turns into a squeeze around breakdown which has not been successfully traversed. Returning to the intersection, there is a choice between an upper breakdown room and the stream passage. This breakdown room is about 50 feet wide and 18 feet high.
>
> From here, a stream sewer, averaging 15-30 feet wide and 3-18 feet high, composes the Southern Passage of the system, and an upper dirt-floored passage leads to the Lone Stalagmite Room, 500 feet farther on. To the left along this upper level passage is a 70-foot active domepit named the Rain Chamber. The Lone Stalagmite Room is 100 feet long and 30 feet high, intersected by a small stream passing through on its way to the Rain Chamber. A single 1½ foot stalagmite in the middle of the room is one of the few speleothems in the cave. However, on the far side of the room is a passage leading northeast which contains some interesting stalactites and other calcite formations along the two stoopway leads which have not been fully explored. A 20-foot intermittent canyon runs southwest from the Lone Stalagmite Room for 500 feet until it is interrupted by breakdown, which might possibly be penetrated.

Figure 8.1. Ray Nelson at the Entrance to Espey Cave. Photo by Bob Biddix, August 9, 2005.

Returning to the Lone Stalagmite Room, there is but one choice – a 10 X 10-foot passage which runs parallel to the lower-level storm sewer for its complete length of 1,700 feet. At the apex of this intersection is a 60-foot wide funnel-shaped room which is connected to both passages by a 4-inch high series of openings. Ahead 250 feet is a 25-foot high by 60-foot wide breakdown room, together with two smaller rooms and a connection with the storm sewer. Beyond this, there is but one large room of note – the Lunch Room, which is 50 feet wide, 200 feet long, and a maximum of 25 feet high in the middle, where the lower level joins. The upper and lower level passages run eastward from this room for 900 feet until the upper becomes too small to get through, and the lower is blocked by a siphon and a 25-foot domepit.

The cave's 6,500 feet take on a variety of forms and shapes from breakdown rooms to dirt-floored walking passages. Like all caves, Asby has those <u>crawlways</u>, but it is not muddy. Altogether, it presents an enjoyable and interesting day of caving, along with the possibility of virgin discovery, since it is seldom visited.[1]

Figure 8.2. Looking out the entrance to Espey Cave. Morgan Brown is the silhouette by the cave stream. Photo by Edward M. Yarbrough, April, 1974.

This is an excellent description of the main passages of the cave and it is nice to know that there are place names. Anyone who has visited this cave can easily recognize the locations in the cave from this narrative.

Barr's Description of the Cave

Espey Cave is described by Thomas C. Barr, Jr. in his book, Caves of Tennessee (1961):

Espey Cave (sometimes called "Jamison Cave") is the largest cave in Cannon County and is well known to the residents of the area. Candled on the ceiling of an upper-level room are names and dates as old as 1847. The cave is mentioned in the Tennessee edition of *Monteith's Comprehensive Geography* (1884). The cave stream once powered a mill a few yards below the mouth. On March 2, 1957, the writer estimated the flow of this stream as 6 cubic feet per second.

The entrance is large and impressive in its beautiful natural setting at the head of a steep-walled hollow which cuts deep into the Highland Rim. A stream flows out this opening, which is 30 feet wide and 15 feet high. The length of the main channel of the cave is 3,500 feet, and the total length of the passages explored by the writer is nearly 2 miles. The amount of overburden attains a maximum of 250 feet or more.

The main cave trends generally eastward but is very sinuous and irregular in shape. At 150 feet from the mouth is a fork to the left which runs for 450 feet northwest, through a large collapse dome 75 feet in diameter. The dome exhibits concentric cantilever breakdown. Beyond this dome the northwest part of the cave averages 50 feet wide and 10 feet high; it ends in a breakdown.

At 900 feet a split into upper and lower levels occurs. The lower level is a dry, gravelly stream-bed crawlway which extends for 1,150 feet before rejoining the upper, larger level. The upper level

---

1 Howard R. White, Jr., "Asby Cave, Tennessee," *Southeastern Caver*, December, 1957, p. 8. Reprinted in the 1957 Speleo Digest on pp 1-16 – 1-17.

Figure 8.3. A caver watches water pour from a hole in the ceiling in Espey Cave. Photo by Bob Biddix, April 23, 2006

Figure 8.4. Erica Sughrue with soda straw stalactites and helictites in Espey Cave. Photo by Bob Biddix, February 22, 2015.

contains a number of large breakdown and formation rooms, and averages 25 feet wide and 15 feet high. On the west side of the main passage in the upper level is a domepit 75 feet high, from which water cascades into a pool 15 feet in diameter. Some small helictites are found in one part of this branch of the cave. Near the end of the cave is a long wide crawlway with large piles of bat guano at the end. The last 300 feet is a low, gravelly stream passage which finally ends in a narrow, water-filled fissure. A crayfish was seen in this pool, and a breeze was flowing through the fissure. In the lower level of the cave the limestone contains many beds of chert, which project as ledges from the walls and contribute to the irregularity of the floor.[2]

The description of the cave is quite accurate, and the accompanying map is of very good quality. It was

2 Thomas C. Barr, Jr., *Caves of Tennessee*, TN Division of Geology, Bulletin 64 (1961), pp 98-99.

prepared by C. K. Barr and T. C. Barr and is dated 1956. But this is a very large and complex cave and the description by Barr covers less than half of the currently known cave, only what would be considered the main passages.

New Year's Day Discovery

Howard R. White wrote the following article for the May 1957 *NSS News* to describe a major discovery by three Nashville cavers:

On New Year's Day, Donald Egbert, David Wilson, and I, all of Nashville, discovered a virgin passage which was to lead to the most spectacular helictites we had ever before seen. We have decided to withhold the location because of the fragility of the speleothems. The entrance to this passage is about four feet in diameter but twenty yards inside the dirt fill has fallen away and the passage becomes a

Figure 8.5. Erica Sughrue in a heligmite forest in Espey Cave. Photo by Bob Biddix, February 28, 2015.

narrow canyon, one-and-a-half to four feet wide and fifty feet high. However, dirt fill forms two to four levels beyond this opening and crawling is often necessary.

As we advanced beyond 200 yards from the mouth of this passage, we noticed a few calcite formations, but the passage soon diminished to a small orifice, one by one-and-a-half feet. I managed to squirm through and on the far side saw the first sample of the spectacular speleothems that lay ahead – graceful, snow-white helictites growing from a wide shelf and spiraling to a height of five inches.

During February and March four parties, made up of two or three members (Tom Barr, Tommy Trabue, Bill Walter, Donald Egbert, and myself) returned to the passage and completed exploration of the canyon. The following is a report of the trip Bill Walter of Louisville, Kentucky and I made on the ninth of March.

We went 300 yards within the canyon and then descended to the bottom, which contains a stream of about 25 gallons per minute capacity. Then we headed upstream through slippery mud, along shelves in the canyon wall for 300 yards. At this point we reached a domepit, 35 feet high, 25 feet wide and 60 feet long, divided into two parts by a steep wall of breakdown. One hundred yards farther, a second domepit of similar size was encountered. Here a waterspout 25 feet above the floor provides one-half of the stream supply while the rest comes from a passage leading from the domepit.

This passage takes on different characteristics from the canyon. It is four feet high and three to ten feet wide with the stream flowing through a three-foot trench which winds down the center of the passage. Banks of red clay, teaming with red gypsum arrows (the flakey crystalline structure), slope toward the trench on both sides. This feature provided the name "Red Gypsum River Passage." This passage contains one outstanding speleothem – a set of three stalagmites, six inches high, which are completely covered with large gypsum arrows an inch long. They resemble some new innovation in subterranean cactus.

The canyon, which we have named "The Grand Helictite Canyon," is controlled by a bedding plane at the ceiling, while the stream has cut the canyon from eight to fifty feet in depth over its seven-hundred-yard course. The helictites occur at the top two or three levels between two-hundred and four-hundred yards from the entrance to the canyon. These levels often meander in wide "S" shaped patterns and several loops are yet to be explored.

Helictites occur on the walls as well as shelves, and one must take great care not to break them. Many beautiful helictites fill the wide shelves near the ceiling. Stalactites and stalagmites between the ceiling and shelves sometimes fuse together to form its sides. Some of the most impressive ones occur on the floor. In one spot the floor sinks to resemble a miniature sunken garden of gnarled, seven-inch helictites. In another spot the massive appendages of a helictite sprawl out seven inches along the floor.

One of the most spectacular features of the canyon is the remarkable variety of color that composes the speleothems. There are white and flesh-colored helictites rising seven inches above

Figure 8.6. Red stalactites in Espey Cave. Scale in photo is 2-inches X 2-inches. Photo by Larry E. Matthews, February 9, 1974.

shelves covered with dark purple flowstone. One small inset in the passage contains one-and-a-half-foot white soda straws, which are trimmed with narrow ribbons of blood-red calcite winding down their surfaces.

In my opinion, the most impressive speleothem in the canyon is a semi-transparent white helictite, which elegantly winds to a height of nine inches. Its branches are sparsely sprinkled with what resembles powdered lampblack, forming a thing a rare beauty.

Except for several loops, the Grand Helictite Canyon has been explored and photographed. Everyone who participated in the exploration agrees that these helictites are the most colorful and the most beautiful of any seen in Tennessee.[3]

The article is accompanied by one photograph of the helictites taken by H. R. White. Although the article purposefully does not mention the cave by name, this discovery was made in Espey Cave. Espey Cave is so large and the entrance to this passage is so insignificant looking, that no one returned to this passage for 4 years.

My First Visit to the Cave

This was another of my friends' and my favorite caves when we were in high school. It was reasonably close to Nashville, the roads were good, and we could get there and spend a lot of time exploring. You would park along a road, where the stream exited Cave Hollow, and follow a trail about a half mile to the entrance. The entrance sits at the base of a huge bluff and is quite spectacular. Ah, those were the good old days.

A few years later, a Yankee purchased the land along the road and put up dozens of "No Trespassing" signs. He would not let you follow the trail to the cave, even though he did not own the cave or the hollow that it was in. To this day, you now have to drive to the top of the ridge above the cave and hike down the very steep slope to reach the entrance, and then hike back up this steep slope to return to your car.

---

3 Howard R. White, "Tennessee's Beautiful Helictites," *NSS News*, Vol. 15 (1957), no. 5, pp 55-56.

Figure 8.7. Jonathan Griffith in a large passage in Espey Cave. Photo by Bob Biddix, November 26, 2005.

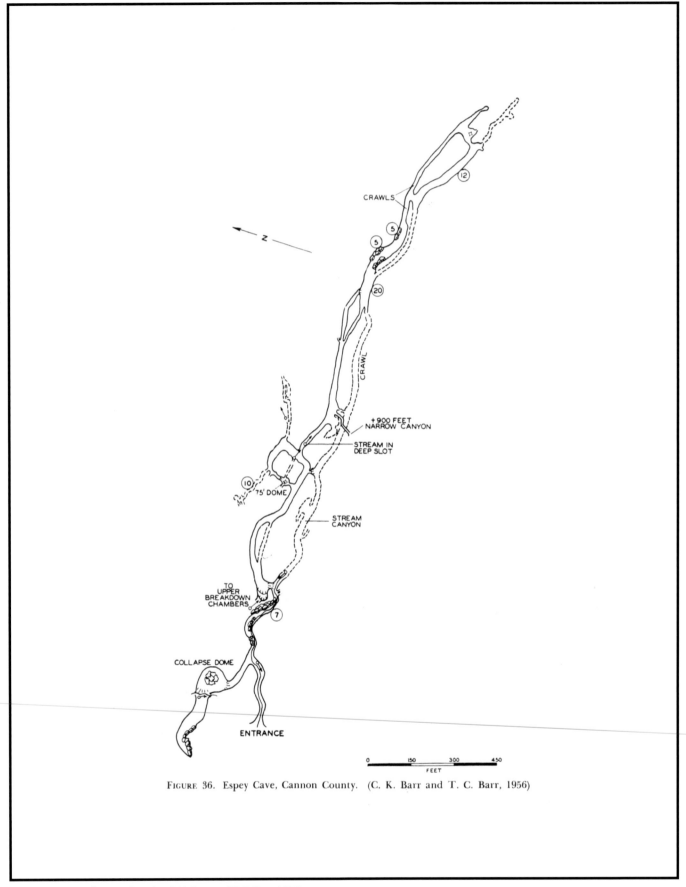

FIGURE 36. Espey Cave, Cannon County. (C. K. Barr and T. C. Barr, 1956)

Figure 8.8. Map of Espey Cave by C. K. Barr and T. C. Barr, 1956.

The Rediscovery of the Helictite Passage

Several of us in the Nashville Grotto in the early 1970s were aware that there was a Helictite Passage somewhere in Espey Cave, but none of us had been able to locate it… yet. On March 9, 1974 a car load of us parked at the top of the ridge above Espey Cave and climbed down the steep slope to the entrance. Based on leads in old issues of the *Speleonews*, we finally located what we thought might be the entrance to the Helictite Passage. The party consisted of Larry Adams, Steve Loftin, Marietta Matthews, and me. At first we explored an interesting canyon passage that showed very little sign of past traffic. A very old, empty carbide can was located in a small side dome. The canyon was sinuous, and you could not see far ahead. This continued for quite a ways. We weren't really sure this was the right passage, but it was very interesting. Finally, we rounded a corner and there on a shelf along the left wall… there they were… hundreds and hundreds of really nice helictites. Of course, the cameras came out and we started taking photographs. The further we went the more profuse and spectacular the formations became. I don't think we even considered leaving until everyone had used up all their film for their cameras.

It was a long trip back to the entrance. It had been a very tiring trip, and we still had that steep hill to climb up to get back to the car. We didn't reach the car until well after midnight. By the time we got back to Murfreesboro we were all starving, but this was back in the day when there were very, very few all-night diners. We did locate one, emblazoned with the sign: "Good Food." Well, that was what we wanted. Even though we had changed clothes, we were still quite muddy and the few people in the place were looking at us sort of funny. We finally got a waitress to come over to take our order. She came back with a big handful of silverware, which she held about three feet above the center of the table, then she dropped them!!! No, we were not really welcome. After a wonderful meal of burgers and fries we continued back to Nashville and did not get home until nearly 3 am. But, it had been worth it. We had found the helictites and they were even better than we had imagined.

Only much later did I find out that Ed Yarbrough and Jimmy Hiett had previously rediscovered the Helictite Passage…thirteen years earlier! They found the passage in May, 1961 and some of the photos from that trip are included in this chapter. Ed informs me that he took Roy Davis and David Smith to see the Helictite Passage in 1962. So, all those years while the rest of us wondered where the helictites were….all we had to do was ask Ed Yarbrough.[4]

Modern Explorations in Espey Cave

Modern cave explorers have access to equipment that the early explorers did not. In some cases, this allows them to push far beyond where previous explorers were forced to turn around. This is especially true of the wetsuit. Joel Buckner describes just such a trip into Espey Cave in 1983:

> Saturday, July 16th, was just too hot and muggy for a surface digging project I had planned so I cancelled that and set up a wetsuit push trip to Espey Cave instead. Don Tebbet and David Parr met me in Woodbury and we were soon at the parking spot above the cave. A few seconds later Paula Ledbetter and Joe Douglas pulled up and after a few more seconds so did Sue Loveless and Jim Hodson. Pretty good timing considering we came separately and were supposed to meet at 10:00 AM and it was then 10:30 AM.
>
> Our goal was a near sump with a breeze described by Tom Barr as being the end of the cave. We hiked down the steep hillside (It was actually kind of a semi-controlled fall) and then into the cave. Along the way, Hodtite kept telling us how he had been to the spot years before and that it was an absolute end with water falling from a dome. He also said there were no pools of water when he was there. "Sure Jim, we'll just take a look anyway since we're here with our wetsuits and all."
>
> Arriving at our destination we saw that there was indeed a dome with water falling and there was also a passage on the left well with about 6 inches of air space above water about 3 feet deep. A strong breeze was ripping out of the passage. We suited up and immersed ourselves as Hodtite rambled on about how he was going to have to get a wetsuit. Sue was also wetsuit-less and remained behind also. Joe was hardcore and plunged in with only wool for warmth.

---

4 Edward M. Yarbrough, Personal communication, February 5, 2019.

Figure 8.9. Beautiful helictites and soda straw columns in Espey Cave. Photo by Edward M. Yarbrough, May, 1961.

The passage immediately opened up and then immediately closed down again to an even lower air space. Only 2 or 3 inches separated the water and ceiling and the wind was so strong it rippled the water surface! After a moment's hesitation we went on through and were rewarded with a great mud slide into deep water on the other side. Even though dry, walking passage beckoned us on, we had to spend about 15 minutes repeatedly enjoying this subterranean playground first.

With great expectations we explored onward through about 1,000 feet of alternating walking, crawling passage. Then the passage lowered and narrowed into a dig with a noticeable lack of air flow. We dug awhile and then poked around until David found an 80-foot high dome with a short, tight passage to a smaller dome off of it. We noticed a few possible high leads, but they were beyond our reach that day. We backtracked and retrieved Hodson (Sue had already vamoosed for a warmer environment) and headed out of the netherworld.

The air has got to be coming from somewhere and we figure it must be one of the high leads. We plan to return soon for a more thorough investigation of this mystery.

Kathy Boozer, David Parr, and I also located another lead with terrific air movement in the cave recently. It is located in a section of the cave that apparently had only been visited by two people previously. They left their names (like a thousand other morons have done in the cave) and blocked up their route into the new section. We came in through a tight climb and exited by their tight crawl. The section contains one of the bigger rooms to a breakdown that blows very strongly. There are three possible ways to get through, but some instant cave will probably be required for penetration.

Hodtite also told us of another good lead; in a remote section of the cave there is what appears to be a walking passage that might be accessible by boosting someone up to it.[5]

5 Joel Buckner, "Espey Exploratory Excursions," *Speleonews*, Vol. 27 (1983), no. 5, pp 68-69.

Figure 8.10. Fantastic helictites in Espey Cave. Photo by Edward M. Yarbrough, May, 1961

The 1990 Discovery

Don Lance gives the following description of the cave, which includes passages not mentioned in Barr's description:

An article on the mapping of Espey Cave by the Tennessee Central Basin Grotto and other TCS members has been written for an upcoming *NSS News*, so only a brief description of the cave's major sections is given here.

The 1847 date mentioned by Barr has not been located, but a charcoal-etched "R. D. McGill, 1840" has been found. Also, there are remains of saltpeter casts and pick marks in Espey's left-hand fork – indicating that saltpeter mining was once in operation.

Immediately north of the main passages depicted in Barr's map are a sinuous set of complex tunnels and crawls. One such crawlway from this area quickly enlarges to roughly 10 feet high and 15 feet

wide and eventually intersects a dome complex with several large, attractive flowstone formations. Leads from this area connect to the Upper Breakdown Chambers to the south and also to Morrison's Hall to the north – a breakdown chamber that measures over 100 feet across, 75 feet wide, and 60 feet high. The main passage from the dome complex continues westward until breakdown puts a halt to further progress. Just prior to the breakdown is a tight, 8-inch crawlway which leads southward and quickly connects to the cantilever dome Barr mentioned in the left-hand fork.

Further north of this area lies Discovery '90, a section first entered by TCBG members Keith Filson and Don Lance in June of 1990. Access to the section is through a tight breakdown crawlway known as the Agony Crawl, which was later shown to run under the breakdown in Morrison's Hall. Immediately past the crawl a tall canyon passage 20 feet wide and 40 feet tall is encountered. This in turn leads to Espey's largest room, the Gosh Room. The Gosh Room measures 230 feet long, 50 feet wide, and is 30-60 feet tall. A stream running through the middle of the room quickly sumps but can be followed upstream and northeastward for over 1,000 feet. Many loops and low, wet crawls are found extending from this streamway.

Immediately south of Espey's main tourist routes is a large confusing set of tall canyon passages which routinely interconnect at 3 to 4 different levels. Although Barr's map indicates "+900 feet narrow canyon," more than a mile of twisting passages have been charted. It is very possible to visit this area many times and never trace the same steps twice. Approximately 1,000 feet into this section is the famous Grand Helictite Canyon (discovered by Howard White, Donald Egbert, and David Wilson on January 1, 1957) where 6-9-inch, multicolored helictites and heligmites spiral from shelves along the walls amid 2-3-foot-long soda straws. This section is typically very muddy but is well worth a visit due to the abundance of exceptional formations. Beyond this area the canyon passages continue on several planes with approximately 50 feet of vertical extent between the highest and lowest level. A steady water flow at the bottom of the canyon can be followed for an additional 800 feet until a 30-

foot dome is encountered. The river passage, named the Red Gypsum River Passage by Howard White and Bill Walter, continues south through another dome for 900 feet until the passage becomes too low to continue. This point, some 1,100 feet east and 1,600 feet south of the entrance is probably close to 2 miles of in-cave travel from the entrance due to the convoluted nature of the passages.

Roughly 200 feet down the main upper level trunk from the beginning of the aforementioned canyon is a windy crawl off to the left. This passage becomes very tight after 50 feet (9 inches high and 3 feet wide), but soon becomes a hands-and-knees crawl for 200 feet. After a small dusty slide through a constriction, a passage leads upward until breakdown is encountered. Chimneying up through the breakdown brings a caver into the Great X Chamber, a waterfall room 80 feet long, 50 feet wide, and 50 feet tall. A promising passage at the top of the room travels 50 feet before ending. Leads from this area have been found to proceed upwards to the highest surveyed point in the cave (130 feet above the entrance). One lead at the bottom of the room takes the caver into a jagged canyon (Fishhook Canyon) which soon intersects a stream passage 10 feet wide and 15 feet tall. Downstream quickly sumps, but only after 100 feet upstream another large room is found. The room, Greater X Chamber, is 120 feet long, 30 feet wide, and between 5-20 feet tall. A 15-foot drop through the room's breakdown leads to at least 300 more feet of nice muddy stream passage and domes.

The water-filled fissure at the cave's end mentioned by Barr was pushed by Joe Douglas and others during 1983. Usually a sump, the water level lowers enough in dry conditions to allow penetration. After 90 feet of relatively low airspace, the cave opens once again and continues for over 1,600 feet as large gravel crawls. The passages in this section are usually 30 feet wide and 4 feet tall, but several breakdown areas and domes reach a height of 20 feet or more. Near the end of this area extends an easy, walking 12-foot tall, 5-foot wide passage that is well decorated with formations resembling candle wax (The Wax Works). The nearby 45-foot TCB Dome is also well-decorated and contains 2-foot-long soda straws and other beauties.

Just beyond the Wax Works, a windy hole in breakdown entices the caver further. An 8-inch irregular hole in breakdown will keep out all but the thinnest cavers. At this point, some 3,000 feet due east of the entrance, water-filled crawls are once again encountered. The passages in this section are typically 30 feet wide and 3 feet high, with 1-foot to 3-inch airspaces. Over 600 feet has been surveyed here, but a push trip has revealed an additional 1,200 feet beyond to add to the map. The passage finally (?) ends in a sump underneath Jakes Hollow. The total amount of cave which lies beyond the sump specified by Barr is roughly 3,500 feet.

As of this writing, the BCBG/TCS survey was still in progress. The survey is mainly the work of Ron Zawislak, Keith Filson, Don Lance, and Marbry Hardin, although they have received assistance from approximately 30 other cavers.[6]

Filson's Tight Crack

The January 1991 issue of *TCB Passages* describes another major discovery in Espey Cave:

The Tennessee Central Basin Grotto first became interested in historical Espey Cave with the arrival of Murfreesboro caver Keith Filson. A seasoned Espey caver of over fifty trips, Keith had many leads in Espey Cave that called for pushing. One particularly gruesome, blowing lead at the end of an agonizing crawl kept him coming back. With caver Marbry Hardin, Keith finally succeeded in squeezing through what today is called Filson's Tight Crack and emerged in a virgin passage forty feet high and twenty feet wide. Wisely, he chose not to continue since Marbry couldn't negotiate the seven-inch slot.

Afterwards, Keith attended the May 1990 TCB Grotto meeting and asked for assistance at the cave, and he also requested that the Grotto take up the survey of well-known Espey. Research revealed that several attempts had been made in the past thirty years by many groups, but none had ever fully surveyed the sprawling cave.

---

6 Don Lance, Tennessee Cave Survey Narrative Series: Cannon County, Tennessee," 1994, pp CN-16 – CN-17. Used by permission from Don Lance.

Nonetheless, this discussion of Espey Cave interested TCB caver Don Lance. He accompanied Keith to the cave on June 3, 1990 and they travelled down the Agony Crawl to Filson's Tight Crack. At the Crack, Keith was able to pass but Don wasn't. Undaunted, they spent the next two hours digging a bypass, and finally Don was able to stand with Keith in the new passage. To this day, no one else has been able to pass through Filson's Tight Crack, save Filson himself.

The ensuing push of this new passage revealed a new, large segment of Espey that had never seen light. Among the discoveries on that first trip were the 230 foot Gosh Room and the thousand-foot-long Streamway, which heads northeast from the rest of the cave and boasts a strong wind. To date, approximately 1,800 feet has been surveyed in the new section's main thoroughfares, and it is expected to reach a total of half a mile unless it contains a few more surprises.

After the initial discovery trip, Don Lance, Jeff Parnell, Jim Freeman, and Drex Freeman began the survey in the appropriately named Discovery '90. Since that time, the surveying has mainly been accomplished by TCB members Marbry, Keith, Don, and MTSU professor Dr. Ron Zawislak. We are very fortunate to have Ron's survey expertise, for we are attempting to incorporate old survey data and we frequently encounter closures and multiple levels in the three-dimensional world that is Espey.[7]

Clearly Espey Cave is very, very complex. I know when I was in high school and college, my friends and I never ran out of new leads to explore. It was a FUN cave. It still is. It would be a wonderful cave for the SCCi to acquire and preserve.

The Surveys of Espey Cave

Espey Cave has been surveyed at least three times, probably more. There is a very good map of the main passages in Barr's *Caves of Tennessee* (1961) on page 99. This map was prepared by C. K. Barr and T. C. Barr and is dated 1956 (See Figure 8.8).

The next survey for which we actually have survey reports and a map was done by the Nashville Grotto in the early 1960s. It appears that they were not aware

of Barr's map. An article in the June 1961 *Speleonews* announced the beginning of the project:

Grotto Project: Mapping Asby Cave

During the May meeting of the Nashville Grotto, the subject of a Grotto Project was discussed. At the previous meeting it had been suggested that the Grotto should do a mapping project on Asby's Cave, near Woodbury, Tennessee; however, no specific action was taken. This suggestion was again brought forth and this time acted on. It was definitely decided to map Asby's. It was also decided that a set of Kodachrome slides would be made up, centered on this cave and would be submitted to the SERA Slide Circle Program.

The mapping project began on May 21, and will continue of June 3 and later dates, if necessary. The mapping will be a "compass and tape" survey, with vertical distances estimated. This type of survey should be accurate enough for our purposes. The map will be as extensive as the group's enthusiasm and crawlway endurance permit.

It has not been decided if the famed Helictite Passage will be included in the map – certain members of the Grotto feel that to include it would open the way for vandalism; this was brought to the attention of the Chairman after the May meeting. A decision will be made on this at the June meeting. The passage in question contains some of the most beautiful helictites to be seen anywhere, but it is known only to a very few people who have very carefully preserved their beauty and location. The Helictite Passage will be included in the slides, as well as pictures of many more beautiful formations, including totems, pillars, and blood-red stalactites.[8]

Progress Report on Asby Mapping Project

The single trip (so far) spent mapping Asby Cave on May 20 has already brought forth some very interesting findings. Some 3,500 feet of cave have been mapped and have now been plotted on a "1 cm equals 10 feet' scale, which makes a three-and-a-half-meter map, which is a lot of map. Which is, indeed, fitting.

7 Don Lance, "Espey Cave, Cannon County, Tennessee," TCB Passages, Vol. 1, no. 1, p. 13.

8 Ken Bunting, "Grotto Project: Mapping Asby Cave," Speleonews, Vol. 5 (1961), no. 2, pp 5-6.

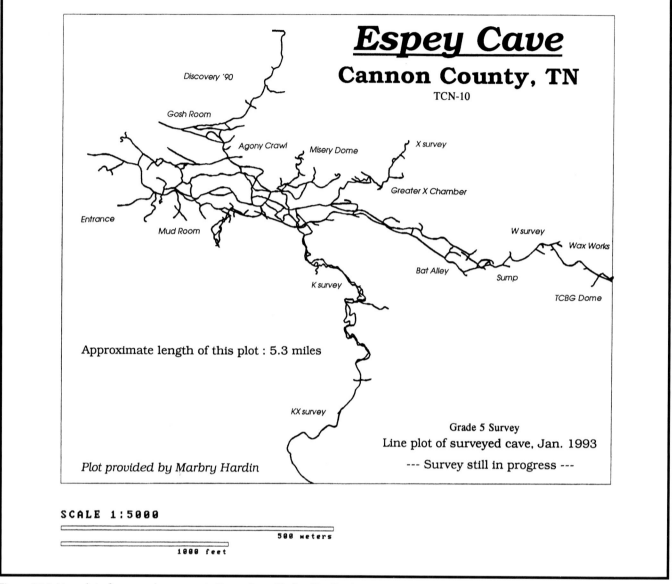

Figure 8.11. Line plot of surveyed passages in Espey Cave, Marbry Hardin, January, 1993.

The most interesting observation one can make of the 3,500 feet already mapped and plotted is that the "C" survey (major right-hand passage out of the second big room) doubles back to the "A" survey passage (main passage). This brings up the strong possibility of one or more connections between these two major passages; this would provide a "loop" which would greatly increase the attractiveness of the cave. As inevitably happens, the stories of "endless passages" have been beaten down by the unstretching tape measure.

On the trip of May 20, the 12 mappers were organized into one photography team and two mapping teams of five men each. Each mapping team was broken down as follows: one compass man, two tape men, one sketcher/recorder, and one team chief/recon man.

Instruments used were: lensatic compass of the military type (estimated accurate to 5 degrees) and tape (estimated accurate to 1%). Since vertical distances were estimated and ignored in the final plotting, the over-all accuracy is estimated to be within 5%.

The small-scale map will serve as a permanent reference; when the mapping and plotting is completed, it will be reduced to 8 X 10 and 1/2 size and published in this journal.

A brief article in the January 1962 *Speleonews* reports that the survey has come to an end and includes a map

Figure 8.12. White heligmites on a ledge in Espey Cave. Photo by Bob Biddix, June 8, 2008.

of the passages that had been mapped. Sally Child wrote the following report in 1962:

Espey (Asby) Cave: Grotto Project

… has come to an end. However, this is not to say the "entire" cave has been mapped; rather this represents that portion which will be of wide use to the careful, cautious, conservation-minded spelunker.

There are passages abound for further mapping which may be a future project for the Grotto, or for an interested person.

We have mapped by means of tape and compass those passages we consider of primary interest and value. Widths and heights of the passages are approximate. Points in the cave, be it on the wall or ceiling of the passage, are not permanent. Total amount of passage mapped: 6,034 1/6 feet.

Thanks go to every Grotto member and visitor for his contribution in the work and finishing of

this project. Articles concerning the last mapping trip and the finished map follow.[9]

Mapping D Passage

There was the usual confusion of deciding what to survey and who was to survey it. The group was divided into two parties equipped with the necessities for mapping. Our group, consisting of five with the purpose of surveying D passage, included Jerry Boynton, Mary Alice, Eric Wilson, a guest, and myself.

After locating a point from which to start, the survey progressed rapidly until we encountered a very tight crawl which slowed us down. D passage is a winding stoop and crawlway with two other passages branching off, both to the left, one ending in a mud fissure and the other winding for about one hundred and fifty feet circling back into D

9 Sally M. Child, "Espy (Asby) Cave: Grotto Project," Speleonews, Vol. 6 (1962), no. 5, p. 2.

passage. This passage was not surveyed, though we did map a little over 600 feet on this trip.

When we arrived at the entrance the other party had not come out, so we had lunch while waiting for them to emerge. When they did arrive, they had mapped a bit more cave than our party. Could be the reason was they had two hours more time.[10]

Mapping the Helictite E Passage

It was about 11:00 a.m. on the day of the May Grotto meeting when our group reached Espey Cave. Our project for the day was to map two of the more beautiful and harder side passages.

As will be seen when the slide circle is completed these passages are to the Totem Pole Room and the Helictite Passage. The Totem Pole Room has several feet of tight crawlway passage to it. You will see this when the map is projected.

However, this is not the part of the cave we want to tell you about. With Kenneth Bunting and Tommy Hutchison to handle the tape and compass, two young women who had doubts but traveled on (in ignorance) went along to take care of paperwork. These were Sally Child on technical data and Mary Jo Bunting on sketching.

The passageway was awkward and tight in several places. We had come to the conclusion that this was going to be just a rough hike until we came to the end of the passage and looked up. There was the Helictite Passage, the beauty of it made the trip worthwhile. We had taken a lower passage, which we believe is actually easier than the upper level. Words cannot tell of the beauty of the Helictite Passage. The Grotto should have a fine slide circle.

Kenneth and Tommy didn't have much trouble maneuvering the passage, but Sally and Mary Jo did. There were several times when they were thankful they didn't eat that extra piece of pie and also they have promised themselves to lose inches and pounds before they go back to the Helictite Passage. There is one thing though to our knowledge, Sally and Mary Jo were the first girls to see the passage. We hope there will be others. The only really bad things about going back there, is the fact that it is hard not to break some of the formations when traveling

through. We want to urge any future travelers of the Helictite Passage to be very careful. It was 5:00 when we staggered out of Espey Cave, our mission completed, two hours later than our prescribed meeting. The girls at least never thought the sun looked lovelier![11]

And so, yet another survey of Espey Cave came to an end. Looking at the finished map, there are several key survey stations shown. Therefore, we know that the A Survey began at the entrance and continued down the Main Passage. The B survey bears left from the Main Passage about 250 feet from the entrance and ends after about 300 feet. The C Survey bears right from the Main Passage where the upper level splits off from the stream level. The Nashville Grotto's 1962 map does not appear to be as complete as Barr's map, but it does show the Helictite Passage.

Louis Hardin mentioned another mapping effort in 1964, as reported earlier in this history of Espey Cave. Whatever became of that map or the survey notes is unknown. It is fair to say that for many large Tennessee caves, at least portions of them, have been surveyed many times, but few finished maps were ever produced.

Another survey was begun in 1979 by Brad Neff and several other cavers after the discovery of a large room named Morrison's Hall. Although this survey was never finished, the Central Basin Grotto members did use that information years later.[12]

The most recent, and complete, map of the cave was made by the Tennessee Central Basin Grotto. The survey began in 1990 and was led by Marbry Hardin and Ron Zawislak. Here are trip reports of several of their survey trips:

December 14, 1990

Don Lance and Keith Filson decided that they shouldn't receive their college degrees without cave dirt in their fingernails. With Marbry Hardin and Dr. Ron Zawislak, another survey/push trip to Espey Cave was scheduled the night before graduation. After searching the east area of the cave for ten-year-old survey marks, it was decided to possibly resurvey the area. After surveying the Funnel

---

10 Homer Martin, "Mapping D Passage," *Speleonews*, Vol. 6 (1962), no. 5, pp 2-3.

11 Mary Jo Bunting, "Mapping the Helictite E Passage," *Speleonews*, Vol. 6 (1962), No. 5, p. 3.

12 Don Lance, "The Mapping of Espey Cave, Tennessee," 2003 SERA Guidebook, pp 7-9.

Room and connecting passages, Ron had to leave and Marbry, Keith, and Don decided to push the N Survey. The only breakthrough was the discovery of an eight-inch virgin crawlway through breakdown. Since the crawlway was across from the formation known as the N-peror (named for the N survey), it was called the N-peror's Pinch. Amazingly, the crawlway connected with the Left-hand Fork of the cave, the first known passage ever known to extend into more cave on that side.[13]

December 28, 1990

Marbry Hardin and Don Lance headed into Espey Cave for an intended 24-hour survey trip. After an almost complete resurvey of the Left-hand Fork of the cave to tie into the N-peror's pinch, they started toward the Discovery '90 section, surveying side leads along the way. At approximately 2:00 am Saturday morning (12/29/90), Marbry reported feeling nauseous and lightheaded. Don noticed he was pale but was showing no signs of hypothermia. Upon Marbry's suggestion, they immediately headed out of the cave.[14]

December 29, 1990

Don Lance returned to Espey Cave with Dr. Ron Zawislak to do more surveying. The N-peror's Pinch was closed with the Left-Hand Fork, and two shortcuts were found and surveyed into a dome area.[15]

Marbry Hardin reports that the final surveyed length of Espey Cave as 6.1 miles. This is the result of 66 survey trips into the cave.[16] A line plot of surveyed passages was prepared by Marbry Hardin in January, 1993 that shows 5.3 miles of passages, but since the map fits on an 8 X 10.5 sheet of paper, there is very little detail. (See Figure 8.11.) Will this be yet another survey where no detailed map is ever finished and published? It certainly looks that way.

Marbry Hardin also notes that the stream crawl heading north from Discovery 90 has good airflow and is not that far from the next ridge over, which contains passage from Haws Spring Cave.[17] Is there a possibility that these two caves might connect?

Saltpeter Mining in Espey Cave

The Upper Level of Espey Cave contains significant evidence of mining for saltpeter. Casts of the leaching vats and pick marks can be found in the left-hand fork of the cave. Like most saltpeter caves, there are few historical records to help us determine exactly when this mining occurred. Saltpeter mining was widespread during the War of 1812 and there was a resurgence of mining during the Civil War. Espey Cave could have been mined during one, or both, of those periods. The lack of dates prior to 1840 may be a clue that this cave was only mined during the Civil War.

Cave Access

This cave and the access to it are located on private property. The current status is unknown. Always be sure you have the owner's permission before entering this, or any other pit or cave.

17 Marbry Hardin, Personal communication, September 21, 2017.

13 Don Lance, "TCB Items of Interest," *TCB Passages*, Vol. 1 (1991), no. 1, p. 7.
14 Don Lance, "Trip Reports," *TCB Passages*, Vol. 1 (1991), no. 1, p. 8.
15 Don Lance, "Trip Reports," *TCB Passages*, Vol. 1 (1991), no. 1, p. 8.
16 Marbry Hardin, Personal communication, September 21, 2017.

Figure 9.1. Kristen Bobo (left) and Mike Moser (right) by a large flowstone terrace in Haws Spring Cave. Photo by Joe Douglas, November 24, 2012.

CHAPTER 9
Haws Spring Cave

Haws Spring Cave is located in Cannon County, Tennessee. It is a very long, complex stream cave. Over 5 miles of passages have been surveyed, with another 2.5 miles explored, for a total length of 7.5 miles

A Description of the Cave

Gerald Moni gives the following description of the initial passages discovered in this cave in 1985 and 1986:

> The 5-foot wide, 1-½ foot high passage slopes down 6 feet to a tight 30-foot long crawl. This entrance can easily fill in, so it may be required to re-dig the entrance ever so often.
>
> The 30-foot crawl leads to a waist-deep pool about 25 feet long. A series of mainly walking passages at stream level and in a dry upper level goes back approximately 4,000 feet. Several side passages and loop-arounds probably bring the total passage length to over 2 miles for this section. This section can be done without a wet suit.
>
> The stream at the end of this section becomes a low bedding-plane crawl for the next 2,000 feet. This easy stream crawl leads to more rooms and walking passages. An 8-inch diameter water pipe drilled from the surface was seen in this area. An 800-foot mud crawl leads to the next section of the cave.
>
> At the end of the crawl, a left passage (walking, stooping, and crawling) was pushed for over 2,000 feet, but the cave continues beyond. The right passage was all walking for over 1,000 feet and some side passages were checked. The end of this passage was not reached either. At this point we were probably over 2 miles from the entrance, and we still had many unexplored side passages![1]

Discovery and Exploration

Joel Buckner wrote the following excellent story on the discovery and exploration of Haws Spring Cave:

Figure 9.2. Roger Haley, Jay Reeves, and an unidentified caver enlarging the entrance to Haws Spring Cave. Photo by Tom Moss, April, 1989.

This saga began in the eighties when Gerald Moni handed me an incomplete Tennessee Cave Survey report form, turned in by the late Peter Williams, that he had been unable to decipher the handwriting on. There was no latitude/longitude information on the form but there was a description and some sketches of a blowing dig near a spring and a natural bridge.

After studying the form a while, I was able to determine a possible location of the lead. So one Saturday, David Parr and I loaded up our gear and headed out for a looksee. We wound our way up a steep, wooded hollow on the Eastern Highland Rim escarpment that seemed to go in the general direction we wanted to go. We came to a fork where the county road turned and went up a side hollow. We noted that a good-sized stream was flowing out of the main hollow while the side hollow was dry. A gravel driveway continued up the main hollow. We headed up it and in a quarter mile or so came up on an old farmhouse with three young fellows lounging about on the porch. We introduced ourselves and explained the nature of our quest.

Sure enough, they said there was a spring and natural bridge a little further up the hollow and we were welcome to go check it out. We eagerly opened the gate they indicated and then four wheeled across

---

1 Gerald Moni, Tennessee Cave Survey Narrative Series: Cannon County, Tennessee (1994), p. CN-25.

Figure 9.3. Gerald Moni at the entrance to Haws Spring Cave. Photo by Joe Douglas, November 24, 2012.

a creek ford and plowed through tall weeds in a small field. On the far side of the field we arrived at a very scenic natural bridge about ten feet high and twenty feet wide with an opening about five feet high and ten feet wide underneath. There was a large spring rising in front of it and a bluff on the hillside behind.

We disembarked and admired the view, deciding that this alone was worth coming to see and anything else would be gravy. To us, the natural bridge was obviously a remnant of a cave passage left behind as the hill eroded back over the eons. Poking around, we immediately found a cave entrance under the bridge on the left that went into a small, irregular room with a pool of water. There was no discernable air flow and it looked like it would crap out.

Behind the bridge, a small rubble slope led up to the bluff. At the base of the bluff, the rubble sloped abruptly back down to a blowing hole, just as Peter

had drawn it on his sketch. The air flow was strong, but the hole was tiny just a few inches across. We figured the air must be coming from a continuation of the passage that made the natural bridge.

We began digging to enlarge the blowhole but quickly encountered a problem. The further down we dug, the more the rubble from the slope above tumbled down into the blowhole. More was falling in than we were digging out so that the hole was actually being filled in faster than we were opening it up! So, we had to change tactics and start at the top of the slope digging in the opposite direction until it was back reasonably far enough that we could work on the blowhole without worrying too much about becoming entombed. This took a couple of trips to accomplish. Finally, we removed enough that we could peer into a very low, perhaps two-inch-high and two-foot-wide, space heading directly back into the hill.

Figure 9.4. Mike Moser wading and Gerald Moni on an inner tube in Haws Spring Cave. Photo by Joe Douglas, November 24, 2012.

Starting to dig at this point was very awkward as you had to lie on your stomach with your head down at the hole and your torso and legs above on the slope. The air flow was so strong it would blow dirt in your face as you dug it up. The hole tended to get plugged by flesh as gravity kept sucking our bodies down the slope to wedge in the hole. Our remedy was a simple but effective, low tech, anti-gravity technique. Someone would hold the digger's feet to stop their slide into the hole as they dug. Gradually, as we dug, we became able to lie slightly more horizontally. Then we only had to contend with not being able to move our arms much ahead in the confined space while trying to push the dirt and rock we dug up back behind us and up the slope for the others to pull out before it slid back in on top of us. We used a variety of trays, buckets, and digging tools with varying degrees of success.

This went on for several more trips till eventually David was taking a turn and got in a body length or so. He reported he could see bigger space a ways ahead and thought it would be easier to just keep digging than to try to back up and out of the

Figure 9.5. Kristen Bobo (left) and Mike Moser (right) in a passage in Haws Spring Cave. Photo by Joe Douglas, November 24, 2012.

very tight hole. So he kept grunting and groaning, worming and squirming, digging his way ahead inch by inch. We did our part by encouraging him ahead from behind with helpful remarks about how the slope seemed to be filling in the hole again, so he better dig faster. Fortunately, for David, he was pretty much immune to such smart-ass remarks due to constant exposure to them over the years.

After about twenty-five feet, he wallered out onto a mud bank in a room about ten feet high and fifteen feet in diameter with a wall to wall deep pool of water. Paul Alexander had accompanied us on the trip and David hollered back that Paul and I should come on in.

Having just heard the ordeal he went through to get there, we hesitated, whimpering back, "How big is the crawl?"

"Big enough" was the only answer we got.

David often digs just enough to get through and that was the case this time. We just barely did manage to cram our bodies through, though there was a lot more whimpering and whining involved. Joining him on the bank, we noticed the right side of the pool appeared shallower, so we waded across only getting chest deep. On the other side, a wide hands-and-knees crawl took off and in a short distance enlarged to a walking passage which then intersected a dome about thirty feet high.

The walking passage continued beyond for a hundred feet or so and then made a hard left and opened up to about thirty feet high and twenty feet wide. A side passage took off to the right. In another hundred feet or so a breakdown appeared to block further penetration. Dave and Paul began poking around the breakdown while I went back to the wide passage. It went a couple hundred feet before ending at a dome about fifty feet high.

Returning to where I had left the others, they were nowhere to be found. While I was contemplating what might have gotten them and what I was going to do with all their gear back in the truck, they suddenly popped up out of a hole in the floor. They reported going through a few hundred feet of walking and crawling passages before being stopped at a short drop off into a much larger passage.

We returned to the drop where you could see ahead a hundred feet or so through an irregular breakdown passage about forty feet high and thirty feet wide. The drop was only about ten feet but unclimbable and a rope would be needed. David said this would be a good stopping point for a return trip, but I was not ready to stop exploration so soon. I noticed a large breakdown block on the right up near the ceiling that offered a possible bypass for the drop.

I climbed up on it and after crawling fifty feet or so, was able to climb back down into the passage. David and Paul quickly followed, but we were soon stopped by another short drop. Luckily, there was a nearby hole by which we were able to climb down and get back to the stream level.

We walked onward, and the passage soon became an unbroken trunk about twenty-five feet in diameter. We sauntered down it with jaws hanging open gaping at the bountiful booty of the pristine ancient corridor before us. A fork appeared, and we eagerly explored up it to another, then another, and then yet another, through a multitude of similar sized large walking passages and loops. After exploring a couple thousand feet or more and running around hooting and hollering like delirious maniacs, we reached a point where the main passage lowered back down to a stream crawl. We finally called it a day here. A damn good day!

On the next trip, we explored many more side passages including one before the first drop. It went several hundred feet as a small passage before intersecting a trunk passage segment that ended in fill. A low and wet blowing crawl led off on the left side. We squirmed up if fifty feet or so digging as we went. It continued ahead but more digging would be required, and we left if for another go later.

On another trip, David and Gerald Moni pushed the main stream crawl wearing wetsuits. They crawled for a couple thousand feet through water before it finally opened back up into some larger passages. They saw a group of flowstone columns there, and David noticed one appeared peculiar before realizing it was a well casing that just happened to come through the midst of the columns. The water crawl continued beyond and they pushed it another eight hundred feet or so to yet another section of larger passages. A later survey showed that the stream crawls were passing under hollows and the larger sections opened up under ridges between.

All in all, we guesstimated we had explored upwards of five miles of mighty fine virgin cave.

The fellows we met at the farmhouse were from Huntsville, Alabama and the property belonged to one of their families. They got interested in caving after we told them of our discoveries and before long they started a survey of the cave. They worked at a company called Intergraph and were members of the Undergraph Caving Club[2], which was pretty active with a large membership for some time.

I ran into Jay Reeves, one of the original three fellows, at a TCS meeting not long after that and he produced a map of their survey of the cave. He said they had mapped everything they could find and had about fifteen hundred feet total footage surveyed. The map looked like a good survey of what they had done.

He asked how much cave we had explored. I said, "Oh, about five miles."

His jaw dropped, "Where is it?" he asked in an understandably plaintive voice.

I pointed to a spot on his map and told him you go down through a hole in the floor there. They had scoured the walls and did some climbs, but it didn't occur to them that the floor was a possibility. I think they were kind of in a 2.5 D mode as they looked left and right, forward and backward, but only up and not down. The hole in the floor wasn't obscure, but they just hadn't been caving long enough yet to learn that a cave can go almost anywhere.

Well, they soon made a beeline back to the cave and started racking up footage. They didn't miss anything else either. Jay later gave me a map with about six miles surveyed. The topo overlay with this article has about five miles of the survey. They mapped the long stream crawl that David and Gerald did to 2,001 feet in length. They named it: "2,001: A Water Crawl Odyssey" which I thought was one of the best cave passage names I've heard.

Most of the cave was relatively dry so they got tired of wading across the pool and being wet for the rest of the trip. They rigged up a cave ferry consisting of a raft of inner tubes and planks lashed together along with a double pull line and pulleys. Then they could hop on to float and pull themselves back and forth across the pool inside the entrance thereby staying mostly dry.

They also returned to the blowing dig we started in the side passage and dug through the rest of the way. They said that beyond they found another mile or so of cave with some of the biggest passages and best formations in the cave. We thought that they deserved some virgin booty after all the time and work they had put in the cave. Unfortunately, a rock later fell blocking off access to this section.

This cave is formed in Ordovician age Bigby Cannon limestone in the Eastern Highland Rim Escarpment physiographic province. It is the second longest known cave in that province. Maybe one of these days we'll get in there and open it back up.[3]

This just goes to prove that you can still find a lot of really good virgin cave if you are willing to put in the time to dig open a promising blowing lead. A worthwhile project now would be for somebody to go in and remove the rock that blocks access to the last mile of the cave that was discovered.

The Survey of Haws Spring Cave

From the TN Cave Survey Files:

A survey of Haws Springs Cave was begun by Roger Haley, Angela Morgan, and other Huntsville, AL cavers, with the effort being led by Jay Reeves. Roger Haley adds that the 2000-foot stream crawl was named: "2001 – A Stream Crawl Odyssey," and that the crawl travels beneath a valley and connects cave in two separate ridges. During the summer of 1993 the cave survey was believed to be ending at around 32,000 feet, however, a recent push trip brought the surveyors through a crawl into yet another ridge with booming trunk! They now estimate that Haws Spring Cave may have in excess of 40,000 feet. Survey trips into the new area are now being planned.[4]

---

2 This was not an NSS Grotto. Tom Moss, Personal communication, September 29, 2018

3 Joel Buckner, "The Discovery of Haws Spring Cave," *Tennessee Caver*, 2013, pp 14-20. Used by permission of Joel Buckner

4 Don Lance, Tennessee Cave Survey Narrative Series: Cannon County, Tennessee (1994), p. CN-25.

Figure 9.6. Bill Hanson by beautiful red-orange stalactites in Haws Spring Cave. Photo by Tom Moss, April, 1989.

The following entries are summaries of some of those surveying trips:

May 6, 1989 Jay Reeves, David Norvell, Angela Morgan, Tom Herring, Phil Kirshtein, and Tom Moss. Tom Moss reports: "We did the mud climb and surveyed to the Wet Felt Room, then to the crawlway with nuts, claw marks, etc., in it. Then we went out to the main passageway and mapped the side passage past the Wet Dream Formation to the Bird Passage.[5]

January 27, 1990 Jay Reeves, Angela Morgan, Tom Herring, Mike Gross, and Tom Moss. Tom Moss reports: "Surveyed the Haystack Heaven area in the Cobblestone Sewer section, then checked out and surveyed leads in the south portion of the main passage, just north of the water crawl.[6]

July 7, 1990 The trip this weekend netted 2,843.7 feet of cave—and a lot of it was virgin! This brings

Haws Spring to a total of 26,008.2 feet (4.93 miles)! We now have the longest cave in Cannon County with no end in sight.

The survey crews (Roger Haley, Pat Smith, Danny Cobb, Jon Brown, Mark Hughes, Rick O'Hara, Don Christman, Jimmy Dawson, and me) started in about 10:30 and proceeded to cover about 3,000 feet of cave in one hour to get to the start of "2001: A Water Crawl Odyssey." This is the 2,000-foot water crawl/swim (with about 1-foot of air space in places) that was surveyed during the last trip. After 2,000 feet of water crawling you come to the first walking passage, the Well Room, so named because an 8-inch well casing drops right into the middle of the cave passage. A crawl through some breakdown brings you into Steel Toe Junction, named for the rusting steel toe found there. There we split into 2 survey crews. Rick, Don and Jim headed south while Roger, Mark, Jon, and I headed north.

A little ways down the north passage we ran upon some formations we dubbed the Popsicles and called

5 Tom Moss, Personal communication, August 30, 2018

[6] Ibid.

Figure 9.7. Mike Moser (left) and Kristen Bobo (right) in a breakdown-floored passage in Haws Spring Cave. Photo by Joe Douglas, November 24, 2012.

this the Popsicle Passage. About this time Danny and Pat joined back up with us with tales of crystals and virgin rooms.

We then picked up a lead heading out of Steel Toe Junction and got into another water crawl. After about 600 feet we were in walking passage again. We had passed up several leads along the way and one of them was large walking passage. We headed south and finally got into a large room with a stream running across it. This room had part of the ceiling drooping down which looked as if at any minute it could go. We started to survey north out of this room and started to notice an abundance of fossils, some quite large. We also noticed some crystals that looked like dog-tooth spar that was all over the ceiling. One room we got into had a ceiling covered in soda straws, orange and white flowstone, stalagmites, stalactites, and rimstones. Reluctantly, we started our long trip out.

Figure 9.8. Kristen Bobo (left), Gerald Moni (middle), and Mike Moser (right) in a passage in Haws Spring Cave. Photo by Joe Douglas, November 24, 2012.

Figure 9.9. Phil Kirshtein by the Wet Dream Formation in Haws Spring Cave. Photo by Tom Moss, May, 1989.

August 18, 1990 There were seven people that did the water crawl to get to the surveying areas, which takes about 3 hours of hard caving to get to. Another group of twelve people were led on a tourist trip in the dry portion of the cave. They poked around near the beginning of the water crawl area for a while and actually got into some virgin cave and found a blowing lead. An extremely large bone was also found in this area and was removed with plans of submitting it to the Red Mountain Museum in Birmingham for identification.

Angela's survey crew (Roger Haley, Pat Smith, and Mark Hughes) headed to the big trunk passage to pick up the survey that we left the last trip. My crew (David Norvell and Ric Haley) resurveyed an area that was surveyed by a new group on the last trip. The reason for this resurvey was incomplete data and a belief that this area was not thoroughly covered.

We started our survey out of Steel Toe Junction. We found a crawl that led to an extremely low room with a crystal-covered floor which was dubbed the Salt Flats due to the white, flaky crystal covering a flat floor as far as we could see. We eventually popped into a large room with upper levels. This room was covered with flowstone. Some areas exhibited orange, white, and brown flowstone, columns, draperies, and soda straws that were quite striking in the contrast of the colors.

We then headed towards the area that Angela's crew should be in doing some lead mopping-up on the way. We found Angela's crew in the big trunk passage still surveying it. They had found a side passage that led to some upper levels that had a lot of fossils and a 50-foot dome. They finished up that area and came back out into the trunk passage and picked up their survey naming a 5-foot long blood-red stalactite the Red Sword. The trunk passage ended with a small, low room that was covered with white, orange, and beige crystalline flowstone, rimstones, columns, and soda-straws that was named Off Limits Grotto. They then surveyed

Figure 9.10. Kristen Bobo in a large passage in Haws Spring Cave. Photo by Joe Douglas, November 24, 2012.

a passage that was named the Bypass that came out into the trunk passage next to a 100-foot dome named Confusion Dome. The teams then started the long trip back to the entrance with the last person out at 10:30 pm.

Totals for the weekend are: Angela's crew 1,237.7 feet, Jay's crew 867.4 feet, for a total of 2,1051 feet for the weekend. The brings the surveyed length of the cave to 28,113.3 feet (5.32 miles).[7]

June 19, 1991 The latest Haws Spring trip netted a total of 2,233.7 feet of cave surveyed. Total surveyed length is now 29,775.8 feet (5.629 miles)

Pat Smith, Roger Haley, Mark Hughes, David Norvell, John Brown, and myself donned wetsuits and headed for the entrance at about 9 am. The survey teams entered the cave and slowly made their way back to the beginning of the 2001 Water Crawl. Water was encountered a lot sooner than usual as it was up a good 3-4 inches. The second, long crawl after Steel Toe Junction was flooded and that made an easy float trip through there, too. The survey area was finally reached 2.5 hours after entering the cave. We surveyed a good ways and came to a couple of splits in the passages. We surveyed into some domes

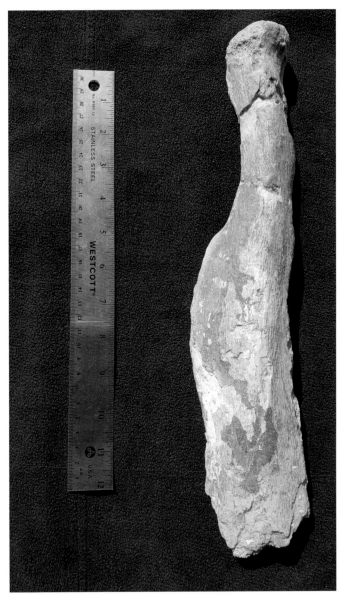

Figure 9.11. Photograph of a Giant Ground Sloth Radius from Haws Spring Cave. Photo courtesy of Donna Cobb, 2018.

that Jon found which we estimated to be around 120 feet high. It was about 8 pm when we started the move out. Both of the water crawls were found to have water levels about 2 inches lower than when we came in, which made for a long trip out as we now had to crawl where earlier we were floating.[8]

April 22, 1992 Jennifer Pinkly, Mike Thurber, Pat Smith, and Jay Reeves were the potential survey crew. Plans were made earlier that morning with people that were going to stay above ground to tap on the well-casing at a predetermined time and make contact with the survey crew below. Plans were also made before hand with the owners of the well to do this. In the conversation the owners

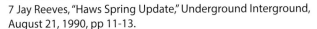

7 Jay Reeves, "Haws Spring Update," Underground Interground, August 21, 1990, pp 11-13.

8 Jay Reeves, "The Damn Thing Is Still Going!," Underground Interground, June 19, 1991, p. 4.

had mentioned a waterfall at the head of the next valley over. They said that it disappeared into the ground in a bunch of boulders. They also told us about another hole in the area that was blowing cold air real hard.

The survey crew entered about 9:30 followed by Paula Ledbetter, Steve Pitts and their trusty cave dog Kellsey. The surveyors lost the tag-alongs in a breakdown area. Jennifer Pinkley had been having trouble with her carbide lamp and her wet suit was beginning to really bother her so she routed for the entrance while Mike, Pat, and Jay did "The Fish" through the water crawl. They arrived at the well-casing about 15 minutes after the above ground crew were supposed to be topside. The surveyors tapped on the well-casing, but no answer. They tapped about every 5 minutes, but there was no response. Then, 10 minutes before they decided to leave came the long-awaited "ping-ping" from above. Contact! We found out later that the crew at the well-casing could hears us yelling; we think it's maybe 50-60 feet down. The surveyors then took off to pick up the survey.

A huge dome found on the last trip (dubbed Surprise Dome) had a high lead that was climbed and found to pinch down very quickly. Then the actual survey was picked up further down the passage. A couple hundred feet were surveyed until an ominous sight appeared: breakdown. The area was scoured for a lead. More passage was seen between the breakdown slabs, but there was not enough space for anyone to squeeze through. Then a small hole leading down was found, but it sumped immediately. The end of Haws Spring Cave had been found.

The surveyors felt they should check the breakdown once more before they left, just to be sure that there was no possible way on. A place was found in the far corner of the breakdown with some loose rocks and boulders. Some digging ensued and… IT GOES!

The survey gear was dug back out of the packs and surveying resumed. They surveyed through some breakdown, through a tight, short crawl, and back into walking borehole again. But not far past this, the ceiling started coming down to about 3 feet

from the floor. From here there were two ways on: a low room that sumped and a lead into a breakdown room. Coming out of this breakdown room was a small stream of water that had created a very unique formation: the bottom of the streambed had a calcified layer in the bottom. The mud under the calcified layer had eroded away leaving an aqua-duct about six inches above the ground which was several feet in length. This aqua-duct was still carrying water! They then surveyed into the breakdown area where it was noted that the whole bedding plane had shifted to about a thirty-degree incline.

We got to the breakdown room with the shifted bedding plane and could not find a way through. The breakdown was very unstable and dangerous. After a few pictures at the end, we headed out, which took 4 ½ hours to reach the entrance.[9]

Unfortunately, no final map of Haws Spring Cave has ever been produced.

The Haws Spring Cave Giant Ground Sloth

Donna Cobb reports the discovery of the radius of a giant ground sloth sitting on top of a little cobble canyon. It was discovered while they were surveying in a small side passage. She says:

> It was in terrible condition and on the next trip I packed it out. I was a preparator at a paleontology museum so, with permission, I spent about six months carefully preserving it with the intention of putting it back in the cave. Sadly, the landowner closed the cave and didn't want the bone, so I still have it and it is beautiful.[10]

The radius is one of the front arm bones. A photograph of this fascinating bone is shown as Figure 9.11. According to Donna, the bone belonged to a young *Megalonyx jeffersoni*.

9 Jay Reeves, "Haw Spring Revisited," Undergraph Interground, pp 2-4.

10 Donna Cobb, Personal communication, August 29, 2018.

Figure 9.12 Closeup of stalactites in Haws Spring Cave, also shown in Figure 9.6. Photo by Dave Bunnell, October 15, 2002.

Cave Access

Like all caves on private property, access varies from year to year. Always be sure you have the property owner's permission before entering this or any other cave. At the time this book went to press, Haws Spring Cave was closed and exploration and surveying were incomplete.

Figure 10.1. Keith Filson at the entrance to Henpeck Mill Cave. Photo by Bob Biddix, August 25, 2006.

CHAPTER 10
Henpeck Mill Cave

Henpeck Mill Cave is located in Cannon County, Tennessee. It is located near Henpeck Mill and the stream inside the cave is the source of the water for the mill.

A Description of the Cave

Henpeck Mill Cave is described by Thomas C. Barr, Jr. in his book, *Caves of Tennessee* (1961):

> This cave is located 0.3 mile north of the old Henpeck Mill. The mouth is 15 feet wide and 6 feet high, irregular in shape, and narrows to a constricted, rock-floored crawlway which extends northeast and east for 45 feet to a stream passage. Downstream the cave is penetrable for only 50 feet, to a silt fill. Upstream there is a pool of water to wade and a low place through which to crawl before reaching the more spacious stream passage beyond. The passage, which continues north-northwest for another 375 feet, averages 8 feet high and 20 feet wide and ends in a deep pool 500 feet from the entrance. At one place the cave rises to 40 feet in height, where vertical solution along a joint has enlarged the passage. Here, several small dripstone formations are present.[1]

Back in the 1950s, wet suits were not available to cavers and cavers didn't have the equipment necessary to safely push these large, stream caves with their cold, 56-degree water. If the passages were big enough, such as in Snail Shell Cave in Rutherford County, Tennessee, rubber rafts could be employed, but these were unreliable and subject to ripping on sharp rocks.

A Major Discovery

Thirty years later, wet suits were available at a reasonable price, and cavers used them to make many significant discoveries. Joel Buckner describes just such a trip to Henpeck Mill Cave:

In *Caves of Tennessee*, Tom Barr described Henpeck Mill Cave as having about 500 feet of passage ending in a deep pool of water. On June 7, 1983, David Parr and I ventured into the wilds of Cannon County on a push trip to HMC. Even though a small stream flows from the entrance, we were hoping that the cave might somehow tie into the hypothesized system feeding the large Henpeck Mill spring located about 1,000 feet away. We had often speculated that there must be a considerable amount of cave beyond the collapse that the spring emerges from. The owner had previously given us permission to explore the cave, but we had never gotten around to it. So when we found out he was selling his house and cave, we figured we'd better take him up on his offer in case the new owner was not so cooperative.

After once again gaining his permission to muddy up his water supply we headed into the cave groaning and sweating clad in full wetsuits and other caving paraphernalia. Arriving at the deep pool we took the plunge and immediately found ourselves swimming. Expecting a sump, we were surprised when the passage forked instead. David swam into the passage straight ahead but judged it not the way after a few feet. I swam into the left passage and was able to find a ledge on the left wall enabling me to walk a hundred feet or so until the water became shallow enough for me to do that anyway. David joined me and we walked and floated through several hundred feet of passage that reverberated our howls quite nicely. We were having a good ole time until we reached a sharp bend in the passage where the water became deep again. Peering around the corner we saw that the ceiling lowered to within a few inches of the water surface at the next turn about 15 feet further. David removed his helmet and swam down to take a closer look. He came back and said that it was definitely low air space and that I should take a look.

My wimp-out alarms were clanging loudly but a fit of madness seized me and I took off my helmet and swam down to the next corner. As I was about

1 Thomas C. Barr, Jr., *Caves of Tennessee*, TN Division of Geology, Bulletin 64 (1961), pp 100-101.

Figure 10.2. Camille Taylor in one of Henpeck Mill Cave's stream passages. Photo by Bob Biddix, July 28, 2006.

Figure 10.3. Pat Yentch (left front) and Keith Filson (right rear) in a well-decorated passage in Henpeck Mill Cave. Photo by Bob Biddix, July 31, 2006. (Above, right.)

Figure 10.4. Pat Yentch in a low-airspace stream passage in Henpeck Mill Cave. Photo by Bob Biddix, July 28, 2006. (Below, right.)

to retreat I noticed a head-sized ceiling pocket that would enable me to get a good look around the corner. I inserted my head into the pocket and saw that there was a 5 or 6 foot stretch with 3 to 5 inches of air space and then the ceiling began to rise again slightly before the passage turned again. While pondering the situation, the realization came over me that by lying back as if in a reclining lawn chair I could leisurely float through and get a good look at the ceiling at the same time! So on I went, feet first and pulling on the ceiling until it opened up again. With a slight feeling of vertigo, I looked back and hollered for David to come on through what I later dubbed the "Roofkisser Pass."

We then proceeded through a couple hundred feet of water passage to a breakdown. Climbing through, we found ourselves standing in a 15-foot diameter passage going two ways. To the left was heading into the ridge so we took off only to encounter another breakdown after a few hundred feet. A wet crawlway led off to one side, so we slithered into it. Somewhere along here David noticed that the water was now flowing into the cave! We had crossed an underground drainage divide! After a ways the water became deep enough for us to float through and just use our hands to pull ourselves along. Then there was a short stretch of bigger passage followed by another crawl.

As we crawled on, we heard falling water ahead. David exclaimed that we were about to find the Henpeck Mill Spring Passage! I thought it was too good to be true. But after a few more feet the water cascaded down into a 14 by 15-foot stream passage which disappeared in both directions. We had done it!

After a short rest, we began walking upstream. And walking… and walking… and walking! The passage was really something; a clean, unbroken trunk that just kept going on and on. Stretches of the passage were decorated with numerous totem pole

Figure 10.5. Camille Taylor in a dome in Henpeck Mill Cave. Photo by Bob Biddix, May 23, 2013

Figure 10.6. Pat Yentch by soda straw stalactites in Henpeck Mill Cave. Photo by Bob Biddix, July 31, 2006.

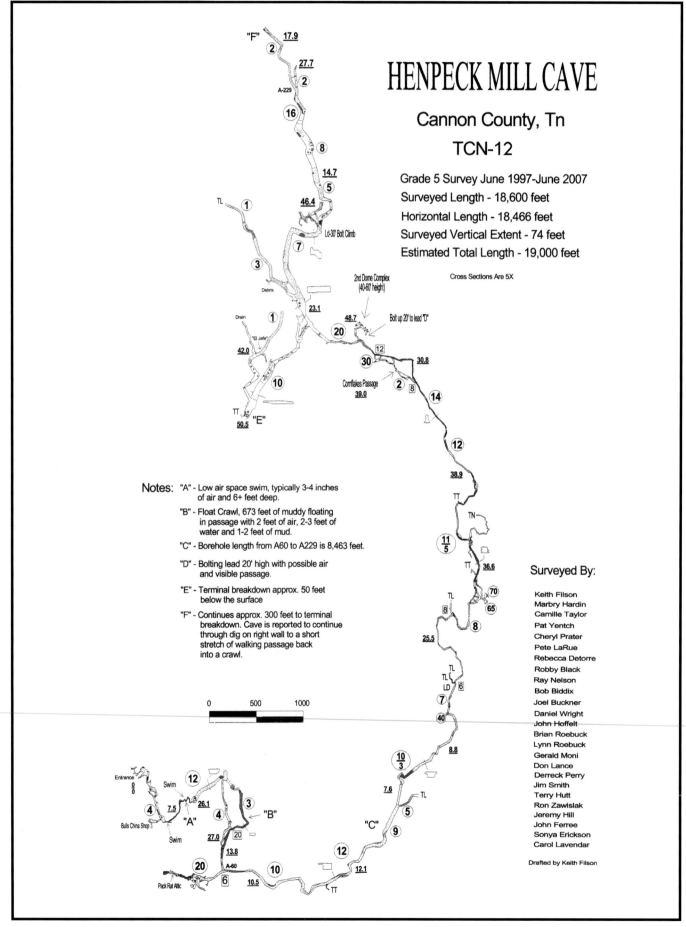

Figure 10.7. Map of Henpeck Mill Cave. Drafted by Keith Filson, June, 2007.

Figure 10.8. Daniel Wright (left), Keith Filson (middle), and John Barnett (right) surveying in Henpeck Mill Cave. Photo by Bob Biddix, August 18, 2005.

stalagmites. We walked at a rapid pace for nearly an hour through a stream averaging about 8 inches deep. We stopped when the ceiling started to lower after a stretch of 40-foot-wide and 10-foot-high passage. We estimated we had covered well over a mile and a half of breakdown-free walking passage from our pop-out point into the stream passage.

Having noticed a number of side leads, we checked out a couple on our way out. One led into a double dome complex we guessed to be at least 80 feet high. Upon reaching the entrance passage again, we headed downstream and after several hundred feet encountered a breakdown which is probably the same one the spring emerges from.

On June 21 we returned to HMC with Brad Neff and found a couple thousand feet of additional passages including a larger and higher dome complex. We pushed upstream at least a thousand feet further through alternating walking and crawling passage which continues as a wet crawl.

As of this writing, an acre of land with a 3-bedroom frame house and the cave entrance is for sale for $19,000. I estimate we have explored at least 3 miles of cave with good potential remaining, especially if we can get into upper levels. So if anyone wants to own a multi-mile cave with one of the longest and neatest walking passages in the state, opportunity is knocking.[2]

Joel Buckner and David Parr had experienced every caver's dream, discovering miles of virgin cave. David Parr continues the exciting story of the exploration of this cave:

The sun was smiling blissfully down upon us as we arrived at the Curly's house to park our automobiles. If there had been any chance of rain "at all" we would have had to postpone this trip to HMC, and choose some other less threatening cave to kill the day in.

After the usual battle with the wetsuits John Hoffelt, Joel Buckner and I were ready to venture into the cave. The purpose of this trip was to check

2 Joel Buckner, "Henpeck Mill Cave: From 1/10th Mile to 3 Miles in 3 Hours (On a Weeknight Yet!)," *Speleonews*, Vol. 27 (1983), no. 5, pp 63-64.

Figure 10.9. Daniel Wright (left front), Keith Filson (middle), and John Barnett (right rear) surveying in Henpeck Mill Cave. Photo by Bob Biddix, August 18, 2005.

Figure 10.10. Camille Taylor by a flowstone-covered ledge in Henpeck Mill Cave. Photo by Bob Biddix, July 29, 2006.

as many side passages going into the cave as we could. On the two previous trips most of our time was spent just trying to reach the upstream end of the main stream passage (which we never did).

We went quickly through the first 500 feet of passage that Barr described and then arrived rather overheated at the deep pool that "was" the supposed end of the cave. We quickly appreciated both the buoyancy and warmth of our wetsuits as we plunged into the deep frigid water. After the 30-foot swim we went through several hundred feet of walkway and then arrived at the Roofkisser. The water level had dropped 2 inches since our last trip, so it wasn't really necessary to kiss the ceiling this time. Beyond we waded with heads held high through a few hundred more feet of passage, crawled over a rimstone dam and then popped up behind a large rock into the first large passage in the cave. This passage looks awesome after emerging from

such a long, low air space passage. 400 feet into this 30-foot-wide, 17-foot-high walkway a lead was spotted high on the right wall. It started out as an easy crawlway and then gradually improved to stoopway with some short stretches of walking. An unclimbable drop-off was encountered 500 feet in; this was quickly recognized as a high lead at the end of the floating crawl. This dry by-pass is really of no use since it would involve rope work. A small hole that led to a large dome was also found but it was much too small to get through.

After retracing our steps we crawled past the drainage divide, floated through the floating crawl and eventually made our way to the Henpeck Mill stream passage. Taking a right we quickly scurried to the downstream end of the cave where a possible high lead loomed overhead.

After we were through admiring "Old Slim" (a 17-foot tall totem pole) John tossed his rope around a projection about 17 feet above the floor. Then he tied one end to a large rock. I ascended the rope and saw that the lead was most likely blind (although I did wimp out before I climbed high enough to truly verify this statement.).

We next started heading upstream. After a few duds and several thousand feet we spotted a promising looking opening high on the right wall. A climb up along a stair-step type ledge led us into this passage. After 50 feet of walking we were stopped cold by a 4-inch crack with blackness beyond. After a bit of search a small opening was found along the ceiling.

The opening was a tight T-shaped squeeze, but it soon opened up to a crawling lower passage and an upper walkway. 40 feet into the passage going "up dip" the upper and lower ways joined forming a nice windy canyon passage 5 feet wide and 15 feet high. In 400 feet the passage broke up into narrow canyons and then continued 200 more feet to where the floor almost met the ceiling.

Backtracking led us to an upper passage that went over the T-shaped squeeze. This passage was followed for 125 feet as a flat-floored walking passage, and then it narrowed somewhat still continuing where we stopped.

After returning to the main passage we washed several pounds of mud off our bodies and then went further upstream to another lead. This lead was found on the left wall about 7 feet above the floor. It was very difficult to get into because the lower part of the climb was very under hung.

The passage up top led to a network of crawls that looped in and out of each other with fine displays of calcite rafts, stalactites, helictites and other such speleothems with eye catching colors. One crawl led back into the main passage about 400 feet from where we made the climb. Several passages were left unchecked in this section.

We were getting quite tired from all our crawling and climbing around but decided to look at one more lead before leaving the cave. Travelling further upstream we came to a major side passage along the left wall with a small stream coming from within.

We had checked this passage before and stopped where it dropped to a hands and knees crawl. This time we boldly went through the easy crawl and popped out into a passage 35 feet wide and 15 feet high. We were astounded as we walked goggle-eyed down this smooth floored borehole.

200 feet in the walls spread to 60 feet apart. At one point we walked by a 20-foot-wide, 8-foot-high side passage along the right wall. This was too good to be true we thought… and we were right! 250 feet past the side passage the inevitable happened, we hit breakdown. A quick look revealed no continuation of the trunk, so we decided to look elsewhere.

We next walked over to an unlikely looking passage sloping upward near the end of the trunk. This passage ended rather quickly and by the time Joel and I had removed ourselves from its tightness, John had already entered the large side passage we had seen on the way in. Joel and I raced over to this lead as quickly as possible and found it to be a very nice walking tube for 300 feet. It then lowered to stoop and crawl for 100 feet and ended at a junction.

John was sitting at the junction contemplating which way to go. The left branch was entered first and went 150 feet to a mud sump. The right-hand branch had a stalactite with blood-colored veins running down its 2-foot length. Beyond the formation the passage got continuously lower for 200 feet and then changed into a low belly crawl which was not followed.

By this time we had seen roughly 3,000 feet of virgin cave and were ready to call it a day. When we arrived at the main passage we ate a bit of food and then took John on a quick tour through 40-foot wide Cannon Corridor. We then made the never-ending walk to the entrance passage and made a hasty retreat to the surface thus concluding a 7-1/2-hour trip in one of Tennessee's most unusual caves.[3]

According to Joel Buckner: "This cave likely has the longest unbroken walking passage in Tennessee. There are literally no breakdowns or obstructions in the Main Trunk until reaching the bellycrawl at the survey end.

3 David Parr, "Henpeck Mill Cave - Trip #3 (August 14, 1983)," *Speleonews*, Vol. 27 (1983), no. 5, pp 64-66.

So this passage still exists as primary cave as it was originally dissolved out without secondary modification by breakdown."[4] What a thrill they had discovering all this virgin cave!

The Survey of Henpeck Mill Cave

The current surveyed length of Henpeck Mill Cave is 19,000 feet (3.6 miles) with a vertical extent of 74 feet. (See Figure 10.7) Joel Buckner reports that the survey was never completed and that they had explored at least a half mile or so more without reaching an end, beyond the point where the survey was stopped. A bellycrawl at that point led to more alternating walking and crawling passage with David Parr finding the cave continued as a bellycrawl at the point of furthest exploration.[5]

Cave Access

Like all caves on private property, access is subject to change at any time. Always be sure that you have the owner's permission before you enter this or any other cave.

WARNING

Do not even consider going to this cave if there is any chance of rain. Do not go to this cave without full wetsuits and floatation gear. Always leave word about what cave you are visiting and what time you expect to return. That way, if you fail to return, there is a chance you may be rescued.

---

4 Joel Buckner, Personal communication, September 11, 2018.
5 Ibid.

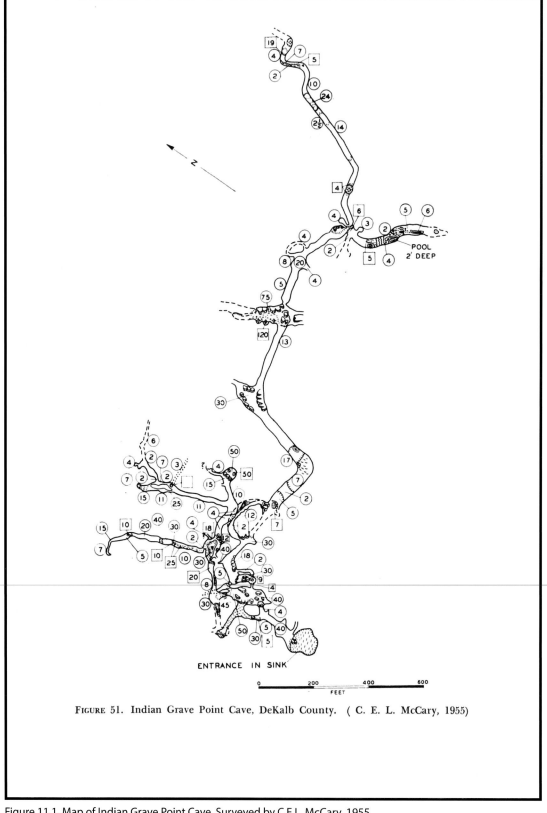

FIGURE 51. Indian Grave Point Cave, DeKalb County. (C. E. L. McCary, 1955)

Figure 11.1. Map of Indian Grave Point Cave. Surveyed by C.E.L. McCary, 1955.

CHAPTER 11
Indian Grave Point Cave

Indian Grave Point is the name of a prominent hill located in Dry Creek Valley in De Kalb County, Tennessee.It contains a large, interesting cave that has been a favorite with spelunkers for many years.

The earliest mention of Indian Grave Point Cave in the caving literature is in an article in the *NSS News*, which announces an NSS National Field Trip. Thomas C. Barr, Jr. had arranged a field trip for the 1949 Labor Day weekend to be held in McMinnville, Tennessee. Six large caves are listed that will be visited. The following description of Indian Grave Point Cave is given as follows:

> Indian Grave Point Cave is about 35 miles distant and consists of an interminable series of huge rooms with pools of water. It has not been well explored by NSS members. In June a domed chamber 150 feet high and 200 feet wide by 300 feet long was reached.[1]

Since Tom Barr was very busy doing research for his *Caves of Tennessee* (1961), it appears that he did not get back to Indian Grave Point Cave for nearly five (5) years. The next printed description of the cave is in the April 1954 *NSS News*:

> The discovery of a spectacular new cave only two hours' drive east of Nashville has set the holiday season explorers all agog, and enthusiasm ran high as one expedition after another plunged into the new monster cavern, led by Tom Barr, Bert Denton, and Bill Cuddington, members of the Tennessee Division of Geology's cave surveying party and also members of the Nashville Grotto. First investigated by Tom Barr and Bert Denton in 1949, the new discovery has already proven to be the most extensive system to be explored since the initial trip into Higgenbotham Cave in 1947. Present investigations indicate that it may surpass Higginbotham in total volume of known passages before the end of 1954. Preliminary explorations on five expeditions have already disclosed a series

Figure 11.2. Erica Sughrue at the bottom of the entrance sinkhole to Indian Grave Point Cave. Photo by Bob Biddix, April 1, 2012.

> of rooms 120 feet in height, half a mile of onyx-studded virgin passage, two tremendous domepits, and an unparalleled assortment of gypsum crystals.
>
> The name applied by Barr and Denton in 1949—Indian Grave Point Cave—will be retained, as descriptive of the location of the cave with respect to natural features. The entrance, a pit-like hole some 40 feet in diameter, is located in a spur of the Highland Rim known as Indian Grave Point. Graves of Indians were excavated in the cave and near the mouth by early settlers in the area. The cavern is developed in the Cannon facies of the Bigby-Cannon limestone and the various facies of the overlying Catheys formation and ramifies throughout the adjoining ridges in surprisingly complex fashion.

---

1 Thomas C. Barr, Jr., *NSS News*, Vol. 7 (1949), no. 8, pp 1, 4.

Figure 11.3. Erica Sughrue at the entrance to Indian Grave Point Cave. Photo by Bob Biddix, April 1, 2012. (Above.)

Figure 11.4. Erica Sughrue in a large passage in Indian Grave Point Cave. Photo by Bob Biddix, May 9, 2018. (Next page.)

Cascade Dome, the present center of exploration, is a gigantic domepit chamber 120 feet high and 200 feet in diameter. To the left of the entrance passage at its juncture with the Dome is a 60-foot climb leading into a section which the explorers named Schoolhouse Gallery, because of its resemblance to the famous West Virginia cave. At the top of the climb 200 yards of virgin passage was discovered leading on the one hand to a precipitous lookout point near the roof of Cascade Dome (the Hodag's Roost), and on the other to two high waterfalls and a 90-foot drop. The climb, originally quite difficult and dangerous if not made with a safety rope, was greatly improved and simplified on the subsequent expedition by moving nearly a ton of loose clay.

Black Gypsum Pass, so-named for the remarkable display of radiating crystals of smoky gypsum, was found to lead into nearly half a mile of virgin passage. One fork was penetrated for 275 yards through travertine terraces, white onyx flows, and a myriad of tiny, delicate stalactites. The other fork leads for 300 yards to a 30-foot drop, which as yet remains unexplored.

Blood-red stalagmites of extraordinary beauty were found along the floor of this route, previously unseen by human eyes. White calcite nodules on the walls sprouted gleaming tufts of delicate gypsum plates. The amazing variety of crystalline forms of the gypsum   plate, fibrous, radiating, and acicular—far exceeded that seen anywhere else in Tennessee.

Two expeditions were made to the cave by five members of the Nashville Grotto during December, during which preliminary reconnaissance was carried out in a mile and a half of the cave. A third expedition of eight other members, led by Tank Gorin and Roy Davis, was undertaken in January. This group traversed the relatively easy 500 yards to Cascade Dome and re-explored Schoolhouse Gallery but were so baffled by the complexity of the system that they failed to locate the opening to Black Gypsum Pass. They spent several hours, however, in

Figure 11.5. Erik Mattson in the Pool Room of Indian Grave Point Cave. Photo by Chuck Sutherland, November 23, 2012.

checking a short tight crawlway, full of the tracks of raccoons and opossums.

Many trips to this cave will be needed before an adequate understanding of its intricate pattern can be acquired, and before it can be mapped and photographed properly. The trunk channels, averaging some 40 feet wide and 20 feet high, connect large breakdown chambers with high, vaulted ceilings, occasionally, as in the case of Cascade Dome, altered by domepit solution. At intervals there are dry, sandy stretches of relatively easy going, followed by low wide bedding-plane crawls featuring soda straws and onyx-rimmed pools.[2]

There can be little doubt that they were very impressed with Indian Grave Point Cave! Just a few months later, the cave was visited by Charles Fort, who wrote the following Trip Report:

We hoped to enter Virgin cave just 200 yards from the entrance of the immense Indian Grave Point Cave near Dowelltown, Tenn. There, a side passage to the left of the main avenue leads steeply up to

a T-shaped junction with a very wet and seldom visited upper level gallery. This is Great Lakes Avenue. To the left, downstream, lies the chain of great lakes, pools of water filling deep depressions in the floor and separated from one another by upraised levels of breakdown . After about 150 feet in this direction the passage is completely blocked by an impenetrable silt and gravel breakdown. This I had to find out the hard way on my first visit to the cave in April after swimming and clambering over breakdowns attired only in my carbide light and helmet. Fifty feet upstream the passage is again blocked, but this time by a steep wall of flowstone descending from what appeared to be a huge upper level extension. For the first 15 feet this wall is sheer to overhanging, forming beautiful cascades of frozen dripstone. It then tapers off at an angle of fifty degrees to rise upward for another 30 feet to the great black mouth of unknown cave.

The ascent of this face was the project that I had scouted out on this first visit, so that on Memorial Day weekend I was back with Lawrence Smith, Carl Schultz, and Jim Johnson from Louisville. We arrived at the entrance about 10 o'clock Saturday morning

2 Thomas C. Barr, Jr., *NSS News*, Vol. 12 (1954), no. 4, p. 3.

Figure 11.6. Ramie Schweers by gypsum crystals in Indian Grave Point Cave. Photo by Chuck Sutherland, November 23, 2012.

equipped with a 15-foot cedar pole, rope, and an alpine hammer. At the flowstone barrier, three of us braced together and holding the butt of the pole at arm's length were able to boost Larry Smith nearly 25 feet of the way up the face. However, the last 20 feet he was on his own up a difficult and dangerous friction climb. Wielding the alpine hammer, he made some slight additional purchases and inched his way to the top. We followed up behind him on a secured line.

Immediately beyond lay a huge circular chamber some 50 yards in diameter, nearly the entire floor of which was covered by an underground lake. This was the largest I have yet seen in a cave. It was even complete with an island, a massive onyx pillar in the center reaching up to meet pendant stalactites high on the ceiling.

On our first view of this beautiful grotto our inspiration for naming this new section was born. This would be Lake Superior, the largest and highest of the Great Lakes complete with Isle Royale. Our climb up the flowstone wall was the Falls of the St. Mary's River and any passage we found beyond we would name the Great Lakes Extension.

Of additional passage there was plenty. We walked down a large gallery which opened from the opposite wall of our room with the underground lake. As we progressed it became drier and we viewed delicate flowers of gypsum with petals three to four inches long sprouting from the walls. We paused to stand on the brink at intermediate levels of two giant dome pits, well over 100 feet in height. After a quarter of a mile we entered a room so large it was like coming outside into the blackness of the night. Continuing on we were brought to an abrupt halt. The smooth level floor that had brought us this far had simply disappeared. Instead was a terrifyingly steep talus slope pitching down at an angle of sixty degrees to the floor, nearly 100 feet below, of an immense circular chamber 200 feet in diameter.

What a spot to turn our backs on, but we had neither the equipment nor the time to make a descent. We could only stare out into the vast space and, with the aid of a burning magnesium flare; dimly see the continuation of our passage on the far side leading on into the unknown.

Figure 11.7. Keith Filson in a large passage in Indian Grave Point Cave. Photo by Bob Biddix, May 5, 2018. (Above.)

Figure 11.8 Erica Sughrue in Cascade Dome in Indian Grave Point Cave. Photo by Bob Biddix, April 2, 2018. (Next page.)

We emerged from the entrance happy in our discovery and already thinking about the next trip, when we would probe further and deeper in this virgin territory.

The Nashville Grotto has been most active in exploring this complex cavern system. Their discoveries are reported in Tom Barr's excellent article in the April issue of the *NSS News*. However, the cave is still so new, even to them, that there are probably many virgin leads left holding promise of rich rewards to the explorer, that no one has yet looked into. We were able to add appreciably to the already known great volume and extent of this cave by trying our luck on just one.[3]

This upper level would turn out to be nearly as large as the main level of the cave and quite beautiful.

A Description of the Cave

Indian Grave Point Cave is described by Thomas C. Barr, Jr. in his book, *Caves of Tennessee* (1961):

3 Charles Fort, *NSS News*, Vol. 12 (1954), no. 10, p. 10.

The cave in Indian Grave Point is the largest cave in DeKalb County and one of the largest in Tennessee. It is apparently almost entirely the product of phreatic solution and is located about 125 feet above the floor of Dry Creek Valley. The original structure has been greatly altered by extensive breakdown, vertical (domepit) solution, and deposition of dripstone.

The entrance is a semi-vertical collapse sink 50 feet in diameter and 40 feet deep. The floor of the sink slopes steeply down toward a low, transverse opening which leads into the cave. Near the entrance are the remains of nitrate hoppers, and farther in the cave are pieces of old wooden ladders apparently used by the nitrate miners.

Most of the cave is damp or muddy. Pools and small lakes have formed in various places, but some of the passages are relatively dry. Gypsum

Figure 11.9. Erica Sughrue by a series of rimstone dams in Indian Grave Point Cave. Photo by Bob Biddix, April 1, 2012.

flowers, plates of dogtooth spar, and thin crusts of gypsum decorate the walls of some of the rooms and avenues. Dripstone is developed in a few spots, but most of it is of small size and is associated with areas where dripping water falls from a considerable height and spatters. Rimstone surrounds several of the shallow pools.

The main passage of the cave, which trends northeastward for about 3,000 feet, averages about 15 feet high and 30 feet wide. It passes through four large breakdown rooms and at two places it drops to a low, wide crawl. At 1,600 feet the main cave intersects an upper-level gallery approximately at right angles. The excavation of three large domepits and extensive breakdown has produced a high, vaulted chamber at this point, 120 feet long, 75 feet wide, and 120 feet high. This tremendous room has been named "Cascade Dome." To the left the upper-level passage extends north-northwest to a series of pits. To the right a very high, narrow gallery extends

southeast, then loops back into the main cave. Directly opposite the observer, as he stands on the brink of the descent to the floor of Cascade Dome, is the continuation of the main cave, which extends at least 1,500 feet farther. There is only one short side passage, leading southeast, between Cascade Dome and the limit of exploration.

Two other parts of the cave branch off from the main passage near the entrance. The first (not shown on the map) opens as a narrow slit immediately to the right of the entrance and is easily overlooked. This branch extends northeastward for about 500 feet and contains few features of interest. The second branch ("Great Lakes Extension") may be entered from the north end of the first large breakdown chamber. There is a lower (southwest) passage which contains two deep pools of water and an upper level system which extends northeast for 500 feet and has two sub-parallel lateral forks. It is necessary to climb up a steep, slippery flowstone to reach the upper

Figure 11.10. Erica Sughrue in the Garden of Eden in Indian Grave Point Cave. Photo by Bob Biddix, May 6, 2018.

part of the Great Lakes Extension. Near the top of the climb is a shallow pool 50 feet long and 30 feet wide.[4]

This description still covers most of the known cave, as the accompanying map will attest. The map of Indian Grave Point Cave that was printed on page 167 of *Caves of Tennessee* (1961) is reprinted as Figure 11.1. It was prepared by C. E. L. McCary and is dated 1955.

My First Visit to the Cave

When my friends and I first began exploring caves in about 1961, we were too young to drive and had to convince our parents to drive us to some of the local caves in Davidson County where we lived. Most of these caves were quite small and muddy, but we still thought they were great. Reading Barr's *Caves of Tennessee* we were fascinated by the description of Indian Grave Point Cave. It sounded so large and so interesting and it was only about 75 miles from Nashville. Soon, we talked one of our parents into driving us over there.

Wow!!! That hill up to the entrance really was *steep*!!! We rigged a safety rope for the entrance slope. The cave just looked HUGE once we got inside, since our eyes had not yet adjusted to the darkness. And, you could WALK !!! We were used to a lot of crawling in the Nashville area caves. We walked right by and over the remains of the saltpeter vats. We did not even recognize what they were, the shape they were in. When we got to the first large breakdown room, we were just amazed how big it was. And, the cave kept getting better and better as we continued on inward. We made it as far as Cascade Dome on that first trip and we were hooked. I lost track of how many times we went back to Indian Grave Point Cave, but it was easily over a dozen times. We pushed every lead we could find, and I assume we saw most, if not all, of the cave.

At one point in time a very large hog either fell into the entrance or was dumped there by the farmer who owned the property. The first time we found it there, the smell of decaying flesh was overpowering. How long does it take a large hog to rot? Many, many months. The hog appeared to have *settled* into the floor a few more inches every time we went. We would take many deep breaths at the top of the entrance slope, hold our breath and run down the slope past the hog and into the cave as far as possible before taking another breath! I think it may have been nearly a year before that dead hog was finally reduced to just bones.

We never did find those remains of old ladders that Barr said had been left by the saltpeter miners. Either they rotted away, or somebody had removed them by the time we got there.

The Survey of Indian Grave Point Cave

It was obvious that the map of Indian Grave Point Cave in Barr's *Caves of Tennessee* (1961) was not complete, nor was it up to modern cave surveying standards. Therefore, several members of the Nashville Grotto began remapping the cave in October, 1978. The primary surveyors were John Hoffelt, David Parr, Joe Douglas, Joel Buckner, Bill Knight, John Cauthen, and Roger Ling. Other cavers assisting in the survey were Johnny Carter, Joe Cauthen, Steve Haynes, David Hoffelt, Larry Johnson, Chrys Kerr, Teri Knight, Mark

4 Thomas C. Barr, Jr., *Caves of Tennessee*, TN Division of Geology, Bulletin 64 (1961), pp 165-168.

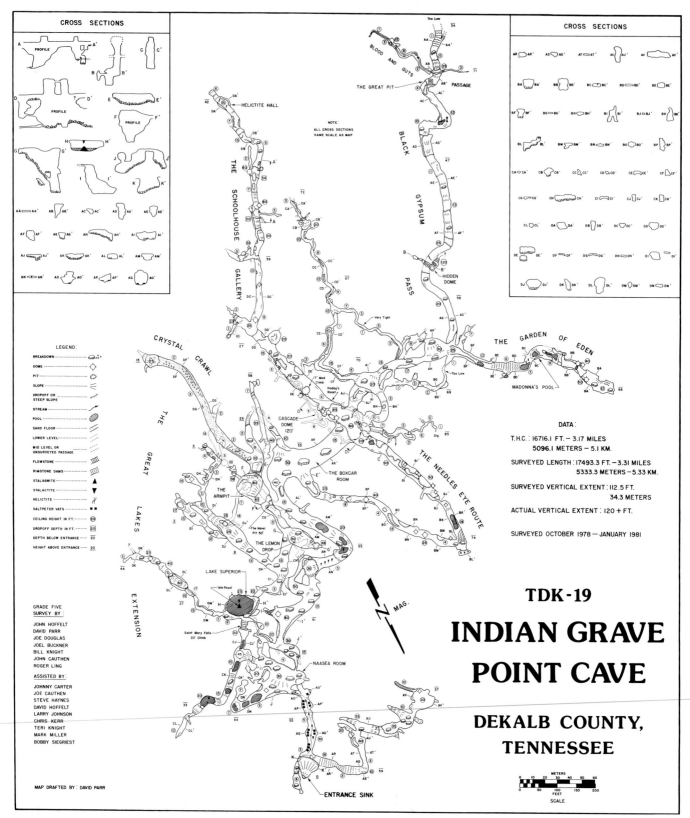

Figure 11.11. Map of Indian Grave Point Cave. Drafted by David Parr, 1981.

Miller, and Bobby Shegriest. The final map was drafted by David Parr. The survey was completed in January, 1981. The final surveyed length was 16,716 feet, or 3.17 miles. The cave had a vertical extent of 112 feet. That vertical extent is based on the survey shots and does

not take into account the ceiling heights. Obviously, if Cascade Dome is 120 feet high, then the vertical extent of the cave is greater than the 112 feet given above.

Several things are readily apparent then you look at this map. First of all, the cave is strongly joint controlled,

Figure 11.12. Ramie Schweers by a large stalagmite in Indian Grave Point Cave. Photo by Chuck Sutherland, November 23, 2012.

and the passages are confined in a relatively small area. This makes for a very complex, three-dimensional cave. The entire cave is contained under a small portion of the southern tip of Indian Grave Point and does not extend into the ridge. In fact, the entire cave fits in an area only 1,200 feet wide and 2,000 feet long. This outstanding map is reproduced as Figure 11.11.

Joel Buckner, one of the principal surveyors, wrote the following observations based on those visits:

> The survey of Indian Grave Point Cave was completed in 1981, so I reckon it is about time the map was published in the *Speleonews*. Since no one else seems inclined to take up the task, I decided to do so.
>
> IGP is an extensive and expansive cave developed in Ordovician limestone. It is largely phreatic in origin except for secondary enlargement by vertical solution and breakdown. The vertical solution has produced about 35 domes ranging in height from 20 to 120 or more feet. The most spectacular of these is Cascade Dome, a triple dome complex located in a large room. An impressive cross section and

profile of the shafts can be seen where they intersect the room. On the Highland Rim, this large room is probably rivaled for size only by Cloud Canyon in John Fisher Cave.

There is not a sizable stream in IGP, although there are a few small streamlets. However it does have a lot of water in the form of pools, particularly in the easternmost section of the cave, the Great Lakes Extension. This section contains the largest pool in the cave, Lake Superior, which has a stalagmite island in its center. The Garden of Eden also has a number of pools although their levels fluctuate from year to year.

The Garden of Eden is named for the profuse flowstone decorating it. While not very colorful, it is attractive especially when the pools are full. Most of the cave does not have much in the way of formations although there are some nice helictites in a couple of passages. Fortunately these areas are located off the beaten path and beyond climbs and pits which have served to protect them from the hoards that descend upon the cave.

IGP is one of the most heavily visited caves in Tennessee and much vandalism has been done by thoughtless visitors. Graffiti mars the walls of many of the easily accessible passages in the cave and a fair amount of trash is present. Much of the graffiti is written on mud coated walls and can be easily wiped off by anyone inclined to do so. A wire brush and some scrubbing can remove most of the rest. Every caver who visits the cave should take a few minutes to remove some graffiti and pick up some trash.

Despite the large traffic flow through the cave, one can still see virgin cave on every trip. Unfortunately that's all you can do because it is in the form of out-of-reach high leads. Four out of the five leads I know of in the cave are high leads and three would require technical climbing to reach. One is a large obvious passage high up in Cascade Dome that is probably a continuation of the Schoolhouse Gallery. It is shown on the map by the question mark in the D--D' profile. Another technical climb is in Hidden Dome in the Black Gypsum Pass. This is an impressive 120 foot, or more, high dome which has never been climbed completely. There are reports that someone climbed to the first ledge about 40 feet up. It seems likely there would be a number of horizontal passages or parallel domes connecting with it. The other technical climb is near the top of Cascade Dome, along the Hodag's Roost. One can climb up to an overlook into Cascade Dome about 80 or 90 feet up. At that point you can look up a wall about 30 feet to a lead at or near the top of the domes. There should be horizontal passages leading off of the tops of the domes. There is also a high lead near the end of the passage leading east off of Lake Superior. This lead could probably be reached with an extension ladder which shouldn't be too hard to get back there. The last good (?) lead I know of is the downstream end of the Blood and Guts Passage. Some enlarging is needed to continue, but David Parr theorizes it will lead either to a small spring on the hillside or intersect a continuation of Black Gypsum Pass which would be very nice indeed.

As you can see from the topo overlay map, there is plenty of room left in the hill for more cave. Since IGP probably formed primarily below the water table (phreatic) before Dry Creek cut down to its present level, it seems likely there is a lot more cave

Figure 11.13. Erica Sughrue in the Garden of Eden in Indian Grave Point Cave. Photo by Bob Biddix, May 6, 2018.

in the ridge. The entire rock strata were saturated with water when the cave was formed, so why would the passages all be concentrated in one area! There should be southerly continuations of Black Gypsum Pass, the Schoolhouse Gallery, the Crystal Crawl, and some of the Great Lakes Extension passages along with more domepit development along them. All that is needed now are some adventurous and determined cavers (with technical climbing skills and/or a fondness for digging). Have at it![5]

When you overlay the 1955 map by C. E. L. McCary on the new 1981 map, you are immediately impressed with the general accuracy of the older map. His map shows only perhaps half of the passages shown in the new map, but still, it is an impressive cave map for the 1950s.

5 Joel Buckner, *Speleonews*, Vol. 29, no. 3, pp 63-66.

Figure 11.14. Keith Filson in a large passage in Indian Grave Point Cave. Photo by Bob Biddix, May 5, 2018.

Saltpeter Mining in Indian Grave Point Cave

As noted in Barr's description of the cave, there are the remains of several saltpeter vats located in the very first room of the cave. This area of the cave is damp, so most of the wood structure of the vats has rotted away, but at least in the 60s and 70s; it was possible to still see pieces of wood protruding from the sides of the dirt mounds that are all that is left from the saltpeter vats. If I had to guess, based on visits made from 30 to 50 years ago, these were probably V-shaped vats, due to their small size. The map shows a total of fourteen (14) vats, lined up on each side of the trail through the middle of the entrance passage. This was a middle-sized saltpeter mining operation. Careful excavation by an archaeologist could probably tell us a lot more about these vats.

We looked diligently for any trace of the ladders mentioned by Barr, but we never found them.

Accidents and Rescues at Indian Grave Point Cave

American Caving Accidents 1976 through 1979 reports the following accident:

February 20, 1977. At about 4:00 p.m. on Sunday February 20, four cavers from West Nashville, Gary Callis (18), Bobby Harrell (24), Larry Hoyal (20), and Doug Wall (16) went exploring in Indian Grave Point Cave near Smithville, Tennessee. After a couple of hours their four flashlights and one lamp began getting dim and it became impossible to find their way out. The cavers settled down to await rescue, burning their rope to keep warm and help pass the time. The rope produced enough acrid smoke that they were forced to move to another room.

Authorities were alerted when the cavers failed to return home Sunday evening. The search began in the Gordonsville area, the cavers' stated destination,

Figure 11.15. Erica Sughrue in a large passage in Indian Grave Point Cave. Photo by Bob Biddix, April 2, 2018.

but at 12:30 p.m. on Monday shifted to Indian Grave Point Cave near Smithville when the lost men's car was found outside. The search inside the cave was pursued by five members of the Nashville Grotto. Forty-five minutes later the lost cavers were found in good condition. They had spent 24 hours in the 56 degrees cave.[6]

Back in 1977 the Nashville Grotto had an active Cave Rescue Team. When the parents of the missing teenagers reported them missing, they told the authorities that they had gone to a large cave near Gordonsville. The police and police helicopters spent hours looking for their car, with no luck. Finally, a newspaper reporter who knew some of the local cavers called Nashville Grotto member Larry Adams and told him the situation. Immediately, he was told that Indian Grave Point Cave should be the first place to look. Based on this information, the police helicopter flew to that location and located the car.

Next the local Rescue Team went to the site and entered the cave. Many hours later, they had not found the lost teenagers and insisted that they had checked the *entire* cave. Reluctantly, the Nashville Grotto Rescue Team was invited to come help. When we arrived and entered the cave, the Dekalb County Rescue Team was still less than 500 feet from the entrance. When asked if they had checked the rest of the cave, they said: "Where is it?" We pointed to the low crawl that led from the room they were in to the Main Passage of the cave. We went through the crawl and 30 minutes later found the lost teenagers in Cascade Dome. They had become lost, and then their batteries in their flashlights had died. They had burned a rope they had with them trying to stay warm.

Ironically, when we led the lost teenagers out of the cave, we were confronted by the head of the local Rescue Team, who insisted that the teenagers were "hiding" and were waiting for us where we could all be on the Front Page of the newspapers. Of course, nothing could have been further from the truth. I suspect it was the Rescue Team Captain who wanted to see his photo on the Front Page. We got not so much as a "Thank You," except from the teenagers and, after all, that was all that really mattered.

Cave Access

At the present time, Indian Grave Point Cave is still open to cave explorers. However, that status is subject to change at any time, so always check to be sure you have the necessary permission from the owner before you enter the cave.

---

6 Steve Knutson, Editor, *NSS News*, Vol. 39 (1981), no. 5, part 2, p. A19.

Figure 12.1. Erica Sughrue in a large passage in Pleasant Ridge Cave. Photo by Bob Biddix, March 30, 2011.

CHAPTER 12
Pleasant Ridge Cave

Pleasant Ridge Cave is located in Cannon County, Tennessee. With a surveyed length of over 13 miles, this is one of Tennessee's longest mapped caves.

Discovery and Exploration

Bobby Higgins sent the following information to Gerald Moni on October 24, 2014. It describes the early history of Pleasant Ridge Cave.

When I was in high school, my mother and father operated the store at the head of Connell Creek. I used to sit in that store reading everything the Woodbury Library had on caving and dreamed of finding a cave. It is funny that the cave I was looking for was just on the other side of the ridge. It is great to see there has been much progress in this cave's exploration. This is the cave I "cut my teeth on."

Before you get into the text below, which you may or may not find interesting, I have a couple of questions. Are there any pictures of the Hall of Dreams? I do remember crystal formations in the upper and dryer portions of the stream passageway. I don't remember anything big, but still there were areas that were pretty much coated, and I do remember finding small sections of Angel's Hair. We never disturbed any formations in the cave and I was selective to whom I showed these upper sections. I hope that they are all still intact.

In case you are interested, I will tell you what I know of this cave. I first found out about this cave while helping the landowner Medford Rich work on his farm. I looked into the entrance and told him it was a cave. He told me it was a groundhog hole. Three of us first entered the cave on Thanksgiving Day, 1972. At the time, we thought we were the first people to explore the cave. This may not be correct as the previous owner, the Morris family, told me they had gone into the cave several years before. It is interesting to see the entrance of the cave as it is now 4 feet tall. When we first explored the cave, we had to crawl in on our stomachs, while out backs

were scraping the roof. Could this be because the sinkhole the entrance of the cave has gotten deeper? That first day we only made it to the entrance of the first room. There is a flowstone formation one has to navigate to climb down into the room. We stopped at the flowstone and shined our 6-volt flashlights into the first room. I had caved some before, but always with someone who was experienced. We were all too skittish to go farther. We eventually became braver and after a few trips made our way to the Great Deterrent. It is great to see the name the Great Deterrent stuck. It took a good bit of time to get past the GD. When we first saw the GD, it must have been a particularly wet season as there was maybe only 4 inches of airspace and we didn't attempt to push it. To my knowledge, the first person to make it past the GD was a local named Alan Gunn. He was exploring the cave, alone, and found this passage dry. I returned with him later that day. This period may have been the only time I ever saw this passage dry. I do remember seeing vegetation stuck to the ceiling of the stream passage a little ways past the GD, so we never explored if there was a chance of thunderstorms.

The rooms off to the left, I think the ones mentioned in your text as halfway back, are located at a wide place in the stream passage which we used as a rest area after navigating a tight passage we called the Hall of Daggers. Early on, our main goal was to try to get to the end of the stream passage, so we passed this section of the cave many times before finding it. A local caver, Burton McFerrin, introduced me to a couple of experienced cavers, Drex Freeman and Lawrence Loveless, who were looking for Tenpenny Cave. I showed Drex and Lawrence Tenpenny Cave and told them about the cave on Pleasant Ridge. I was caving with Drex, Lawrence, and Drex's brother whose name I think is Jimmy. This was in 1976. Again, we were trying to push the stream passage and were taking a moment to rest when Jimmy climbed up and in the rooms.

I am confident Jimmy was the first one to see those rooms. As a side note: While exploring those rooms that day I fell and broke the bone in my left cheek. I was able to walk out, and it was a good thing as the other people in the party were not familiar with the cave and were unsure of the route.

Drex was a member of the NSS at the time and wanted to officially report the cave. Up until that time, we referred to the cave as Med Rich's Cave. Years before a friend and I used to joke and wonder what we could do to make Pleasant Ridge famous. When we were thinking of a name for the cave, I remembered those conversations and decided on the name Pleasant Ridge Cave. So…it pleases me to see this cave on the Longest Cave List.

Drex, Lawrence, myself, and a couple of others started mapping the cave. I do not remember how far we got and have not seen Drex for many years. He was active in the NSS at the time and may still be.

Does any passage in the Hollins Cave go north? The reason I ask is that there was a local logger named John Preston who was riding a mule down a hillside and the mule stumbled into what John called a groundhog hole. As the mule struggled, the ground gave way and the mule fell into a pit. Luckily, John fell down the hillside and did not fall into the pit with the mule. John was one of our customers at the store at the time. I am not sure what year this happened, but we only operated this store from 1970 to 1975. I saw the pit and the mule. It was maybe thirty feet deep and less than 10 feet across. The walls were not limestone but were dirt. There was a limestone crack at the bottom. The thing that makes this interesting is that it happened close to Hollins Cave. If one travels north on Highway 53, leaving Hollins Cave, the next hollow to the left has a road going into it. If I recall correctly the pit was on a hillside off to the right side of this road. I was only there that one time. Someone rappelled into the hole, got John's gear off the mule, and claimed there was passage below the mule. I was told that a year later the hole was no longer there as the dirt sides had collapsed. One would think this would leave a sink, so this may be something someone could find. There are three hollows to the right of the road. If

Figure 12.2. Erica Sughrue in an incised canyon in Pleasant Ridge Cave. Photo by Bob Biddix, December 20, 2011.

I wanted to look for this, I would start looking at the first hollow as I remember walking back into a hollow and turning left to get to the dead mule.

A few years ago, Willie Roy Womack told me he had found a cave in his hillside that one would need rope to explore. I had not been caving in a long time and no longer have equipment, so I did not check it out, but this may be interesting because Willie Roy's place is roughly between Pleasant Ridge Cave and Blow Hole Cave. His house is on top of the ridge just before the road goes down Sycamore Hill. I throw this out in case you are looking for leads and I don't know of a caver who isn't.

It looks like Willie's house, as the crow flies, is roughly half way between PRC and BHC and slightly north, but his property is behind his house, so this reported cave, if it exists, may be more in line with the two. Willie Roy is now deceased, but his family still lives there.[1]

Bobby Higgins and his friends were the first serious cavers to enter and explore Pleasant Ridge Cave.

1 Bobby Higgins, Letter to Gerald Moni dated October 24, 2014.

Figure 12.3. Carol Lamers in a muddy crawlway in Pleasant Ridge Cave. Photo by Bob Biddix, April 28, 2012.

A Description of the Cave

The following description of Pleasant Ridge Cave comes from the 1991 SERA Cave Carnival Guidebook:

Pleasant Ridge Cave is a long, challenging, but rewarding cave. The entrance is a small hole which leads to a short crawl passage and then becomes larger. There is a climb-down on the left side of a drop-off and then a corkscrew passage down to the stream level. Look for a gravel-floored belly-crawl, which seasonally has a pool, doing downstream. This crawl is known as the Great Deterrent, although it soon opens up into a narrow stream canyon. The stream passage, the A-series, goes for many thousands of feet. At stations A-80 and A-100 one can climb up into large, phreatic, upper levels. These upper passages contain rooms, domes, and alternate routes farther back into the cave. Eventually, one must return to the stream level to continue. The main stream goes past a small waterfall and eventually lowers to a crawl. Around station A-180, on the right before the crawl, is a dry, side passage, the Hall of Dreams. This passage contains large and locally rare crystal chandeliers. The main passage

Figure 12.4. Erica Sughrue by the Cave Apple located in Pleasant Ridge Cave. Photo by Bob Biddix, March 31, 2011.

Figure 12.5. Erica Sughrue in a joint-controlled passage in Pleasant Ridge Cave. Photo by Bob Biddix, August 14, 2018.

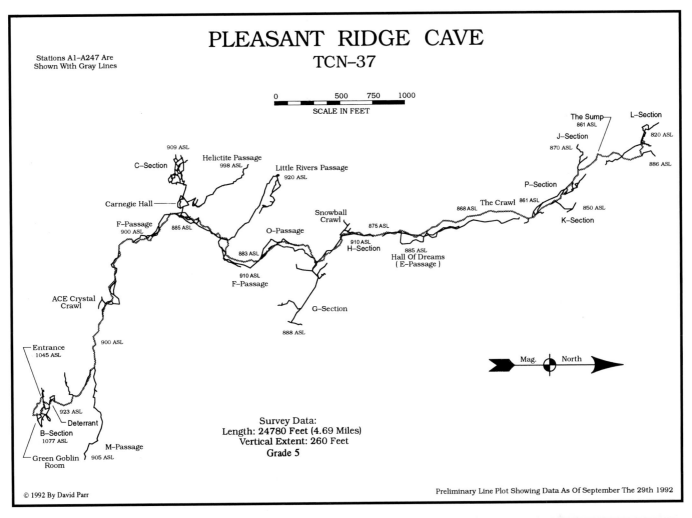

PLEASANT RIDGE CAVE
TCN–37

Stations A1–A247 Are
Shown With Gray Lines

SCALE IN FEET
0   500   750   1000

Survey Data:
Length: 24780 Feet (4.69 Miles)
Vertical Extent: 260 Feet
Grade 5

© 1992 By David Parr

Preliminary Line Plot Showing Data As Of September The 29th 1992

Figure 12.6. Map of Pleasant Ridge Cave by David Parr, 1992. (Above.)

Figure 12.7. Erica Sughrue by helictites growing on stalactites in Pleasant Ridge Cave. Photo by Bob Biddix, December 9, 2013. (Below.)

opens up again after the crawl and leads to a pool one must crawl through. The stream passage closes down around station A-230. Although the cave trends northwest, the water changes to an easterly direction and resurges in Connell Creek. This cave has not been completely surveyed and if it ever were it would be at least six miles long. Wool or polypro is recommended.[2]

Since the current surveyed length of the cave is over 13 miles, clearly this description is out of date.

The Survey of Pleasant Ridge Cave

According to the Tennessee Cave Survey, Pleasant Ridge Cave has a surveyed length of 59,240 feet (11.2 miles),

2 Anonymous, "Pleasant Ridge Cave," 1991 SERA Cave Carnival Guidebook, p. 24.

Figure 12.8. Erica Sughrue stands in the entrance to John Hollins Cave. Photo by Bob Biddix, February 2, 2017.

making it the seventh longest cave in Tennessee. Joel Buckner, however, reports that the surveyed length is now over 13 miles.[3]

The initial survey of Pleasant Ridge Cave was begun by David Parr in the late 1970s. That survey eventually reached over 4 miles with many leads remaining. Among those, he noted a dig with air flow at the furthest point of exploration, a couple of miles from the entrance.[4]

John Hollins Cave

John Hollins Cave is located in this general area and is mentioned in the narrative by Bobby Higgins earlier in this chapter. Although it is not a large cave, it is well known locally. Tom Barr gives the following description:

> The John Hollins Cave is named for a former owner, who was shot and killed in the barn across the road from the cave mouth. The cave is developed along the axis and in the southeast limb of an anticline. The mouth is 18 feet wide and 8 feet high. A passage of the same dimensions extends along the axis of the anticline W. 10° S. for 100 feet to a room 30 feet high. The west end of the room is blocked by a huge mound of flowstone. The cave continues, southeast, following the inclination of the limestone, which dips at about 15°. For 90 feet the average dimensions are 10 feet high and 25 feet wide. The floor is strewn with small pieces of broken rock and flowstone, but no permanent stream is present. At 190 feet the cave slopes downward sharply for 50 feet to a deep, stagnant pool.

Bobby Higgins sent the following information about this cave to Gerald Moni in 2014:

> Not trying to be a know-it-all, but part of the text you sent me is incorrect. John Hollins (or John Hollingsworth) did own the property and a killing

3 Joel Buckner, Personal communication, March 12, 2018.

4 Joel Buckner, Personal communication, March 12, 2018.

Figure 12.9. Erica Sughrue inside John Hollins Cave. Photo by Bob Biddix, January 28, 2017.

did take place at the barn, but John Hollins was not killed there. The story goes like this: In 1897, John Hollins shot and killed my great-grandfather, Jim Higgins. Jim Higgins is buried at Pleasant Ridge Cemetery. Hollins then disappeared. My great-grandmother won a judgement and the Hollins place was to be auctioned off and the proceeds were to be given to her (she was pregnant with my grandfather when her husband was killed). On the day of the auction, John Hollins reappeared and with his son started shooting people. John Hollins then escaped and lived for several years in Oklahoma under the alias of Bob Logan. I am not sure how the name was shortened to Hollins or lengthened to Hollingsworth. I have heard the original name was Hollins and got changed after the killing, but the newspaper articles I find use the name Hollingsworth.[5]

John Hollins Cave has now been connected to Pleasant Ridge Cave and is no longer a separate cave. The following section of this chapter describes this discovery.

The John Hollins Extension

At some point during the late 1970's while David Parr and others were surveying Pleasant Ridge Cave; they believed that it was possible that Pleasant Ridge Cave was hydrologically connected to nearby Blowhole Cave. In order to test this hypothesis, geologist John Hoffelt ran a dye trace. However, to everyone's surprise, the dye trace to Blowhole Cave was negative and the dye was actually detected at a creek bed spring rise in Connell Creek near John Hollins Cave and a couple of miles from the known end of Pleasant Ridge Cave.[6]

Sometime in 2005 or 2006 Joel Buckner took Marbry Hardin to John Hollins Cave and showed him the pool at the end of the cave. Marbry stuck his head underwater

5 Bobby Higgins, op. cit.

6 Joel Buckner, Personal communication, March 12, 2018.

Figure 12.10. Erica Sughrue by massive flowstone formation in John Hollins Cave. Photo by Bob Biddix, May 23, 2009.

Figure 12.11. Derek Wolfe, the primary surveyor and cartographer of both Blowhole Cave and Pleasant Ridge Cave. Photo by Bob Biddix, February 19, 2018

and thought it looked like a good lead to dive. He later brought Forrest Wilson and TJ Johnson to take a look at it, too.[7]

One early July, during the extreme drought of the summer of 2007 Joel returned to John Hollins Cave with Hal Love and Jason Wyatt after a survey trip in Henpeck Mill Cave. They found the pool lower with strong air flow![8] Joel Buckner describes their next visit:

We returned the next weekend accompanied by Marbry Hardin, David Parr, and Trey Caplenor. With Marbry leading the charge, we pushed through a spot in the pool about 4 feet deep and with 4 inches or so of air space into a muddy chamber about 30 feet high and wide.

A walking passage led on for a ways to a low, sloppy crawl that Marbry declared had to be the remains of the second sump. Shortly past that, we

turned a corner and emerged into a virgin canyon passage about 40 feet high and 20 feet wide. That went for 700 or 800 feet to another crawl with a 10-inch high low air space where the air flow rippled the water surface. Just beyond, however, we encountered bleak looking breakdown. Poking around though, we saw a couple of possibilities for digging further. On the next trip, we successfully penetrated the breakdown into continuing trunk passage and explored at least a couple thousand feet or so of large passages.

Subsequent exploration and survey trips found thousands and thousands more feet of complex, multi-level canyon passage that was well decorated in places with various formations. Eventually, a blowing crawl off in a side passage was dug open to connect with the blowing dig that David Parr had found so many years before in the back of Pleasant

7 Joel Buckner, Personal communication, March 8, 2018.
8 Ibid.

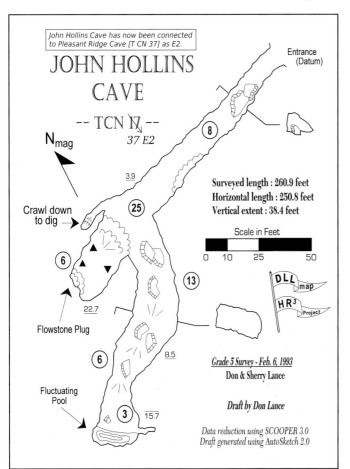

John Hollins Cave has now been connected to Pleasant Ridge Cave [T CN 37] as E2.

JOHN HOLLINS CAVE

-- TCN 17 --
37 E2

N mag

3.9

Crawl down to dig →

25

Surveyed length : 260.9 feet
Horizontal length : 250.8 feet
Vertical extent : 38.4 feet

Scale in Feet

0   10   25   50

6

Entrance (Datum)

8

13

22.7

Flowstone Plug

DLL map
HR³ Project

6

8.5

Grade 5 Survey - Feb. 6, 1993
Don & Sherry Lance

Fluctuating Pool

3   15.7

Draft by Don Lance

Data reduction using SCOOPER 3.0
Draft generated using AutoSketch 2.0

Figure 12.12. Map of John Hollins Cave by Don & Sherry Lance, February 6, 1993.

Ridge Cave. Exploration and survey have continued intermittently since and the Pleasant Ridge/John Hollins Cave System survey is over 13 miles at this time.[9]

Marbry Hardin recalls one of those trips:

> In the nice borehole section between the second initial sump in John Hollins Cave and the breakdown water crawl at the end of that which had to be dug open, there was a small, elevated room to one side. It was very faint, but there was possible evidence of modern footprints.
>
> We speculated at the time that someone in the past may have come through during a similar dry period of low water. But it is certain that no one had been past the breakdown crawl in the stream after that.

The initial exploration, when it was still sumped, we put Forrest Wilson and Tom Johnson through the first sump. They saw the second sump but weren't inclined at the time to carry their gear across the very muddy breakdown in-between to try and dive it.[10]

So, the exploration and survey of the Pleasant Ridge/John Hollins Cave System has spread out over 50 years. And, it is not finished, yet.

Cave Access

This cave is located on private property and access may vary from year to year. Always be sure you have the owner's permission before you enter this or any other cave.

10 Marbry Hardin, Personal communication, September 22, 2018.

9 Joel Buckner, Personal communication, March 12, 2018.

Figure 13.1. Erica Sughrue by massive formations in Hayes Cave. Photo by Bob Biddix, January 26, 2012.

CHAPTER 13
Prospect Hill Cave

Prospect Hill Cave is located in Cannon County, Tennessee. It was discovered in January, 1967 by Harry White.

A Description of the Cave

Prospect Hill Cave is described by Larry E. Matthews in his book *Descriptions of Tennessee Caves* (1971):

Prospect Hill Cave was discovered by Harry White in 1967. The entrance is a semi-vertical opening 150 feet long, 75 feet wide and 75 feet deep. The opening narrows to only 10 feet wide after a descent of 50 feet. A rope is needed to descend the last drop, which is a 10-foot vertical pitch followed by a 15-foot slope. A handline is useful, but not necessary, for the top 50 feet of the entrance.

The entrance room is 50 feet in diameter and 10 feet high. Several domes in the ceiling at this point are as much as 40 feet high. A passage averaging 10 feet wide and 15 feet high leads for 400 feet to a fork. The right fork continues for 300 feet before abruptly narrowing to a crawl through mud and water. The left fork is 25 feet wide, 5 feet high and 450 feet long. A small room and a low, wide, side passage were noted. The passage ends at a breakdown. By going to the left of the breakdown and up, one enters a large breakdown room 150 feet long, 75 feet wide and 40 feet high. A large stream, the Sculpin River, is encountered at this point. By following the stream one enters a passage 40 feet wide, 5 to 10 feet high and 250 feet long. At this point a huge canyon, called White's Canyon, is intersected. This canyon is 200 feet long, 30 feet wide and 60 feet high. The stream passage continues across the canyon, averaging 10 feet wide and 7 feet high for 125 feet. The passage appears to end in a breakdown, but by crawling through the breakdown along the left wall for 25 feet, one may continue into the cave. A passage 15 feet wide, 10 feet high and 80 feet long leads into a tremendous breakdown chamber 150 feet in diameter and as much as 70 feet high. A huge canyon that leads northeast from this room averages 20 feet wide and 60 feet high for 150 feet to a fork. The left fork is a passage 50 feet high, 25 feet wide and at least 80 feet long. Its floor is occupied by a deep lake.

Hanging above the lake is a flowstone cascade 20 feet long which ends in a 20-foot-long drapery. Also noted was a 15-foot stalactite hanging above the lake. The right fork trends east for 150 feet and ends in several small crawlways and mud-filled passages. This farthest point reached in the cave is only 200 feet from the large spring that feeds Hill Creek and the associated Hill Creek Cave. The Sculpin River inside Prospect Hill Cave is almost certainly the source of the water issuing from this spring.

From the first breakdown room, another passage leads southwest for 560 feet and averages 10 feet high and 8 feet wide before ending abruptly in a dirt fill. This passage is rather dry in most places, and some of the walls have thin crusts of gypsum. Gypsum crystals were noted in the dry, loose dirt at several places.

Several short side passages were also explored. The cave has a surveyed length of 3,290 feet. A number of sculpins were seen living in the cave stream. The stream flow has been estimated at 2-3 gallons per second on several visits during various seasons of the year.[1]

A map of the cave is included in the book. (See Figure 13.4) In 1988 caver Doug Plemons reported the discovery of approximately 2,000 feet of additional virgin cave to the TN Cave Survey, however no map or description of these passages was included. This new discovery would make the know cave approximately one mile long.

---

1 Larry E. Matthews, *Descriptions of Tennessee Caves*, TN Division of Geology, Bulletin 69 (1971), pp 32-33.

Figure 13.2. Erica Sughrue by large stalagmites and pool in Hayes Cave. Photo by Bob Biddix, January 26, 2012.

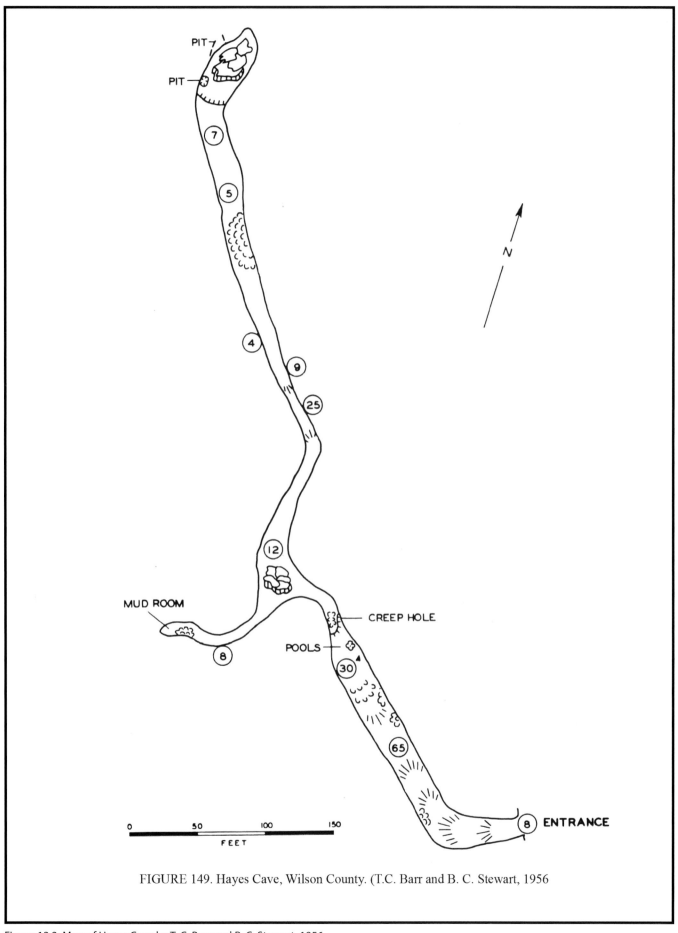

FIGURE 149. Hayes Cave, Wilson County. (T.C. Barr and B. C. Stewart, 1956

Figure 13.3. Map of Hayes Cave by T. C. Barr and B. C. Stewart, 1956.

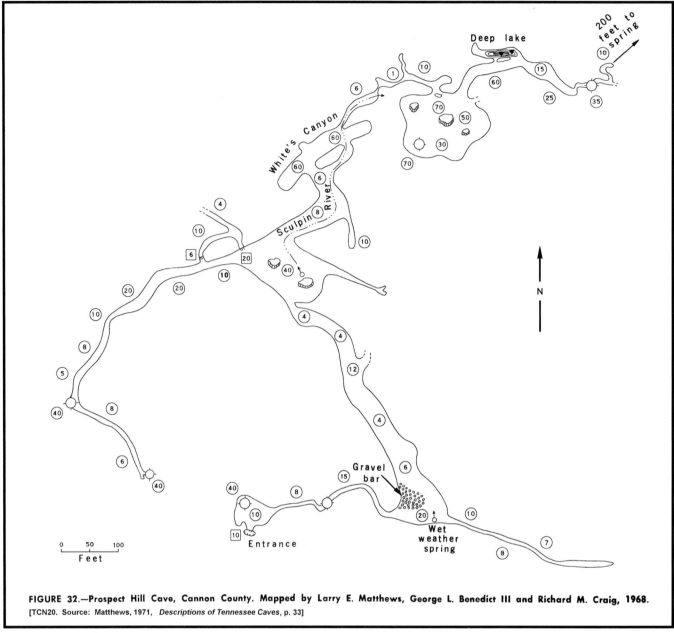

FIGURE 32.—Prospect Hill Cave, Cannon County. Mapped by Larry E. Matthews, George L. Benedict III and Richard M. Craig, 1968.
[TCN20. Source: Matthews, 1971, *Descriptions of Tennessee Caves*, p. 33]

Figure 13.4. Map of Prospect Hill Cave, Cannon County. Mapped by Larry E. Matthews, George L. Benedict III, and Richard M. Craig, 1968.

My First Visit to Prospect Hill Cave

My first visit to Prospect Hill Cave was sometime in mid-1967. We may have been the second group to enter the cave, since its discovery by Harry White a few months earlier. The cave was totally clean, so it has had little, if any, previous exploration prior to its discovery by Harry White.

The Survey of the Cave

The surveyed length of Prospect Hill Cave is 3,290 feet. It was surveyed by Larry E. Matthews, George L. Benedict III, and Richard M. Craig in the summer of 1968. The map is shown as figure 13.4.

Hill Creek Cave

Hill Creek Cave is located 5 feet above a large spring which is the principal headwaters of Hill Creek during dry weather. This spring is probably the emergence of the stream encountered in nearby Prospect Hill Cave. The entrance to Hill Creek Cave is 8 feet wide and 3 feet high. A passage 10 feet high and 4 feet wide leads for 30 feet to a sump. A side passage to the northwest is 20 feet long, 4 feet high and 3 feet wide.[2]

Hayes Cave

Hayes Cave is located in Wilson County. Although it is not a long cave, it is very large and well-decorated. It is

2 Matthews, op. cit., p. 30.

Figure 13.5. Erica Sughrue by a "Fallout Shelter Starts Here Sign" in Bob Williams Cave. Dozens of caves were designated as fallout shelters during the Cold War. Photo by Bob Biddix, March 11, 2018.

described by Thomas C. Barr, Jr. in his book, *Caves of Tennessee* (1961):

> The entrance gallery of Hayes Cave—65 feet high, 25 feet wide, and 150 feet long—is one of the most impressive sights in any Tennessee cave. The mouth is 12 feet wide and 8 feet high, and the floor slants sharply downward into the high gallery. Flowstone on the walls and large columns and stalagmites at the inner end add to the grandeur of the scene. Near the end of the gallery it is necessary to scale a 15-foot cliff or crawl through a small slit known as the "Creep Hole" in order to reach the back part of the cave. The remainder of the cave is readily traversable but is considerably smaller. It ends in a breakdown room 700 feet from the mouth. The general trend of the cave is north-westward. One short side passage was noted.[3]

A map of the cave by T. C. Barr and B. C. Stewart, dated 1956, accompanies this description and is shown here as Figure 13.3.

My First Visit to Hayes Cave

When I was in High School the Interstate Highway system was still under construction, so we were limited to slow, two-lane roads for our caving trips. This limited how far we could go on any given day. Hayes Cave was relatively close to Nashville, the description by Barr sounded great, so it was one of the first caves outside Davidson County that we visited. We went sometime in 1963 and we were not disappointed. As you can see from the accompanying photographs, it is a beautiful cave. Due to its huge size and beautiful formations, it has always been a favorite of Nashville cavers.

---

3 Thomas C. Barr, Jr., *Caves of Tennessee*, TN Division of Geology, Bulletin 64 (1961), pp 525-526.

Bob Williams Cave

Bob William Cave is another very long Cannon County Cave. It was initially described by Thomas C. Barr, Jr. in his book, Caves of Tennessee (1961):

This cave is located 275 yards south of the former site of the Bob Williams home, which once stood at the forks of the hollow. The mouth is 30 feet wide and 6 feet high and opens into the side of a gallery 8 feet high and 6 to 8 feet wide. This galley extends south for 275 feet, gradually becoming smaller toward the end, and north for 175 feet to a fork. The west fork of the north branch is 40 feet long and leads into a low room 40 feet in diameter. The east fork of this branch extends up into a room 40 feet long, 25 feet wide, and 15 feet high. This east room contains a drip pool, some flowstone, and a stalagmite 8 feet high. A crawlway which extends northward from the room is 150 feet long, averaging 5 feet wide and 3 feet high, and leads to a second entrance to a cave—a small hole 20 feet above the bottom of the hollow, 80 yards north of the main entrance. Beyond the second entrance the crawlway continues for 75 feet, divides into two branch crawlways, and becomes quite muddy.[4]

The TCS files report the following further exploration of this cave:

On April 11, 1987, Tennessee Central Basin Grotto (TCBG) members Jeff Parnell, Drex Freeman, and Jim Freeman were looking a for a "Saturday cave"—a cave that could be surveyed in one day. They chose Bob Williams Cave because, from the description, they expected about 1,000 feet of passage. After surveying that first day, however, they had netted 3,000 feet and the cave survey was still incomplete. After three additional trips, an additional 1,000 feet was added.

On January 13, 1990, TCBG members Jeff Parnell, Don Lance, Marbry Hardin, Greg Johns, and Pat Arnold ventured into Bob Williams Cave on what was billed as the last survey trip. After surveying the last lead to an unpromising, low-airspace water crawl, Greg Johns donned a wetsuit top and pushed ahead. After a very cold 100 feet, he broke out into borehole. A quick inspection revealed stream passage, calcite and gypsum formations, and leads everywhere! He returned to the group to report his find, but the other cavers did not have wetsuits to combat the melted snow-water. They exited the cave.

Successive surveys after this initial find pushed ever deeper into the cave. On September 22, 1990, Jeff Parnell, Jim Freeman, and Raleigh Marlin surveyed an incredible 5,320 feet during an 8-hour trip into the new section. In one day the length of Bob Williams Cave had doubled. A later trip on October 10, 1990 by Jeff Parnell, Tony Baker, and Ian Anderson mapped an additional 1,400 feet in a 3-hour trip. The cave continues, but no additional survey trips have been undertaken.

The new section is only accessible by wetsuit via the water crawl. Like most of the wet Highland Rim caves, cavers entering this section should be wary of the weather. The water crawl and a substantial section of the surrounding cave floods in any kind of rain.[5]

This is another great exploration story of how persistent cavers pushed a 1,000-foot long cave to over two miles of mapped passages.

At some point during the Cold War, Bob Williams Cave was one of a number of Tennessee caves that were designated to be Fallout Shelters. Figure 13.5 shows a sign indicating the beginning of the area to be used as a Fallout Shelter.

Cave Access

All of these caves are located on private property. Their current status is unknown. Always be sure you have the owner's permission before entering these, or any other caves.

---

4 Thomas C. Barr, Jr., *Caves of Tennessee*, TN Division of Geology, Bulletin 64 (1961), pp 95-96.

5 Don Lance, TCS Narrative: Cannon County, Tennessee, p. CN-4

Figure 13.6. Carol Lamers in the main passage of Hayes Cave. Photo by Bob Biddix, January 26, 2012.

Figure 14.1. Mike Moser by a ladder leading to the middle entrance to Robinson Ridge Saltpeter Cave. Note the walled-up lower entrance at the bottom. Photo by Joe Douglas, November 26, 2011.

CHAPTER 14

Robinson Ridge Saltpeter Cave

Robinson Ridge Saltpeter Cave is located in Cannon County, Tennessee. It was first located by organized cavers from the Nashville Grotto in 1968.

Back in the Golden Age of Tennessee Cave Exploration, you could scan 7.5-minute topographic maps and find caves marked on them that were not in Barr's *Caves of Tennessee* (1961). This is how I first located Robinson Ridge Saltpeter Cave. Following is my description of that first trip to this cave:

This cave is marked on the Beech Grove Quadrangle and is located in Cannon County about 0.5 miles north of Burk Cave which is in Coffee County. Since this cave is not in Barr and we could not find anyone who had ever been to it, Marietta and I decided to go explore it on Wednesday, September 11. We drove to the farmer's house and secured his permission to explore it. He said that he had been in it and that it was quite long, but that I would need a ladder to get down the entrance. Since we were already there, Marietta and I decided to go take a look anyway, figuring that we might be able to climb in or chimney in.

After hiking to the cave we could see that it had three entrances, arranged in a vertical row in a cliff. The lowest entrance had a stream flowing out and was only about 1 foot in diameter. Closer inspection showed that the lower entrance had been partially walled up, although this is not easily discernable due to the age of the limestone block wall. At one time, it would have been possible to crawl into the lower entrance. The middle entrance is located about 15 feet above the lower entrance and it is possible to reach it by means of a ledge coming around from the right side of the cliff. The upper entrance is another 10 feet above the middle entrance and would be difficult to reach without ropes. It is about 3 feet high and 1 foot wide.

The middle entrance is about 4 feet high and 5 feet wide. It is very rectangular in shape. In fact, it is so rectangular in shape that it made me wonder if it was natural or artificial. A close inspection showed several very weathered drill holes. Either this entrance is entirely artificial, or, more likely, it was a smaller entrance which has been enlarged by someone. By now Marietta and I were getting quite excited but we could not enter the cave because only 5 feet inside the middle entrance was a 12-foot drop which was slightly overhanging. We could see that we were entering the side of a passage which was at least 30 feet high and 10 feet wide. To the right it appeared to end after only 15 feet, but to the left it went upstream out of sight and we could distinctly hear a waterfall.

Reluctantly, we left and returned to Nashville, determined to return in a few days with my cable ladder and find out how large the cave was. Especially exciting, was the possibility that this might turn out to be a new saltpeter cave. The drill marks at the entrance were similar to those found in Big Bone Cave, Calfkiller Cave, Cave Hill Saltpetre Pits, and others.

We returned on Saturday, September 14, with Ron Zawislak, Jeff Gardner, and Bob Cook. We quickly rigged the entrance with my cable ladder and climbed in. Once inside, we found ourselves in a room 35 feet high, 15 feet wide, and 75 feet long. At the far end of the room, the cave stream was falling 8 feet out of a high, narrow passage into a pool of water 5 feet deep. We all got rather wet climbing up, only to find we faced another deep pool and a 5-foot waterfall climb… to another pool and a 4-foot climb. At this point we were in a well-decorated, high, narrow stream passage. This continued for about 200 feet, then opened up into a

Figure 14.2. Beautiful formations in Robinson Ridge Saltpeter Cave. Photo by Kristen Bobo, November 25, 2011. (Above, left.)

Figure 14.3. Gerald Moni on the ladder at the first waterfall climb in Robinson Ridge Saltpeter Cave. Mike Moser standing in the foreground in a red caving suit. Photo by Joe Douglas. November 26, 2011. (Above, right.)

stream passage averaging 15 wide and 10 feet high. The passage continued to be well-decorated with flowstone formations. We excitedly followed this passage for several hundred feet to a fork.

We first took the left fork for several hundred more feet and many more formations. It finally dropped to a hands-and-knees crawl through the stream. Marietta and I went ahead to check it out. It soon opened to stooping passage, but after two or three hundred feet it again lowered to a stream crawl. I was starting to turn back when Marietta decided to go ahead and look around the next corner. The passage opened up! We were in a medium-sized room with walking passage apparently leading in three directions. The one passage I climbed up to had dry dirt, a trail, and rotted wood. Now I was more sure than ever that we had found a saltpeter cave. But did the miners come through the stream crawl like we just had? We decided to retrace and get the others before we explored further.

After talking with the others, we decided to go half way back to the entrance and try the right fork, which we had not checked yet, in hopes that is would bypass the stream crawl. The right fork was also a stream passage. We followed it as walking passage for several hundred feet, then as stoop passage for another couple of hundred feet, then I pushed on down a hands-and-knees crawl for a final 250 feet before I decided to turn back.

We retraced and went to the room through the crawl like Marietta and I had originally done. After climbing up to the dry passage where we had turned back we immediately found five (5) casts of saltpeter vats. About 99% of the wood had rotted away and the casts themselves had started to crumble, but they appear to have been square vats. They were rather small, only 5 feet long, 4 feet wide and 3 feet high on the average. We continued down the passage which forked, then rejoined after 100 feet in a medium-sized room. Jeff and I explored an upper lead off of this room which was 3 feet high, 8 feet wide and 75 feet long. The passage had clearly been dug out, and shovel marks were still plainly visible in places. After 75 feet a dirt wall where the miners had stopped digging blocked further exploration in this direction,

Continuing down this Saltpeter Passage, we came to the stream passage again. We followed it upstream as a stoop way for 200 feet, then it opened up to 20 feet wide and 15 feet high for several hundred feet. Finally it began to lower and after several hundred more feet we turned back when it dropped to a crawl. While returning to the junction of the upper saltpeter level and the lower stream level, Jeff and

Figure 14.4. Mike Moser in a stream passage in Robinson Ridge Saltpeter Cave. Photo by Joe Douglas, November 26, 2011. (Above, left.)

Figure 14.5. Mike Moser in a well-decorated passage in Robinson Ridge Saltpeter Cave. Photo by Kristen Bobo, November 25, 2011. (Above, right.)

Figure 14.6. Kristen Bobo in a well-decorated stream passage in Robinson Ridge Saltpeter Cave. Photo by Joe Douglas, November 26, 2011. (Left, below.)

I explored a side passage for several hundred feet, although we could have continued further. Marietta and Ron found another upper lever passage which was about 300 feet long and also showed signs of digging. From the junction Bob and Jeff pushed the stream passage downstream, while Ron, Marietta, and I took a rest. Bob and Jeff returned after exploring several hundred feet of low passages and a high, narrow, intersecting canyon.

We returned to the place where we had originally entered the upper level. One of the other upper passages connected with our Saltpeter Passage as a high lead after about 200 feet. The other lead required climbing up a beautiful and gigantic flowstone formation 40 feet high and 30 feet wide with occasional rimstone pools on its steeply sloping face, which enabled Bob and me to climb it. At the top we found that it joined the ceiling and that any passage in this direction had been blocked.

We were all getting tired by this time, and the only remaining leads were crawlways. We figured that we had explored well in excess of 3,000 feet of passages… possibly as much as 4,000 feet. Ron took several photographs on the way out and we returned home.

Looking at the topo map we see that the entrance of Burk Cave is located about 3,200 feet south of the entrance of Robinson Ridge Saltpeter Cave and about 250 feet higher in elevation. A wet weather stream flows into Burk Cave and a stream flows out of Robinson Ridge Saltpeter Cave. It seems possible that the two caves may be connected by pushing the hands-and-knees crawl at the explored end of one of the two branches of the cave stream.

Mapping of the two caves would make looking for a connection easier.

Robinson Ridge Saltpeter Cave is almost entirely free of vandalism and is well worth exploring and photographing. Future visitors should strive to keep this cave in its clean, natural state.[1]

It was an exciting find and the cave seemed to have much more potential.

A Description of the Cave

Robinson Ridge Saltpeter Cave is described by Larry E. Matthews in his book *Descriptions of Tennessee Caves* (1971):

The lower entrance to Robinson Ridge Saltpeter Cave has been walled up so that a hole 1-foot square remains through which the cave stream flows out. Another entrance is located 15 feet above the stream exit and is accessible by a ledge. This entrance is 4 feet high and 5 feet wide. Old drill marks in the mouth of this entrance indicate that it has been artificially enlarged by blasting, probably by the Civil War saltpeter miners. A rope is necessary to negotiate a 15-foot drop from this entrance into the main passage of the cave.

From the entrance a stream passage averaging 10 feet wide and 15 feet high leads for 500 feet to a fork. The right fork was followed for at least 500 feet, averaging 10 feet high and 15 feet wide at its beginning, but diminishing to 1 foot high and 5 feet wide at the limit of exploration. The left fork continues for 300 feet with walking dimensions, then drops to a 200-foot crawl through the stream. After 200 feet, this stream-crawl intersects an upper lever, which contains several hundred feet of dry walking passages with crawlways leading off to the sides. Near the beginning of the upper level are the remains of five saltpeter vats. Most of the wood has rotted away in the humid atmosphere of the cave, but the casts show that the vats were of the square type, 5 feet long, 4 feet wide, and 3 to 4 feet high. Pick and shovel marks are visible in the dirt in this area.

The upper level intersects a continuation of the stream passage, which may be followed both upstream and downstream. It may be followed upstream for at least 600 feet with maximum dimensions of 20 feet wide and 15 feet high, until it lowers to a crawlway where exploration was halted. Downstream it may be followed for several hundred feet before becoming a crawlway. One side passage off the stream passage was followed for several hundred feet to a breakdown and appeared to continue on the other side.

In all, more than 3,000 feet of passages was explored, and several leads remain to be checked. The stream that flows out of this cave may be the same one that flows into Burk Cave 3,300 feet farther south and 250 feet higher in elevation. If so it may prove possible to connect the two caves by exploration.[2]

As it turns out, future exploration would prove that Robinson Ridge Saltpeter was much larger than the initial 3,000 feet described above. Due to the shape of the entrance, this cave has also been known by the name Window Cave.

New Discoveries

Don Lance reports on the further exploration of Robinson Ridge Saltpeter Cave:

Past the point in the right-hand side mentioned by Matthews, the stream passage continues with walking, stooping, and crawling dimensions for over 3,000 feet. After about 1,000 feet, a stream passage is encountered on the left whose water joins the main cave stream. This branch leads to cave which drains Hettie Hollow. Continuing upstream for about another 1,000 feet, a small maze area from which three passages extend is found. All three contain water; two of these terminate after about 300 feet. Several beautiful white helictites and heligmites were located in this area and inspired the name "Medusa Maze." One lead in this area led upwards into a narrow, slick canyon which contained a lot of moving air, but it could not be negotiated safely.

The main stream can be followed for about another 800 feet until several domes, dry loops, and breakdown areas appear. A hazardous climb upwards in the breakdown in this region brings the

1 Larry E. Matthews, "Robinson Ridge Cave," *Speleonews*, Vol. 12 (1968), no. 5, pp 66-69.

2 Larry E. Matthews, *Descriptions of Tennessee Caves*, TN Division of Geology, Bulletin 69 (1971), p 34.

Figure 14.7. Denis Smith in a well-decorated passage in Robinson Ridge Saltpeter Cave. Photo by Kristen Bobo, November 25, 2011. (Above, left.)

Figure 14.8. Mike Moser in a beautiful flowstone-lined passage in Robinson Ridge Saltpeter Cave. Photo by Joe Douglas, November 26, 2011. (Above, right.)

Figure 14.9. Kristen Bobo climbing out the ladder leading to the middle entrance of Robinson Ridge Saltpeter Cave. Photo by Joe Douglas, November 26, 2011. (Below, right.)

caver into the North Galaxy Room, where Homer Green's Upper Entrance can be found. A nice 70-foot dome lies just beyond a crawl which is downstream from the climb. Also nearby is a smallish dome with an invisible lead in the wall. This lead goes for 1,400 feet as a crawl until it intersects another set of impressive domes called the Methuselah's Tomb.

Overall, much of Robinson Ridge consists of long stream crawls which branch from the two forks mentioned by Matthews. The passages typically travel for hundreds of feet before terminating. (First you will have 300 feet of stream crawl that is 3 feet high, then 300 feet of stream crawl that is 2 feet high, then 300 feet of stream crawl that is 1 foot high….) Most of the cave is developed at the stream level, with the exceptions being the upper levels in the left-hand side and the upper breakdown chambers and crawls in the area of Homer's Upper Entrance.[3]

So, even though this is a significantly long cave, much of the cave consists of low, stream crawlways.

3 Don Lance, TN Cave Survey Narrative Files, 1991.

Homer Green's Gold Mine

A nearby resident, Homer Green, based on stories by his father, believed that the Confederate Army had buried gold on his land during the Civil War. In 1985 Green hired a bulldozer to excavate for this buried gold on a section of hillside on his property. As luck would have it, he intersected the large, upper levels of Robinson Ridge Saltpeter Cave! Perhaps there was a sinkhole at that point, or some other indication that made him pick that point to excavate. We may never know. Caver Don Lance tells more of this incredible story:

The story of the appearance of Robinson Ridge's Upper Entrance is something to hear. Jeff Parnell remembers his first through trip at Robinson Ridge on August 25, 1985, and he recalls seeing a bulldozer parked about a hundred feet inside the entrance. They came to find out that a long time ago Homer's father had told his son that the Confederates had buried gold in a cave on their land. Although no indication of a cave existed, Homer hired a bulldozer to excavate a section of the hillside. Amazingly, he intersected the large, upper levels located deep in Robinson Ridge Saltpeter Cave. When he journeyed inside his new entrance, he found several old Tennessee Central Basin Grotto survey stations and became convinced that they were placed there by the Confederates during the Civil War.

This both helped and hampered the survey. Although the new entrance was very convenient, Homer did not want anyone using it for fear of someone finding the rumored gold cache – so he would not hesitate (and still doesn't) to shoot at someone on his land. He simply refused to believe that he had intersected an existing cave, even after having been told so. In time, however, relations improved somewhat and he will now only let familiar TCBG cavers use his entrance occasionally.

Homer Green has become somewhat of a celebrity these days, having been featured in newspapers and on TV with his Appalachian folk art that decorates his yard. He is also notorious for being distrustful at times and cursing with every other breath. He has shot at TCBG members exiting from his entrance late at night, as several people can fully attest.[4]

Bob Biddix recalls the story of the first time he met Homer Green:

Seeing this photo reminds me of the first time I had asked Homer Green to visit Pleasant Ridge Cave. Ray Nelson and I knocked on the door for permission knowing that Jeff Parnell had softened him up weeks earlier by bringing him home made pies. I asked Homer to go to the cave and he said he would need to get Grandmaw's permission first. Ray looked at me and I shrugged my shoulders at Ray as we followed Homer to the barn to meet Grandmaw. Once inside there was a pine box casket in the center elevated just beyond waist high. Homer said we should stand back a bit until he got her attention so we stood just out of visual range of the interior of the casket as he opened the top portion. "Grandmaw there's some boys here that want to go in the cave" he yelled down in the pine box. "What's that Grandmaw" he said with his back turned to us? "You want them to come closer"? Come over here boys, Grandmaw wants to speak to yuns" And it was at that moment as we approached Homer stepped and pulled a lever that operated a spring loaded wooden Grandmaw complete with painted face and wig, that rose quickly and set upright in the casket! The noise of the spring action and the speed at which Grandmaw arose (not to mention the hideous face) would make any one jump out of their boots! Homer got great pleasure at seeing us jump out of our skin and laughed a deep "heh, heh, heh, heh," as he cranked Grandmaw back down into position. After that we could now go in the cave.

This Upper Entrance to Robinson Ridge Saltpeter Cave is located in Coffee County.

More than one Highland Rim cave owner has had a history of shooting at people on his land. Is there something in the water? We may never know. But, you have been warned! No trespassing means no trespassing. Always be sure you have permission before you go on any private property.

The Survey of the Cave

The Tennessee Cave Survey lists the surveyed length of Robinson Ridge Saltpeter Cave as 19,516 feet (3.7 miles) and the vertical extent as 365 feet.

---

4 Ibid.

Figure 14.10. Homer Green's "No Trespassing" sign. Photo by Bob Biddix. Circa 1989.

Caver Don Lance gives a history of the early survey efforts in the cave:

Robinson Ridge Saltpeter Cave and Tennessee Central Basin Grotto (TCBG) cavers Jim and Drex Freeman go back a long way. They first visited the cave with John Smyre in 1968, when the only entrance was Sam Butcher's Window Entrance. By 1973, they had begun a survey using a Boy Scout compass. This survey, however, was not the first. Research indicates two previous main surveys – the first attempted by the original Tennessee Central Basin Grotto in the 1950's.

The final survey of Robinson Ridge began with Drex Freeman and Jeff Parnell on June 14, 1986. After the many surveys in many different areas, it was decided to begin a resurvey and to use old survey notes to collaborate the current calculations. They began in the large, upper levels far from the Window Entrance but close to Homer Green's new Upper Entrance.

Since 1986, many TCBG cavers have spent many hours surveying the long, torturous waterways that comprise the cave. Primarily, the survey has been the work of Raleigh Marlin, Drex Freeman, Jim Freeman, and Jeff Parnell, although they have been assisted by Mark Moore, J. D. Toliver, Clint Adams, Don Lance, and many others.

The last big survey trip in Robinson Ridge occurred on November 4, 1990. On that trip, Mark Moore, David Parr, Jeff Parnell, Drex and Jim Freeman surveyed the Hidden Passage for 1,400 feet. After passing through the Crystal Crawls (where well-formed 3-inch gypsum needles occur), they came across two domes: a large dome approximately 70 feet tall and another smaller 25-foot dome. There appeared to be two large passages near the top of the larger dome. Because of the strong wind in the Crystal Crawl, these passages are believed to either connect with similar domes nearby or lead to more cave. A later ridgewalk above this area found no trace of an entrance.

The above-mentioned domes were the site of a series of climbs during 1991 by TCBG members Raleigh Marlin, Jim Freemen, Jeff Parnell, and others. Using bolts and mud pitons, over 60 feet of height was gained, but the passages could not be reached safely.[5]

In 1994 Robinson Ridge Cave was the deepest cave in Cannon and/or Coffee County, with an overall vertical extent of 337 feet. The surveyed length of the cave at that time was 19,516 feet (3.7 miles). Apparently, no further surveying has occurred in this cave since that time. Despite all the time and effort spent surveying this cave, apparently no finished map has ever been produced.

Saltpeter Mining in Robinson Ridge Cave

The five casts of saltpeter vats found in this cave and the evidence of dirt mining in the upper lever clearly show that this cave was mined for saltpeter. Whether it was mined during the War of 1812, the Civil War, or both is

unknown and the poorly preserved wood near the vats would probably be unsuitable for either C-14 dating or dendrochronology.

Cave Access

This cave is on private property. Before entering this cave be sure that you have the owner's permission. There are two entrances, and they are owned by different people.

5 Ibid.

CHAPTER 15
Short Mountain's Pits

Short Mountain is located in Cannon County, Tennessee. It is perhaps the most conspicuous topographic feature in Cannon County and is home to three (3) well known pits. One other pit on adjacent Little Short Mountain and two other Cannon County pits are also included here for convenience.

As Bob Biddix so correctly pointed out, technically Short Mountain is not the edge of the Highland Rim, but an outlier of the Cumberland Plateau that sits on top of the Highland Rim. However, due to its location, I am ignoring this fact and including these pits with the Highland Rim Caves. Since they are a relatively short drive from Nashville, they have always been some of the favorite pits of the Nashville Grotto members.

Blue Crystal Well

Blue Crystal Well is described by Thomas C. Barr, Jr. in his 1961 book *Caves of Tennessee*:

> Blue Crystal Well is on the south side of Big Short Mountain, 150 feet below an old logging trail near the top of the mountain. It is developed in the Ste. Genevieve-Gasper limestone.[1] The entrance is a hole 10 feet long and 5 feet wide. The well extends downward vertically for 110 feet. A series of interconnecting domepits which average 60 feet high may be entered from the bottom of the entrance shaft. The horizontal length of the cave is only 65 feet. The sides of the shafts are coated with flowstone, all of which has a bluish color.[2]

Back when we were in high school, my friends and I spent several days searching for Blue Crystal Well, without success. We later learned that a tree had fallen over the entrance and the entrance was not visible. Here is an early trip report from Richard Bilbrey:

> On the afternoon of December 22, 1963, my mother and father, Mike Phillips, and I traveled to Cannon County, Tennessee, to descend into Blue Crystal Well. As we arrived on the mountain the sky was bleak and foreboding. After driving to within about one-half mile of the pit, we loaded ourselves down with rope and other gear and walked to within about one hundred feet of the pit. This was my third visit and second descent into the pit, but I spent about ten minutes hunting for the entrance due to some logging operations on the mountain.

> When I finally found the entrance, I discovered that someone had felled a large tree directly across it. We spent about fifteen minutes breaking tree limbs and clearing a path through the tree-top. Then I tied the rope to a nearby tree which was still standing and fed it into the pit. I threaded my rappel spool and descended to the bottom of the pit. Mike soon followed me, and we set out to see the sights of the cave.

> The whole pit is coated with flowstone some of which has a light blue tint with sparkling crystals in it, hence the name of the pit. Some of the other colors we observed were black, brown, and white. As we finished making pictures of the formations, my father called down to me that it was snowing. By the time I finished making a sketch of the passage at the bottom of the pit and prussiked back up, it was dark outside and snowing hard. On the last fifteen feet of the prussiks, snow was falling on us and the slope just inside the entrance had a light skif of snow on it. There was about three-quarters of an inch of snow on the ground. We retrieved the rope and headed for the car. I think we each fell about a half-dozen times before we reached the car. The drive off the mountain was the most dangerous part of the trip. An hour and a half later we drove into Murfreesboro. There was almost three inches of snow on the ground and it was snowing like mad.[3]

---

1 This geologic unit is currently known as the Monteagle Limestone.

2 Thomas C. Barr, Jr., *Caves of Tennessee*, TN Division of Geology, Bulletin 64 (1961), p. 102.

3 Richard Bilbrey, "Vertical Views," *Speleonews*, v. 7 (1963), no. 5, pp 47-48.

It is always interesting to go back to these earlier trip reports and look at the variety of vertical gear and other caving equipment that was in use in those days.

An excellent plan view and profile view of Blue Crystal Well by Don Lance and Marbry Hardin is included as Figure 15.1.

Devil's Hole

Devil's Hole is described by Thomas C. Barr, Jr. in his book *Caves of Tennessee*:

> The Devils Hole is a double-shaft swallet hole, 20 feet long and 8 feet wide at the surface. In transverse section the shaft is dumbbell-shaped. It extends downward vertically for 159 feet. About 100 feet down, the shaft bells out into a chamber 65 feet long and 30 feet wide, the main axis of which runs perpendicular to the long axis of the shaft.
>
> For nearly a hundred years the Devils Hole has been the center of local rumor and legend. More than one missing person is supposed to have vanished into its depths.
>
> Fifty yards east of the Devils Hole is the entrance to Jacks Cave an opening 25 feet wide and 10 feet high. After only 75 feet the cave narrows to a rocky crawlway leading to a horizontal fissure from which a strong blast of air issues during the summer. A sink, some 50 feet in diameter, is immediately below the entrance to Jacks Cave.[4]

As Barr states, the Devils Hole has been well known locally since at least the mid-1800's. We may never know who the first person was to set foot on the bottom. It has long been a favorite of cavers. Here is a trip report by Kin Moore from 1964:

> On Saturday, February 22, Kirk Holland, Bob Bradley, Ed Alexander and I all piled into Ed's Ford and headed out Murfreesboro Road toward Short Mountain. Upon arriving at our destination, we found that the mountain was well covered with snow, about three inches. There were gasps and shivers as we donned our cold boots and coveralls. At last, we assembled our gear, took a last look at the map and began our futile search for Blue Crystal

> Well, which lasted about two hours, and ended with cold hands and numb feet.
>
> Since we were to meet Louis Hardin and George Benedict at 12:00, we decided to give up the affair. Ed, however, took time to inquire at a resident's house, and the man said that he would gladly lead anyone to both Blue Crystal Well and Melton Hole on a nice day. (His house is located at the top of the horseshoe curve on the road to Short Mountain Camp). We advise that future cavers contact this man before looking for the pit.
>
> We arrived at the meeting place early and decided to relax by the warmth of a stove in a small grocery. Our unusual apparel caused curiosity and the typical questions. It wasn't long before we realized that the 160-foot Devils Hole, our next stop, was well known locally. One old timer said that several Nashville cavers (I'm anxious to find out who.) went to the pit with 1,100 feet of rope; and you can guess the rest: It didn't reach the bottom. (Editor's Note: It was only 460 feet of rope and I never found the pit.) Upon learning our intentions to descend the pit we were given explicit directions.
>
> Finally we gave up on Louis and Benny, who were visiting Espey Cave to take pictures. We left the warmth of the stove and bounced down the road to Little Short Mountain. The Devils Hole is located amidst some outcroppings about half way up the hill, just above the point where the cedar trees give way to deciduous timber. It is almost directly north of the house of a Mr. Anderson.
>
> Somehow, I was elected to carry the 340 feet of 5/8 inch Manila rope. After a grueling climb, we located the hole. I took pictures as Bob, Ed, and Kirk rigged for the descent. Kirk rigged his Swiss seat and carabiner, snapped the rope into place, and made his rappel to the bottom of the shaft.
>
> I was to rappel next, and soon after getting over the edge of the opening, I found that the rope did not slide easily over my make-shift shoulder pad. I spent several hair-raising minutes in pushing the rope over my shoulder. Finally, I began to move and made a spinning descent for the remaining seventy feet and landed dizzily on the floor.
>
> Bob and Ed did not have my problem and made routine rappels. After determining that there were no passages I attached my prussiks and began the

---

4 Thomas C. Barr, Jr., *Caves of Tennessee*, TN Division of Geology, Bulletin 64 (1961), pp 96-97.

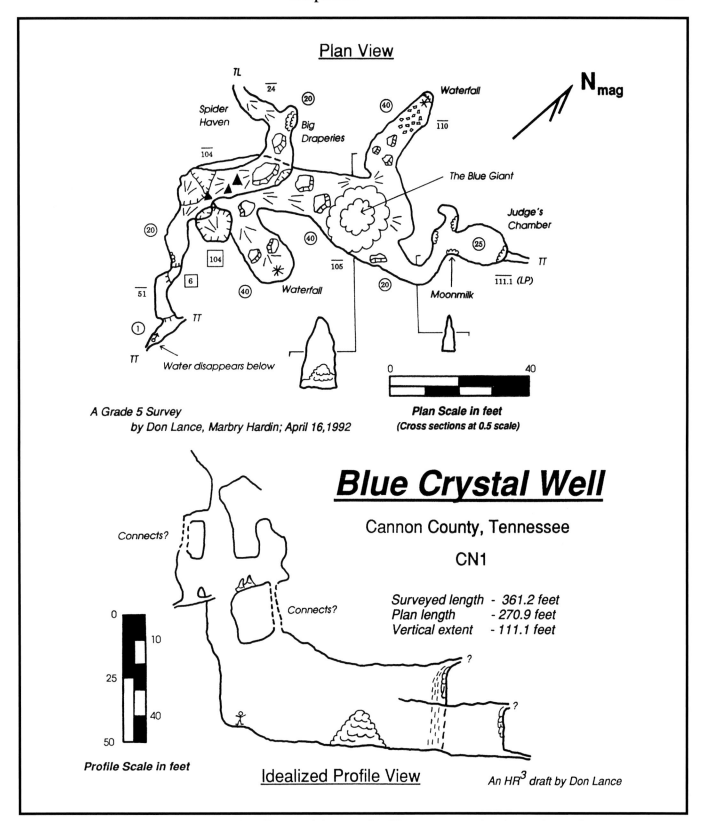

Figure 15.1. Survey showing the plan view and profile view of Blue Crystal Well by Don Lance and Marbry Hardin, April 16, 1992.

ascent. About half way up I heard Benny and Louis, who had just arrived at the Hole. They gave their remarks and lent moral support. I made my prussik in fifteen minutes, and climbed out into the cold air, hot and tired.

Kirk and Ed prussiked out next; Kirk's time, eighteen minutes and Ed's thirty. Then we yelled to Bob to come up. There was no answer. We continued to bellow and scream for about five minutes before getting a feeble reply, "You woke me up!"

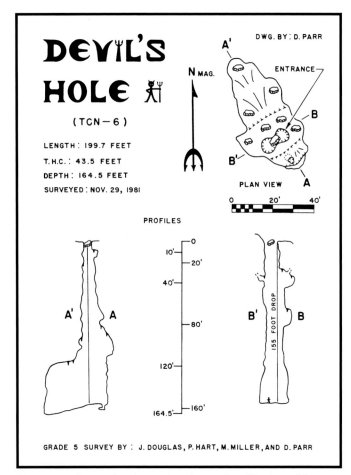

Figure 15.2. Survey showing a plan view and profile view of the Devil's Hole by David Parr, November 29, 1981.

Figure 15.3. Carol Lamers rappelling into the entrance of the Devils Hole. Photo by Bob Biddix, August 28, 2012.

Bob prussiked up in twenty-four minutes and arrived on top as the sun was about to set. We coiled the rope, gathered our equipment, took one last look in the Hole and started down the mountain. We stopped at the store to inform the people of its true depth, and then we started the haul home.

It was nearly seven o'clock before we reached Nashville. We were all tired and dirty, but very satisfied with our successful adventure into one of Tennessee's beautiful caves.[5]

The rappelling method described by Kin involved a home-made Swiss seat, made from a single length of webbing, a single locking carabiner, and some type of a shoulder patch. The Manila rope was run through the carabiner, over the shoulder, across the back, and down by the opposite leg. Braking and control were accomplished by pulling on the rope and increasing friction across the back of the jacket and the trouser leg. Ouch! Very uncomfortable and, by today's standards,

incredibly primitive and dangerous. Modern caving ropes and the now ubiquitous rappel rack would not be invented for several more years.

An excellent plan view and profile view of the Devil's Hole by David Parr is shown as Figure 15.2.

Melton Hole

Melton Hole is described by Thomas C. Barr, Jr. in his book *Caves of Tennessee*:

Melton Hole is on Big Short Mountain, near the head of Gunner's Hollow. It is developed in the Ste. Genevieve-Gasper limestone. The entrance has a natural bridge across the top of an oval-shaped well 10 feet wide and 30 feet long. The first pitch, 15 feet, drops to a balcony which overlooks a huge well 40 feet in diameter and 120 feet deep. No horizontal development has taken place at the bottom of this drop.[6]

5 Kin Moore, Vertical Views, *Speleonews*, v. 8 (1964), no. 1, pp 5-6.

6 Thomas C. Barr, Jr., *Caves of Tennessee*, TN Division of Geology, Bulletin 64 (1961), pp 102-103.

Figure 15.4. Carol Lamers on the bottom of the Devils Hole. Photo by Bob Biddix, April 11, 2013.

Figure 15.5. Erica Sughrue rappels into the entrance of the Melton Hole. Photo by Bob Biddix, December 16, 2012.

A couple of weeks after I graduated from high school, Kirk Holland, Kin Moore, and I visited Melton Hole. Kirk describes this visit in one of his trip reports:

> On June 13, 1964, Larry Matthews, Kin Moore, and I made another visit to the Mountain to descend into the Melton Hole. We contacted the man who had previously promised to take us to it on a nice day. This man turned out to be none other than Mr. Melton, after whom the pit is named.
>
> To our surprise, Mr. Melton told us of another deep pit about three-quarters of a mile past the Short Mountain Youth Camp. Of course we didn't believe all this at first, but when he volunteered to lead us to the new pit our interest was renewed. Because the camp was being prepared for opening, we had access to the gates and were able to drive Larry's invincible VW to within a quarter mile of the cave. On the thirty-minute search which ensued, we learned from Mr. Melton that Richard Bilbrey of the Central Basin Grotto (Murfreesboro) had descended into the hole a few weeks earlier, reached the 150-foot level, and still did not see bottom. Swearing Mr. Melton to secrecy, he prepared for another descent which culminated the week before our visit with the total descent into the abyss. He claims it is over 250 feet deep with about seventy feet of horizontal passage at the bottom.
>
> So it was with dubious expectations that we found the shaft, but we also found that our fears of a hoax were groundless. It certainly was a deep pit. We only had 150 feet of tape with which to plumb its depth and this did not reach bottom. From the sound of rocks thrown into the hole, the depth exceeds 150 feet by a good margin. We also noted that there appeared to be a ledge about 110 feet down. A future expedition was quickly planned for the following week, and the results of this venture will appear in a future issue of the *Speleonews*.

Figure 15.6. Erica Sughrue on rope in the Melton Hole. Photo by Bob Biddix, December 16, 2012.

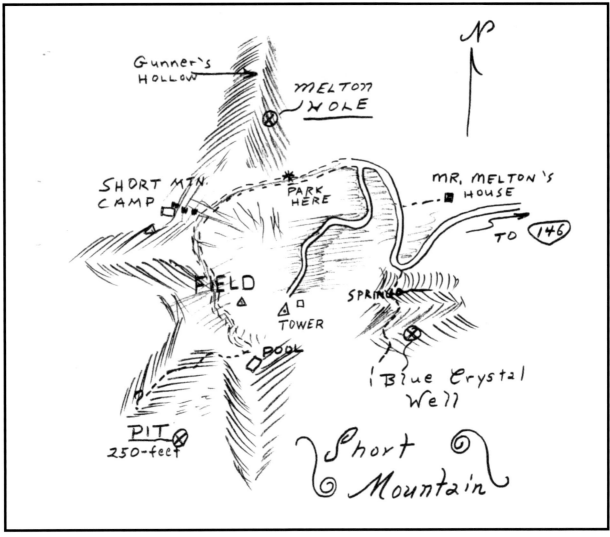

Figure 15.7. Map of the summit of Short Mountain and location of pits by Kirk Holland, 1964

Our next stop was our original destination, the Melton Hole. Under Mr. Melton's guidance we had no trouble finding the entrance and soon the pit was rigged with five-eighths inch Manila rope. I was nominated to descend first. Larry rappelled in next, and he was followed by Kin. We noted that the pit was formed by vertical solution along a crack which formed a double shaft. The wall which separated the shafts had long since disintegrated, leaving a twenty-foot talus slope at the bottom and a natural bridge at the top. Rocks have washed down the hillside and become wedged in the smaller shaft, leaving a very unstable looking, but solid, jumble of rocks at the top. A quick reconnaissance revealed that the pit was completely devoid of interest except for a carrot-shaped flowstone formation on one wall, so I attached my Prussik loops and ascended to the surface. Kin quickly joined me at the top and, after

a while, was followed by Larry. We then hauled the rope up and headed back to Nashville.

There are a number of small caves on Short Mountain as reported by Dr. Barr but none of these have been located on a topo sheet. (Short Mountain Quadrangle was not complete at the time of the original Tennessee Cave Survey.) One of these, Summit Cave, runs under Short Mountain Youth Camp, and another is said to have an opening at the base of the Mountain and is penetrable to a forty-foot falls for which a ladder is needed for further exploration.

Short Mountain should not be ignored as a possible site for new discoveries in the future. It is, in fact, probably one of the best locations for virgin cave. Much more exploration is needed before Short Mountain will give up some of its best secrets.[7]

7 Kirk Holland, "Vertical Development on Short Mountain," *Speleonews*, v. 8, (1964), no. 3, pp 28-29.

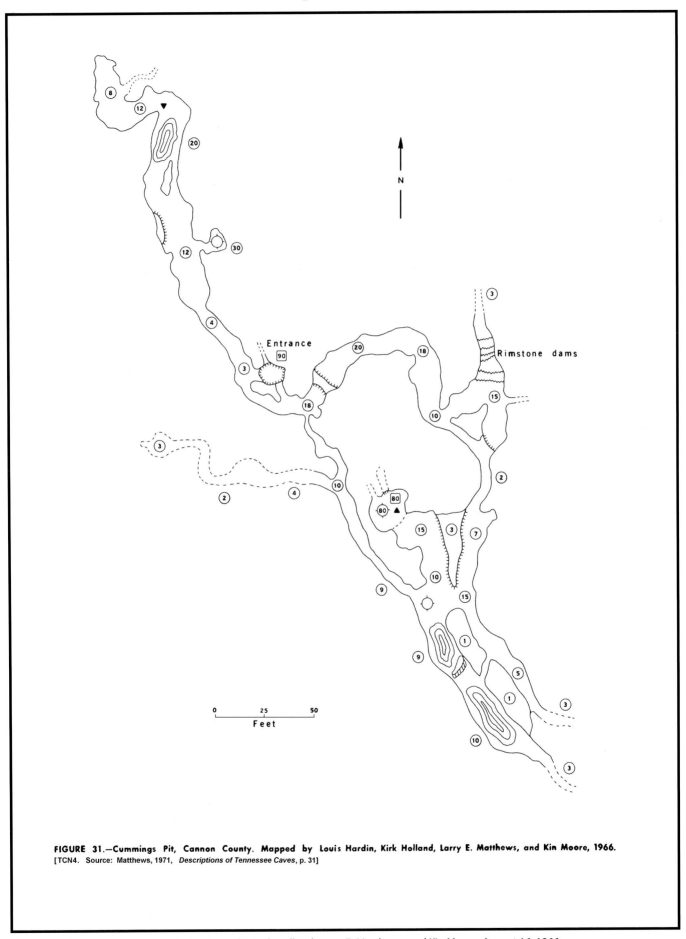

FIGURE 31.—Cummings Pit, Cannon County. Mapped by Louis Hardin, Kirk Holland, Larry E. Matthews, and Kin Moore, 1966.
[TCN4. Source: Matthews, 1971, *Descriptions of Tennessee Caves*, p. 31]

Figure 15.8. Map of Cummings Pit by Louis Hardin, Kirk Holland, Larry E. Matthews, and Kin Moore, August 16, 1966.

Despite Kirk's optimism, no really large cave has ever been discovered on Short Mountain, but it has some very nice pits.

Young's Pit

Young's Pit is described by Larry E. Matthews in his book *Descriptions of Tennessee Caves* (1971):

> The entrance to Young's Pit is 8 feet high and 10 feet wide and extends horizontally for 10 feet to the lip of the pit. The pit is 240 feet deep and has a major ledge developed 80 above the floor. The first 160 feet of drop is partly free and partly against a flowstone-covered wall. The remaining 80-foot drop from the ledge is entirely against the wall. A rather large room is developed at the bottom of the pit, and a crystal-clear lake covers part of the floor. Several albino crayfish were observed in this lake. A passage which can be entered from the ledge 80 feet above the floor is 30 feet high, 25 feet wide, and 150 feet long. This passage contains draperies, flowstone, and dripstone, as does most of the pit.[8]

Kirk Holland's report earlier in this chapter on our first visit to Melton Hole noted that Young's Pit was discovered by Richard Bilbrey in 1964. Unfortunately, we do not have a report from Richard Bilbrey of that discovery and the first descent. Kin Moore wrote the following trip report of a trip to Young's Pit the following year:

> On New Year's Eve Kirk Holland, Louis Hardin, and I (Bob Bradley was also along, but not listed in the original trip report) made a pilgrimage to Cumberland Caverns by way of Holland's haulin' Dodge. Kirk was to meet several cavers from Indiana for a day of pit exploring on Short Mountain. Our plans were to visit Young's Pit, a 240-foot pit recently discovered on the Mountain. But as it turned out, the Indiana Boys had been there the day before, so they set off to Devil's Hole, and we decided to carry on with our previous plans.
>
> We had no trouble locating the pit since Kirk and I had been to the entrance before. We were joined by the *Speleonews'* favorite Editor, Eddy Yarbrough, and it wasn't long before we were on the bottom.

Figure 15.9. Kirk Holland at the entrance to Young's Pit. Note the rappel spool and the thick, 5/8-inch Manila rope. Photo by Ed Yarbrough, December 31, 1964.

> The pit is quite unusual. Portions of the drop are against flowstone covered walls, with a free drop about halfway down of forty feet or so. This drop brings the explorer to a large ledge which slopes off to the edge of the remaining drop of eighty feet to the floor. A passage about 150 feet long goes off from the ledge. Its dimensions are about thirty feet high and twenty-five feet wide. This area is covered with draperies, flowstone, and dripstone, as is most of the pit. On the bottom, a high fissure about twenty-five feet wide extends for an undetermined distance. A crystal-clear lake covers the floor of this portion, (which, incidentally, is claimed to be a fine swimming hole by the Indiana cavers.) Bob and I noted several albino crayfish in the lake.
>
> Eddy started up after taking several pictures. We had planned to go up to the eighty-foot ledge and then get off Prussik to see the passage. So without much difficulty Kirk, Bob, Louis and I reached the ledge and soon Kirk began the climb out. Bob went out next and experienced some difficulty with slipping knots. (By this time the rope had become soaked with a muddy mess.) Bob managed to get over the slick spots though, and I started out next. Since my knots were 5/16 instead of 3/8-inch rope they stuck instead of slipping and required loosening before every step. But I was out in a short time and Louis began the climb. He also had slipping knot problems, but we managed to drop him a safety and hold him on belay over the slick places.
>
> By the time he got out it was pitch dark and raining, but we coiled up the rope and started back

[8] Larry E. Matthews, *Descriptions of Tennessee Caves*, TN Division of Geology, Bulletin 69 (1971), pp 34-35.

Figure 15.10. Erica Sughrue at the bottom of Young's Pit. Photo by Bob Biddix, April 22, 2018.

Figure 15.11. Keith Filson at the bottom of Young's Pit. Photo by Bob Biddix, May 4, 2018.

Figure 15.12. Robby Black on rope in Cummings Pit. Photo by Bob Biddix, April 11, 2005.

up the mountain. Due to an unforgivable sin the only light we had was what was left of the carbide in Kirk's lamp. Needless to say we lost the path and ended up well confused, bewildered, and in a word LOST on the mountain. But with Kirk's rapidly fading lamp we reached a road and finally found the car. Ah, how sweet it was.

We all felt that we had experienced a very exciting day but regretted the failure to take enough carbide. None of us relished the idea of spending the night on the mountain with the rabid foxes and no light. But as the old saying goes, "Live and learn," and we certainly learned the hard way.[9]

So, within a matter of months, Young's Pit had become one of the most popular deep pits in Tennessee

There are also a number of small caves located on Short Mountain. Two of them are described as follows:

Gunter Cave

Gunter Cave is located of the southeast slope of Big Short Mountain near the head of Mountain Creek. It was described by Jim Hodson in 1974:

> The cave stream emerges from breakdown just below the cave entrance, which is 5 feet high and 12 feet wide. One meets the stream just inside the entrance, where the passage lowers to a meandering stream crawl with wall-to-wall water. The passage averages 3 feet high and 6-10 feet wide. After 300 feet one emerges in a room 12 feet wide, 25 feet long, and 40 feet high. A stand-up room in the crawl gives access to an upper level passage which also leads to this room.
>
> Climbing to the top of the room, one enters a passage 7 feet high which may be followed in two directions. Towards the entrance is a breakdown slope 50-60 feet long. In the other direction is a stream passage averaging 6 feet high and 8 feet wide. This passage was explored for 800 feet to two rooms. The first of these is sandy-floored, with a waist-deep pool at one end through which one must wade. The second room, the Waterfall Room, is 15 feet in diameter and also has a pool, with the cave stream forming a waterfall. Harry White is reported to have climbed this waterfall and to have explored 200 feet of stream crawl. A high, blowing lead just before the Waterfall Room was explored for 100 feet as a crawlway. A total of about 1,500 feet of cave was explored.[10]

Summit Cave

Summit Cave is described by Thomas C. Barr, Jr. in Caves of Tennessee (1961):

> Summit Cave is on the north side of Big Short Mountain, beneath a ledge of sandstone near the top of the mountain. The sandstone is of Pennsylvanian age and forms the roof of the cave, which is developed in the Glen Dean limestone. The cave is only 100 feet in length, and the walls are deeply grooved by vertical solution.[11]

9 Kin Moore, "Vertical Views," *Speleonews*, v. 9 (1965), no. 4, pp 41-42.

10 Jim Hodson, TN Cave Survey Narrative Files – Cannon County, TN (1994), Written and edited by Don Lance, p CN-24.

11 Thomas C. Barr, Jr., *Caves of Tennessee*, TN Division of Geology, Bulletin 69 (1971), pp 102-103.

Figure 15.13 Above. Erica Sughrue at the entrance to Gunter Cave. Photo by Bob Biddix, April 1, 2018.

There are quite a few other small caves located on Short Mountain, but they will not be discussed here. If there is a big cave under Short Mountain, no one has discovered it yet.

Other Caves and Pits in This Area

There are several nearby pits that are also of interest. They include Cummings Pit and Sadlers Well.

Cummings Pit

Cummings Pit is located very close to Short Mountain and, therefore, is included in this chapter for convenience. Nashville caver Kirk Holland describes his first visit to this pit in 1966:

> This pit was located by Harry White of the Nashville Grotto about a year ago. It has seldom been visited and supposedly there was an interesting cave at the bottom. So it was with great vigor that we piloted our cars the 55 miles to Woodbury, where we picked out a likely looking farmhouse at the base of the Highland Rim to question for the whereabouts of the pit. We turned out to be quite fortunate, for the pit was located about 300 yards behind the farmer's

house. Mr. Mayo, the farmer, told us we could drive closer by a dirt road off the highway, which leads to property owned by Mr. James H. Cummings, a Woodbury lawyer. The cave is on his land, and thus the pit has been named in the classic manner.

After getting our "originals" on and all our gear together, we huffed and puffed up the steep hill for about 500 feet until we came to the somewhat dubious opening at the base of an elm and a hackberry tree. We were amazed at the proximity of the pit to US Highway 70-S in full view a few hundred yards away, which we had travelled so many times – completely unaware of this small opening on the cleared hillside which now beckoned us. Since we had come prepared for the Conley Hole (175 feet deep), we were forced to rig the pit with a 290-foot length of ½ inch braided Goldline. One end was used as the rappel line and the other end was utilized as an auxiliary sling to keep the rope from abrading itself on the rock walls at the top of the shaft.

After a few pictures were taken, I threaded my trusty rappel spool and rappelled into the pit, noting

Figure 15.14. Erica Sughrue rappels into the entrance of Sadlers Well. Photo by Bob Biddix, March 16, 2018.

its features on the way down. It is a classic solution shaft, somewhat elliptical, although irregular, in shape. The flowstone wall is at the caver's feet for the entire ninety feet, which is its plumbed depth. I landed on a fairly level bottom, which was about 20 feet in diameter and represented the maximum diameter of the shaft above. Two passages and a rocky crawl exited from this room. I climbed into one of the passages to get out of the way of falling rock and waited for the next person to descend. Kin soon joined me on the bottom, disappointed in that it was not a longer drop and saying that he was just getting started. Jim was next down, and he was followed by Bill. Jim and Bill were impressed with the pit, partially on its own merits and partially on the fact that it was one of their first pits.

While Bill Took pictures, Kin prussiked back out, since he had Louis' light and Louis wanted to use the spool. Meanwhile I "scoped out' the passages leading off from the bottom of the drop. One ended after about 150 feet in a collapse, obviously from the surface, and the other, which actually

was a continuation of the first passage with the pit intersecting it, led through a muddy passage to a series of spectacular domes about 80 feet high. I then returned to the rope since my electric light was fading fast. Since Louis was still not quite ready to descend, I attached my prussik slings and returned to the world of sunlight above.

After several more pictures, Bill and Jim on the bottom set out for the farthest reaches of the cave in search of pictures. Louis joined them on the bottom and after a quick look-see into one of the passages, he heard Kin yelling about a thunderstorm. This convinced Louis that it was time to break off reconnaissance and ascend. Prodded by our instant weather reports, Louis soon reached the surface and was greeted by dark, menacing clouds. Jim and Bill were told we would wait for them at the cars and, whenever they finished taking pictures and had ascended to de-rig and join us at the base of the hill.

Forty-five minutes and one thunderstorm later, we were reunited at the base of the hill, with two very wet cavers casting sinister glances at the three of us in the dry comfort of our car. However, they took their unexpected shower very good-naturedly and, after retrieving the rope and other pieces of equipment, we parted company.

The next trip to Cummings Pit occurred on August 16, 1966. On this trip Kirk Holland, Louis Hardin, Kin Moore, and Larry E. Matthews planned to map the cave. This trip was made on a Tuesday night, after work, and the occupants of the house at the base of the hill were quite astonished that we were actually going into a cave at *night*. The group entered the cave at about 8:00 pm at exited the cave after midnight. For some unknown reason (we *were* new at cave surveying) the surveyed length of the cave does not appear on the map. The map does show the cave to be somewhat longer and more complex than Kirk's earlier description, with a total surveyed length of approximately 1,000 feet. (See Figure 15.8)[12]

12 Kirk Holland, "Vertical Views – Cumming's Pit," *Speleonews*, v. 10 (1966), no. 4, pp 53-57.

Sadlers Well

Sadlers Well is another very popular pit in this area. It was first reported in the caving literature by Daniel E. Bloxsom, Jr. in the Cumberland Grotto publication, *The Troglodyte*:

> Sadler's Well and Cave is situated at the headwaters of Carson Creek in Carson Cove, where the Highland Rim drops to the Nashville Basin, Cannon County. The Well is a very pretty one, with flowstone algae-covered walls dripping from the spring that probably made the well. The roof has only recently (geologically) fallen in (but not in the memory of anyone living there since 1900), and there is an 8-foot talus pile of rocks, leaves, and trees at the bottom. Crawlways at the bottom all but pinch off.
>
> The cave has about 1,000 feet of tightly knit vadose maze passage, very few formations, and narrow dimensions, in Bigby-Cannon Limestone, at the bottom of the Cove from the well.[13]

The owner of the property at the time was Mr. David Sadler, where the Tullahoma cavers parked their car. Barr gives the following description:

> Sadlers Well is a vertical pit 12 feet in diameter and 100 feet deep. A spring emerges near the hole and falls into the pit. An 8-foot pile of talus is at the bottom. A few small crawlways open near the bottom of the shaft.[14]

As Barr's footnote explains, this description is by D. R. Bloxsom, Jr. Barr did not personally visit this pit.

Since this pit is close to Nashville, very attractive, and not too deep, it is a popular place to take persons new to vertical work.

Cave and Pit Access

Some of these caves and pits are located on private property. Their current status is unknown. Young's Pit and Gunter Cave are reported to be on the state-owned Headwaters Wildlife Management Area. It would be unwise to go here during hunting season. Always be sure you have the owner's permission before entering these, or any other pits or caves.

A 500 acre privately owned Natural Area is located on the top of Short Mountain. It is named the Short Mountain – Jim Cummings Scenic-Recreational State Natural Area.

---

13 D. Bloxsom, Jr., "Sadler's Wells and Cave," *The Troglodyte*, v. 1 (1955), no. 5, p. 4 (unnumbered).

14 Thomas C. Barr, Jr., *Caves of Tennessee*, TN Division of Geology, Bulletin 64 (1961), p.102.

Section 3: Southeast and South Section: Bedford, Lewis, Maury, and Moore Counties

Figure 16.1. Erica Sughrue at the entrance of Bishop Cave. Photo by Bob Biddix, January 13, 2019

Figure 16.2. Paul Bull Snook by "Father Time" in Bishop Cave. Photo by Paul Bull Snook, 2008.

CHAPTER 16
Bishop Cave

Bishop Cave is located in Bedford County, Tennessee. It has been the site of several rescues over the years. It has a surveyed length of 2.1 miles, but no finished map has ever been produced.

The Cumberland Grotto Explores Bishop Cave

The first, modern cavers to visit Bishop Cave and report their findings in the cave literature were the Cumberland Grotto of the National Speleological Society located in Tullahoma, TN. They refer to the cave as both Clendenon Caverns and Pete's Cave, because it was first located by a local caver named Pete Clendenon. Cord H. Link provides the following information:

As near as we know, Pete Clendenon began caving in 1952 or early 1953. He was completely independent at first, going whenever and wherever he could find a companion. Frequently, this friend was Casey. Very early in their search for caves they found the entrance to a cave no more than 50 yards off US 41-A, and subsequently Pete has been back to it about a dozen times and has not yet run out of traveling room. The names Pete and Casey appear often in the cave. In the fall or winter of 1953, we were with a party of six, including Whitesell, Folk, Clendenon leading, and the Bagbys. Pete failed to show off the cave this trip, but led directly to areas he wished to probe, mostly crawlways.

Pete's Cave has been revisited, and our earlier ideas of it have been drastically changed. It is definitely a significant cave. This cave is in Rippey Ridge, having its entrance approximately 0.8 mile south of the Rippey Ridge Cave. It appears that Pete's Cave will surpass Rippey Ridge Cave in passage length, in volume, and in complexity. The possibility of a junction of these two caves under the ridge is not to be considered unlikely.

At about 9:30 pm, Saturday, January 19, 1957, the foursome piled out of the car beside Highway 41-A. Link, for whom this would be the fourth visit

Figure 16.3. Photo of the end of a soda straw stalactite showing growing calcite crystals. Photo by Paul Bull Snook, 2009.

(one time the cave entrance was full of water and impassable), led the way, followed by Jimmy Thomas and his friend John (didn't get the last name), and Bob Nygaard.

The trail follows a line of trees extending up the hill about 50 yards along a small wash. At the head of the wash is the stooping entrance. One immediately finds bare walls and about 60 yards of walking passage. The floor of wet mud bears the prints of hundreds of coons, it seems, a trail that leads under a ledge, into a muddy, wet crawl, sometimes a stoopway, seldom standing room. Then a pool which can be straddled, and more crawling in a gravelly stream. After perhaps 100 yards there is an opening in the roof of the passage, to the right on entering, and through this rocks and dirt spill from chambers above. Put your head through this hole and look up a small dome, small in diameter, perhaps 5 feet, but perhaps 75 feet high. Look around and climb into the huge room, the first big one. It appears to be a connected series of domepits, making a chamber some 200 feet long, 30 to 40 feet wide, and some of the fluted vertical dome-lets rise perhaps 80 feet. This large chamber roughly parallels the entrance crawl. Going on in the in-bound direction, after

Figure 16.4. Robert Sewell lights up the main borehole passage of Bishop Cave. Photo by Paul Bull Snook, 2009.

traversing perhaps 500 feet, through half a dozen separate rooms, the passage shrinks and eventually fills with large stream deposited gravel. The party starts back out….but there is a large passage leading to the left (outbound) and this passage proceeds much like what we have been through but further and we begin to see massive flowstone formations. Three-foot high piles of bat guano are found, and the ceiling bears roost sign of a hundred square feet in one location, and there are dozens of roosts in ceiling solution domes, like large inverted bird baths. But there are no bats here anywhere, nor are there any fresh droppings. Are the bats hibernating elsewhere in the cave? Have they migrated for the winter? Great holes and chasms in the roof invite one to fly up. Branch passages lead in all directions. Here and there one find "Pete" and "Casey" smoked on the wall, and "DANGER" near a 30-foot pit in mid passage.

The floor rises and falls away, hill after hill. The four cavers choose a passage and work to its mucky end. Then Bob Nygaard climbs 40 feet, reports big rooms, and all make the tricky climb into upper passages. Here the formations are white and small forests of helictites grow. Fringe after fringe of soda straws crisscross the ceiling. A white straw feeds a stubby black, yes black, stalagmite. There are fine examples of pale brown and pink bacon rind. Across a chasm one sees the roof goes up higher. This must be 100 feet above the stream at the entrance. We are well back under a prong of Rippey Ridge.

We take some photographs. It is now after 1 o'clock on Sunday morning, January 20. We have only about 4 loads of carbide left, so we start out, stopping a few times for photos and to rest briefly. We miss a turn and walk one room too far. We find the great dome-series room and the crawlway out. We all get out at about 2 a.m.[1]

---

[1] Cord H. Link, Jr., *The Troglodyte*, Issue No. 20 (February, 1957), pp 1-4.

Figure 16.5. Robert Sewell in the Register Room of Bishop Cave. Photo by Paul Bull Snook, 2009. (Above, left.)

Figure 16.6. Roger Wilson in Brian's Breezeway in the upper level passages of Bishop Cave. Note the beautiful helictites in the upper right corner of the photo. Photo by Paul Bull Snook. (Above, right.)

Figure 16.7. Steve Hambrick in the Double Dead-End Crawl in Bishop Cave. Photo by Paul Bull Snook, 2009. (Right, middle.)

Figure 16.8. Robert Sewell in the East Dry Passage, leading to the Throne Room in Bishop Cave. Photo by Paul Bull Snook, 2008. (Right, bottom.)

It is clear from Cord Link's Trip Report that they were very impressed with what is now known as Bishop Cave.

Barr's Description of the Cave

Bishop Cave is described by Thomas C. Barr, Jr., in his book, *Caves of Tennessee* (1961):

> Bishop Cave, although quite large and only 300 feet east of US Hwy. 41-A, is seldom visited and is little known locally. The mouth, in a shallow sink at the foot of a hill, is an arch 15 feet wide and 4 1/2 feet high. A small passage, which averages 5 feet high and 6 feet wide but includes some crawlways, leads back into the hill for 510 feet in an easterly direction and intersects a large, apparently phreatic cavern developed along a joint. At the point of intersection extensive domepit solution has enlarged the cave to 15 feet wide by 60 feet high. The main cave is about

1,000 feet in length and trends east-southeast. At 600 feet is an upper-level passage of large dimensions, which extends S. 20° W. for 750 feet. At the end it drops into a low stream passage, which makes a horseshoe bend and emerges in the main cave again. A few formations are present, but most of the cave is rather dry. Helictites are seen in a few places. The whole cave appears to be constructed along joint sets that strike N. 20° E. and S. 60° E.[2]

My First Visit to Bishop Cave

My first visit to Bishop Cave was on January 25, 1967. Lots of large passages, breakdown, and mud are my best recollection. I was accompanied by Louis Hardin. The cave was much larger than we had expected, based on Barr's description and was extremely complex.

The Survey of Bishop Cave

Gerald Moni reports that Bishop Cave has been mapped at least twice.[3] Unfortunately, none of these groups ever produced a finished map after all that work. The official TN Cave Survey surveyed length for Bishop Cave is 10,982 feet (2.1 miles), based on the survey notes.

An Accident in Bishop Cave

On May 26, 1986 a caver had to be rescued from Bishop Cave. It is believed that this person descended into a 30-foot pit, then discovered he did not have the strength to climb back out hand-over-hand. At this point, one of his companions left the cave and the local Rescue Squad was notified. When the local rescue squad arrived, they lowered a Manila rope to the trapped caver, who then tied the rope around him. The rescue squad then attempted to pull the trapped person out of the pit, pulling the rope over the edge of the pit. No pulley was used. After raising the person about 25 foot, the rock edge of the pit cut the rope and the caver fell back to the bottom of the pit. This totally inept rescue squad had injured what was previously an uninjured person!

Fortunately, at some point a Cave Rescue Team was contacted and cavers Jim Lawrence, Larry Adams, and Judi Lawrence from the Nashville Grotto arrived on the scene. Ironically, the local rescue team had again tried

to raise the trapped person from the pit and had been successful the second time. Jim Lawrence reports what they found when they entered the cave:

18:23 HOURS - First truck with J. Lawrence, Judi Lawrence, Adams on scene. Conference with local authorities reveals that the local rescue squad had been successful with a second attempt raising patient. This was done again with Manilla rope with no patient assessment before either attempt.

18:59 HOURS - It is decided all three of the first arrivals will enter the cave. Local rescue squad team was encountered just after they had started to try to move patient through the cave. Patient was strapped in a wire Stokes Basket with a rain coat thrown over him. Also an oxygen mask had been placed on his face with the tank laying on the patient. All extra Manilla rope was also laying on top of the patient. A local EMT was with the patient but wanted to get him out of the cave before making an assessment of his condition. A laceration to the forehead had been bandaged.

Judi Lawrence, paramedic, ordered the stretcher stopped and started a complete patient assessment. She also ordered all freight removed from the Stokes. Larry Adams immediately went out of the cave to bring in a rescue basket and exposure bag. The cave was wet and muddy and the patient had now been disabled for five hours.

Patient was repackaged and local rescue squad was formed into a stretcher team coached by Jim Lawrence. The patient was moved down a twenty-foot mud slope with a simple brake system. Progress was slow but fairly steady.

19:42 HOURS - Other Nashville Grotto Rescue Team members on scene and enter cave. Local Rescue Squad relieved.

23:00 HOURS - Patient is out of cave. Cave is being cleared of equipment, and personnel. Patient transported to hospital.

23:30 HOURS - Mission declared closed. The patient, Scott Allen, 18 years, from Shelbyville, TN stated he had been caving on previous occasions and considered himself to be a caver. He was accompanied by one other person on this trip who was only identified as Ashley during the rescue operation. Neither person had any sort of caving gear or seemed familiar with such equipment. The

2 Thomas C. Barr, Jr., Caves of Tennessee, TN Division of Geology, Bulletin 64 (1961), p. 64.

3 Gerald Moni, Personal communication, August 21, 2017.

Figure 16.9. Erica Sughrue in a stream passage of Bishop Cave. Photo by Bob Biddix, January 13, 2019.

patient was asked at the hospital if he would go into another cave and he stated most strongly that he would.

Lack of further information is the result of cave rescue units arriving during the middle of the operation. Local authorities did not have any real organization set up for entrance control and did not really know who they had in the cave. No information had been compiled about patient. A very severe scalp laceration was the only injury visible. Patient could not tell us whether he had lost consciousness. No information on why the first attempt to raise the patient failed and the rope broke.[4]

Unfortunately, this is a typical scenario when a local Rescue Team attempts to make a cave rescue. Even though they are well-trained for surface rescues, they usually do not have any training for cave rescues and do not have the equipment needed for cave rescues.

Caves Access

This cave is located on private property. Caver Paul Snook reports that this cave is closed at the current time and that the owner does not allow permission for anyone to enter this cave. Please respect the owner's wishes.[5]

WARNING

Ken Oeser reports that the passage into this cave is sumped shut during the wet seasons.[6] You would not want to enter this cave if there is heavy rain in the forecast. You could get trapped for days… or longer.

4 Jim Lawrence, "Bishop Cave Incident," NCRC Newsletter, Edition 7 (July – August 1987), pp 2-4.

5 Tag-Net Digest #7612, October 14, 2018.

6 Ken Oeser, "The Long Caves Of Tennessee: A Review – Part II," *Speleonews*, Vol. 36 (1992), Summer, pp 5-11.

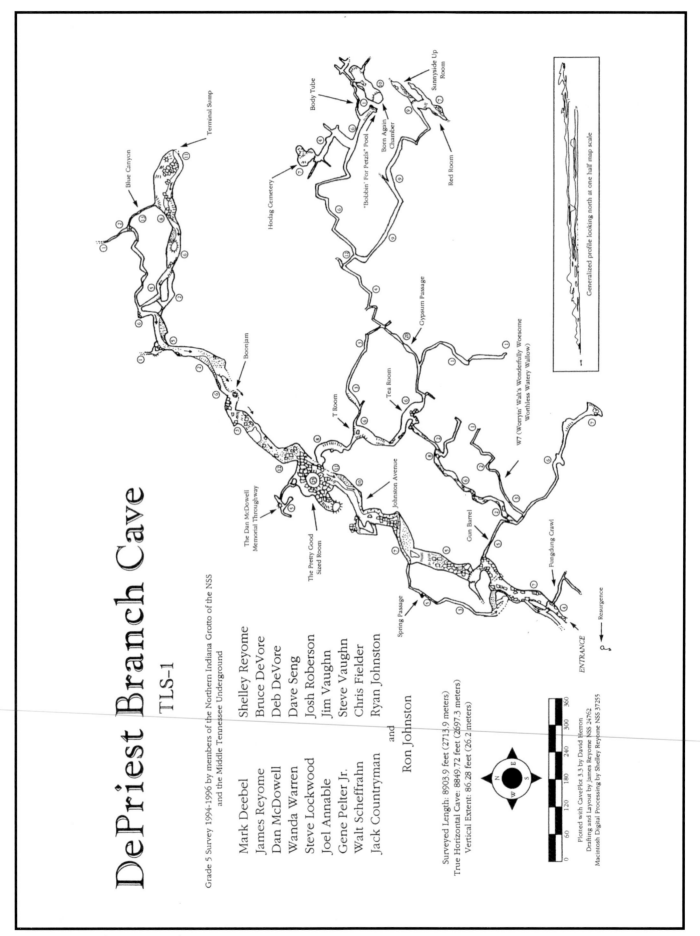

Figure 17.1. Map of DePriest Branch Cave.

CHAPTER 17
DePriest Branch Cave

DePriest Branch Cave is located in Lewis County, Tennessee. It has a mapped length of 1.7 miles. Without a doubt, it is one of the most beautiful caves in Tennessee

Barr's Description of the Cave

DePriest Branch Cave is described by Thomas C. Barr, Jr., in his book, Caves of Tennessee (1961):

> DePriest Branch Cave is a joint-pattern cave modified by slab breakdown and cantilever-dome collapse. A secondary stream has found its way into the cave and excavated a saw-cut gorge in one of the passages.
>
> The mouth, which is 5 feet high and 12 feet wide, opens above the large spring where the cave stream emerges. A passage of slightly larger dimensions than the mouth extends northeastward for 300 feet to a fork. The left prong extends northwest for 60 feet, then doubles back to the cave stream, and continues northeast for another 600 feet, at which point breakdown impedes further penetration. A large cantilever breakdown dome, some 60 feet in diameter, is developed at this point.
>
> The right prong of the cave heads northeast for 160 feet through a stream channel passage 5 feet high and 18 inches wide. This turns east abruptly for 35 feet, and then opens out into a passage 15 feet high and 6 feet wide, which continues east and northeast for another 465 feet. An upper-level, somewhat drier passage averages 4 feet high and 5 feet wide for 160 feet; it contains small crystals of gypsum.[1]

It is interesting to note that this is the only cave in Lewis County reported by Barr. Even today, the TN Cave Survey only lists twelve caves for Lewis County.[2]

Prehistoric Visitors to DePriest Branch Cave

DePriest Branch Cave has stoke marks located on the walls throughout the cave. We know that prehistoric people visited here using cane torches. (See Figure 17.10.)

Even today, the entrance area around DePriest Branch Cave is a beautiful campsite. I can imagine Indians camped there thousands of years ago, enjoying the cool, clear spring water and the cool breeze from the cave entrance. Because this is a wet, active stream cave, it may be impossible to find any charcoal for a C-14 date.

The Survey of DePriest Branch Cave

DePriest Branch Cave was surveyed by the Northern Indiana Grotto and the Middle Tennessee Underground from 1994 through 1996. Nineteen different cavers participated in the survey. The total surveyed length was 8,903.9 feet, of which 8,849.7 feet was true horizontal cave. The vertical extent was 86.3 feet. The finished map shows two main sections, a main level stream channel with a relatively wide passage and a more complex upper level with more narrow passages. (See Figure 17.1.) Dan McDowell and Jim Reyome recall how the survey began:

> Dan: In February of 1993 I called Mike Bose of the Cumberland Valley Grotto (CVG) in Tennessee about getting together for a caving trip the following month. Mike arranged for a trip into DePriest Branch Cave in Lewis County, Tennessee. A CVG member, Ron Johnston of Hohenwald, owns the cave.
>
> On March 24th, Jim Reyome, Jack Countryman, and I attended the trip led by Ron into his cave. During the five-hour trip we saw several thousand feet of passage. Combined with some really attractive formation areas, it was definitely a nice cave.
>
> Jim: So nice that I knew I had to go back, if for no other reason than to take pictures. I had left my

1 Thomas C. Barr, Jr., *Caves of Tennessee*, TN Division of Geology, Bulletin 64 (1961), p. 290.

2 Gerald Moni, Personal communication, July 3, 2018.

Figure 17.2. Ron Johnston, the owner of DePriest Branch Cave at the entrance. Photo by Kristen Bobo, February 18, 2013.

camera in the car this trip and kicked myself for months after.

The seeds for the survey were sown on that first trip. Ron made it known that he wanted desperately to have a really good map done of the cave, and Dan and Jack indicated their interest. I was interested too, so in the next few months, I got in touch with Mike Bose and other Cumberland Valley Grotto members trying to get something started. Despite some early interest, it seemed that most of the CVG people primarily concentrated on working up on the Cumberland Plateau—who could blame them, right? Progress toward a full-blown survey project came to a dead stop for a full four months.

Later that year a bunch of us (as I recall, Dan and Jack, Dean and Eddie Tendick, Steve Lockwood, Tom DeCamp, among others) ventured out to Camps Gulf Cave. Laying around that night the topic of a survey at DePriest was brought up and tossed

around again, but like with any other suggestion of this sort, the need had to be demonstrated to those who would put forth the effort. Show us the cave, in other words, and we'll decide if it's worth surveying.

Dan: Later in the year Jim and Shelly invited the NIG down to their home in Lyles, Tennessee over the 1993 Thanksgiving holiday weekend. This developed into "SpeleXpose," and the Reyomes published a guidebook listing some thirty local caves. DePriest Branch was the featured cave of the weekend, and Ron led a dozen NIG members on another five-hour trip into the cave on the Friday after Thanksgiving, while on Saturday we visited several other nearby caves.

The existing maps of DePriest, one of which was printed in the SpeleXpose Guidebook, were rather poor. The printed map was also quite a bit incomplete. After some discussion with Ron, we were given the opportunity to survey the cave.

The SpeleXpose map showed 3,295 feet.[3] Another map supposedly showed around 8,000 feet. The Tennessee Cave Survey had a figure of 6,000 feet listed.

Jim: Shell and I were more than happy to offer our home again as "Survey Central." Caving and NIG had been more than gracious to us and we wanted to, in some way, give a little something of ourselves back to the sport and the people who made it what it is.

Plus, we'd already made a close friend of Ron Johnston, a genuinely nice guy (even if he might never admit it) and the caver's wet dream as a cave owner: concerned, protective, yet eager to show off his cave. And we wanted to do it for Ron. So, it would be done.

Dan: The Reyomes again provided us with their home as our base of operations. It sure was nice, coming out of the cave after a day of surveying, to have hot showers and a nice place to sleep.

March 5, 1994: Mark Deebel, Shelley Reyome, James Reyome, Wanda Warren.

It began about the way I figured it would. Certainly nothing historic, as one might well expect for such a grand venture. Mark staggered in late and crashed on the sofa bed, which still hadn't quite recovered from the last time Dan had slept on it. We were all awake waiting, of course, a little keyed up for the day to come but ready to go to work.

Our initial goal was to shoot as far as the Big Room. Judging by the Ledbetter map the distance was somewhere between 700 to 1,000 feet. That, I figured, would be a good day's work for the rookies and would give us a general trend to work from. We picked an obvious point of reference at the entrance, mainly the big rock everybody sits on just before going in, as zero station. From there we shot into and through the gate, and we were on our way.

Things went pretty smoothly, "as well they should've." I'm sure I can imagine some of you would be thinking just now. Okay, so we scooped some of the bigger parts of the cave. Hey, we had to start somewhere, right? And it wasn't all a picnic. The low portions between the Gun Barrel and the stream trench are never fun, and Shell took one

look at the slick climb going up into the Big Room and decided she'd pass. So, we turned around and headed back for the entrance after four hours and just shy of 800 feet of survey in the book.

We stopped for a rest at the stream trench, and Mark and I looked at it, looked at each other, and kind of mutually decided that it would be a shame to not at least start a survey into the Spring Passage. We did seven shots, about a hundred or so feet, scouted ahead until it got a bit gross, then turned around and rejoined Shell and Wanda.

We got that same feeling upon reaching the Gun Barrel. Knowing as we did that the better part of the loop trip was through that uniquely shaped vadose canyon, we decided that we needed to start a trend here too, at least through to the other side. For everyone who had previously thought of the Gun Barrel as interminable, here are the facts: it is 82 feet to the right angel turn, then another 30 feet out into the walking passage beyond. Not very far at all when you think about it, unless you are as monstrous as Dan and I or behind a bean eater. Anyway, we shot through and set a station on an obvious point, then decided we'd had enough fun for one day and toddled on out after five joyful hours underground.

On the surface, everyone changed while I totaled the day's footage. I'd have been happy with 900 feet, but I was pleasantly surprised to find we'd done over a thousand, 1,016 to be exact.

March 19, 1994: Jack Countryman James Reyome, Wanda Warren.

When Wanda finally did arrive it was about noon. We had already decided that we were going to confine ourselves to the area around the entrance, there being at least three leads nearby that I could think of that needed to be looked into.

The first room in DePriest Branch gives you three options. The most obvious one of course is straight ahead under "Death Rock" and down the main passage. To the left lies the link to the Spring Passage and to the right…well, at that time we really didn't know what was down that way. Today was the day to find out. We tied into station 2 and shot up into a fairly spacious crawl we knew had little chance of going anywhere significant, as it seemed destined to head back toward the hillside.

---

3 This map was drawn by J. Ledbetter. It is printed on page 21 of the Guidebook for the "First Annual SpeleXpose," November 25-28, 1993.

Figure 17.3. Erica Sughrue in DePriest Branch Cave. Photo by Bob Biddix, December 16, 2017.

It wasn't bad, but it wasn't very good either. Ron's gate does a pretty fair job of keeping trespassing humans out, but it won't stop the varmints, and it seemed that they had made this particular crawl their underground home. I remembered a cave in Indiana called Fungdung, and it only seemed appropriate to dub this crawl the same.

It ended undramatically at a sand fill. Digging to the left would only gain a little bit of unneeded width but to the right a low opening did appear to go on. I managed to move enough dirt and rock to be able to slide in, and found a crawl continuing, not far, but it would have to be surveyed. The little passage ran at a right angle to Fungdung and ended pleasantly in a room decorated with delicate rimstone and stalactites.

With a little bit of time left we looked briefly, very briefly, into the Spring Passage, if for no other reason than to say that we did it. It didn't look like the kind of fun we'd had in mind when we set off that morning, so we passed it by and walked deeper into the cave. At station 4, I peered down into another connection into the stream, but by golly, that didn't look like all than much fun either. Another couple of stations and another lead passed by later we ended up at the Gun Barrel and figured, what the heck, let's shoot a few more stations down the Loop. We started the L Survey and did seven shots and called it a day with 337 feet in the book.

March 20, 1994: Jack Countryman, Dan McDowell, Jim Reyome, Wanda Warren.

This trip on Sunday afternoon was the third survey trip. The first two trips had netted over 1,300 feet.

A short distance beyond the Gun Barrel we picked up our survey at Station L-7. From here we had only 150 feet or so to the end, all easy walking cave. From there it was back to the end of the Gun

Figure 17.4. Danja Mewes by stalagmites in the Born Again Chamber. Photo by Kelly Smallwood.

Figure 17.5. Erica Sughrue in the Gun Barrel in DePriest Branch Cave. Photo by Bob Biddix, December 16, 2017.

Figure 17.6. Avis Moni, Shari Lydy, and Lynn Buffkin in DePriest Branch Cave. Photo by Kelly Smallwood. September 22, 2012.

Barrel again, Station GB-4, and from there we started the RL survey into the Upper Level Passage.

Anyway, this was the Real Loop Passage that connected into the Sunnyside and Gypsum (Rose) Passages. Pretty dry, mostly walking or stooping with a couple of short crawl sections. If I remember right, there was a short climb-up at station 11 and a bit farther, station 16 was a T-junction. To the right was the Rose Passage. Left from the T led a few stations to another T which was the Sunnyside Passage. A final half-dozen stations to the left we were tied into the Big Room. This room is about 900 feet from the entrance. From the Gun Barrel, through the RL Passage and into the Big Room, then down the Main Passage back to the Gun Barrel makes for a 2,000-foot loop. I don't have the exact figures from the notes, but we set around 33 stations and surveyed a bit over a thousand feet.

March 22, 1994: Joel Annabel, Bruce DeVore, Deb Devore, Dan McDowell.

We entered the cave at about 11 am (Indiana time). It took us about an hour to get back to

Figure 17.7. Erica Sughrue by beautiful formations in DePriest Branch Cave. Photo by Bob Biddix, December 16, 2017.

the place where we were to start our portion of the survey. We had climbed up over breakdown, crawled, and walked in stream passage.

We started the SS Survey, named for the Sunnyside Up Room. Dan was doing the book and the sketching. Deb was on front tape and worked with Joel on measurements and compass readings. We surveyed crawling passage mostly to the entrance of the Sunnyside Up Room. The plan was during the week to survey the passages to the formation packed rooms and let the weekend people take the time necessary to survey the rooms themselves.

We went into the Sunnyside Up Room to reap our reward for a couple hours of crawling survey. Words cannot adequately describe how beautiful the room is. There are formations of all different colors, sizes, and types. What really impressed Deb were the red stalagmites. The room was overwhelming. As you enter the room, the walls on either side are covered with stalactites, stalagmites, and totem poles six to seven feet tall. The formations are very active, everything is wet, and the colors are vivid.

We went on to the Hodag Cemetery, another room full of pretties. That was one of the different things about this cave. Most of the passages were unremarkable; some with an array of gypsum flowers, but for the most part the passages were dry and dusty. The cave has three main areas with all the formations: the Sunnyside Up Room, the Hodag Cemetery, and the Born-Again Chamber at the end of the Body Tube. I think that last is one of those places I will never see! We finished the day with just under 1,000 feet,

March 24, 1994: Dan McDowell, Joel Annabel, and Mark Deebel.

When Mark Deebel, Joel Annabel, and I went out to the cave Thursday morning it was still raining

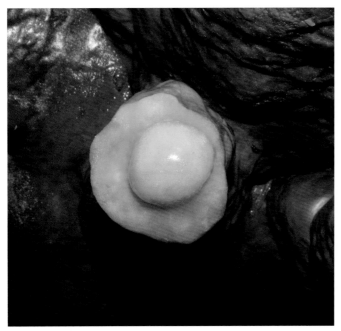

Figure 17.8. Fried Egg formation in DePriest Branch Cave. Photo by Kelly Smallwood, September 22, 2012.

Figure 17.9. Justin Hydrick by orange stalagmite in DePriest Branch Cave. Photo by Kelly Smallwood, 2018.

Figure 17.10 . Stoke marks on the wall near the T Room in DePriest Branch Cave. Photo by Kelly Smallwood, July 22, 2018.

quite hard. Fortunately, it let up a bit and we made a run to the entrance without getting too wet. I unlocked the gate, and then for some reason I told Mark to bring the key on into the Entrance Room and put it on a ledge. We had been leaving it under a rock on the floor near the gate.

For this trip we were to begin to survey some of the smaller passages of the cave. We wanted to leave some of the good stuff for the surveyors coming in on the weekend. Mark knew of a small circle passage off the west side of the Main Passage at station 18. In eight stations we had tied back into station 19 with a bit under 200 feet. This slightly upper level passage was high open cave turning into a breakdown before reentering the main stream passage.

Afterwards, we moved into the Big Room. I believe this room will be designated as the Pretty Good Size Room (PGS Room) on the map. We needed to make some splay shots to get the correct configuration of this room. The room is roughly circular and something like 60 to 75 feet across, maybe more in the north-south direction. The breakdown is some 20 feet high, and the ceiling is another 20-25 feet higher. We set another station less than 20 feet from the previous survey junction so that we could set better splays of the half-dozen shots taken from the center of the room. Four of these shots led into other passages.

The northeast end of the PGS Room opens 15-18 feet above the continuation of the Upstream Passage. Here we established the beginning of the US (upstream) survey. We surveyed upstream in some of the largest passage in the cave: 25 feet wide and 15 feet high. A large stream of water over knee-deep was flowing pretty good. After setting eight stations for some 250 feet we hit a crawl section.

Figure 17.11. Nancy Aulenbach by beautiful red flowstone in the Born Again Chamber of DePriest Branch Cave. Photo by Kelly Smallwood, September 22, 2012.

Beyond the Gun Barrel, I met up with Mark and Joel again. They told me that the entrance room was flooded waist deep and there was only ten inches of airspace going out the entrance. It was a good thing we had put the key on the ledge. The water was two feet deep and fifteen feet wide flowing from the entrance. When we returned at 10:30 am the next day, the cave entrance and the entrance room were virtually dry.

March 25, 1994: Gene Pelter, Jr., Dan McDowell, and Walt Scheffrahn.

By Friday morning the 25th there was 4,300 feet of cave surveyed as two more teams entered the cave. Mark Deebel and Steve Lockwood made up one team, headed for the Body Tube and the Born-Again Chamber. Dan McDowell, Walt Scheffrahn and myself were to close the loop in the Gypsum Passage and then move on to the Hodag Cemetery. With these objectives accomplished we headed out of the cave following Mark's Petzl Plunge— thanks, Mark.

Back at Jim and Shelley's Jim was eager to get the data into the computer to see what the new line plot looked like. The new surveyed length of the cave was now 5,800 feet.

March 26, 1994: Gene Pelter, Jr., Walt Scheffrahn, Mike Walsh, and Wanda Warren.

Saturday morning the 26th saw Jim, Dave Seng, and Steve Lockwood head out of the Big Room, upstream to the siphon. Mark, Steve Vaughn, and Jim Vaughn headed off for a side lead off the Gypsum Passage I had scouted for about 100 feet on Friday, while Walt, Mike Walsh, Wanda Warren, and myself were off to the Sunnyside Up Room. The Water Puppies did in fact find the siphon as well as a going side lead, while Mark and company picked up 250 feet of crawlway only to be stopped by a low spot that needed to be dug for about ten feet before it would open up. Walt's Waltzers made it to the Sunnyside Up Room to dance among the varied formations and around the haystacks. On the western end of the formation room there is a going lead with formations. This lead will require very slender cavers to push. There is potential for this lead to connect with the Born-Again Chamber, with is possible judging by the description of a

Figure 17.12. Shari Lydy, Jason Hardy, and Stephen Collins in DePriest Branch Cave. Photo by Kelly Smallwood, September 22, 2012.

corresponding lead in that room. If that does happen it would produce the third loop in the cave.

On the way out we mopped up a number of rather large mud plugs. There seems to be a lot of passages that end in mud fill. Some of them appear to be rather large leads, too. On the way back to the Gun Barrel we met up with Mark and the Vaughns. The Vaughns headed out and Mark stayed with us. Before entering the Gun Barrel to exit the cave we walked around the corner to take a break and cool down. While sitting there we noticed a small stream crawl coming out of the wall. After Mark and I had looked down it a few times we decided it at least needed to be measured, so Mark dropped his pack and picked up the tape.

One of Mark's last comments before entering the crawl was "If it goes, we survey." I said yes with some reluctance, since we'd all stayed dry except for the water puppies at the siphon. Mark was gone for just a moment then shouted back that it went. He set the first station as I took the readings and Walt kept book. The first 20 feet is combat crawl that you

Figure 17.13. Erica Sughrue by orange stalagmites in DePriest Branch Cave. Photo by Bob Biddix, December 16, 2017.

Figure 17.14. Nancy Aulenbach by flowstone formations in DePriest Branch Cave. Photo by Kelly Smallwood, September 22, 2012.

can just keep your chest dry in. After this point it becomes a meandering stream passage two and a half to three feet high by about the same width. We picked up about 200 feet of passage with a narrow water crawl side lead and going passage ahead. Back at the Reyome's, Jim started entering data. The final total was 7,674.9 feet THC.

Comments from Walt Scheffrahn on the same day: Our objective was to complete the Gypsum Passage survey back to the Real Loop. Our survey team consisted of Dan McDowell, Gene Pelter, and myself. The passage was small, low, and contained many gypsum crystals along the walls and ceiling. They were brownish in color and there was no brilliance to their glitter. In many places they appeared to be almost hidden from view. Along the survey we encountered a deep valley and surveyed down to the bottom and up the other side. At the bottom appeared to be a passage that was to be surveyed later. Then we continued and closed the Real Loop.

Next we went to the Hodag Cemetery. This survey went well since we could walk most of the time. This made it easy. We also managed to get several long straight survey shots. At the very end we came into the large massive flowstone/formation room. This area is photogenic. As we started out we surveyed a couple of loose ends consisting of small, short side leads. Even though they didn't go anywhere, they would give the cave extra footage and give the map more "character." Besides, every little bit helps. After 7 pm we came out of DePriest with nearly 1,000 feet surveyed.

The following day, Saturday, I went back to DePriest Branch with the others to survey the Sunnyside Up region and mop up other side leads. This trip consisted of Gene Pelter, Wanda Warren, Mike Walsh, and myself.

Instead of taking the Gun Barrel as we did the day before, we went along the River Passage. It was large and wide, but very low and muddy in places. Toward the back we climbed a breakdown pile and into the Real Loop Passage. From there we crawled, stoop-walked, and walked to the end of the previous day's Hodag Cemetery Passage. Here we began surveying in a long, narrow, canyon passage. Later the passage

Figure 17.15. Justin Hydrick by a flowstone grotto in DePriest Branch Cave. Photo by Kelly Smallwood, 2018.

turned into a hands and knees crawl with a couple of twists and turns which finally ended up in walking passage. We surveyed up the flowstone/formation area known as the Red Room. It is worth bringing a camera to photograph all these formation, draperies, and helictites. At the far end was a tight squeeze that appeared to go on. I thought this was the most beautiful section of the cave. Near the Red Room on the opposite side was another flowstone/formation slope with more beautiful formations.

Upon completing the main surveys, we did as we did the day before, mopping up small side leads. As we were leaving, we headed out towards the Gun Barrel to survey a small stream passage. Prior to this time I was fortunate to keep myself relatively dry. Now we had to lay in the stream passage and simultaneously explore and survey. It was cold! It was less than two feet high, wet, and with a gravel floor. Approximately 120 feet in it got a little larger, say three feet high, and made an S-curve. It is slow to survey laying in water, keeping the tape stretched out, without touching the passage walls and to accurately read the compass. Three of us laying in

water! With extra effort I was able to keep the survey notebook dry, so our efforts were not lost.

Well, we had committed ourselves to be out by 6 pm, so Mark put a permanent marker in the stream crawl, then we started to head out. Again we had surveyed over 1,000 feet of passage, and the computer produced another updated map totaling over 7,600 feet of cave.

March 26, 1994: Steve Lockwood, James Reyome, and Dave Seng.

The Water Puppy brigade left the station Saturday morning ready for just about anything. None of us really knew what to expect as we'd never been to the sump before, but we were certainly prepared. Steve was wearing his wetsuit, Dave was wearing mine and, ever the optimist, I settled for polypro inasmuch as I'd had too many bad experiences wearing the wetsuit.

We chugged along; leaving the rest of the day's parties behind at the Gun Barrel and went non-stop to the Pretty Good-Sized Room. Here we encountered our first problem—we didn't know which way to go. Down, we reckoned, so we picked our way through the breakdown, calling to each other as we went, until we finally managed to find the right way and regrouped in an impressive airy passage below, certainly one of the biggest passages in the cave, the stream gurgling in its channel about six feet below the rock choke we stood on.

The big passage didn't last long, mud fill and breakdown eventually making things interesting. Not surprisingly, this was where Dan, Joel, and Mark had left off a few days prior. We worked out way through a small bit, then come into larger passage again, with the stream visible ahead. Stopping to rest, we broke out water and candy bars, and as we did, I happened to look back the way we'd come and down a little bit, and there, virtually hidden in a little alcove and circled by a clear pool was a beautiful pair of tall columns.

On we went, down to the stream and past another mess of formations, some of them quite nice. The surroundings were wonderful, but a look ahead is all one needs to tell what you need to go through to actually reach the sump. The ceiling lowers dramatically, to a height of maybe two to two and a half feet, and this was in water too, of course.

Anyway, it might have been a pleasant little slog but for the floor which was composed of cherty gravel. Coming around a corner of the low, wide passage and seeing the Phantom Ship, another white formation seemingly a-sail in the stream, almost made me forget the pain. Like the rimstone Grotto beyond Fungdung, it's not worth the trip, but it's worth a look if you have to be there anyway.

The passage width began to narrow a bit ahead, but the ceiling rose. Good thing too. We had decided at the beginning of the trip to get to the sump and then map our way back to tie into Dan's US survey, and seeing that the low, grim portion of the mapping wasn't too awfully long gave us some cheer, and the fact that just down the passage we could walk again helped too. A right angle turn in deep water with a lead taking off the far wall came next, then the water became shallow and the passage broadened, eventually ending in what I think is the most impressive room in the cave, and, not coincidentally, the end.

In terms of volume the Bitter End is not as big as the Pretty Good-Sized Room, but it is just as long and certainly wide, and it's quite an eye opener after the low water crawls. Sadly, this would seem to be the end, as the stream rises from under the wall at the southernmost point of the room, with no apparent way. Perhaps in lower water….

So, we shot our way out. The first few hundred feet were easy, in good sized passage. At the big bend to the southwest we took a couple of shots into the dry lead to get a head start, then we got to the low ceiling and were forced into the water. The mapping went smoothly, no problems, and it wasn't long before we were tying into Danny's last station. Time to go home.

Not so fast. We were in unfamiliar territory down here. We figured we'd get out the easy way, by following the US survey flags, and at first that plan worked pretty well…until we got to what should've been the connection to the Pretty Good-Sized Room. We looked everywhere for the next bit of flagging tape. No joy. Time to fight the breakdown pile again, only this time gravity was definitely not on our side. It was a struggle, but eventually the slickest breakdown it's ever been my misfortune to battle yielded and we made it up, and eventually out, with nearly 850 more feet in the book.

March 31, 1994: Mark Deebel, Steve Lockwood, James Reyome, and Wanda Warren.

The first object of the day was to finish W7, a stream crawl, which is located near the end of the Gun Barrel. After we all stood at the nasty looking entrance to W7 for a moment I crawled in first and found the last survey station which I had placed the weekend before. A far as anyone knew this passage was virgin, so anything could lie ahead. We began surveying. Crawl, crawl, crawl. Survey, survey, survey. You get the idea.

I finally came to a crack in the ceiling where I could manage to almost sit up and decided to wait for Jim and Steve to catch up while Wanda waited somewhere back along the crawlway. They reached me a few minutes later with Jim commenting on how tight it was. I then went on ahead to find that the gravel floor came to within two inches of the ceiling only forty feet from where Jim and Steve were waiting. One last survey shot was made and that was the end of W7.

I turned around and started to crawl out while Jim tried to sit up in the crack in the ceiling and turn himself around. This took quite a while, and unfortunately since I was the first one in the passage, I was going to be the last one out. Jim finally did get turned around and we exited, vowing never to go back.

We then went back through the Gun Barrel and began to survey the downstream water passage. It starts as a canyon five feet wide and six feet high, with the water usually up to your knees. We found where the first survey had stopped and began, following the passage for a few hundred feet. It keeps getting lower. It keeps getting deeper. It keeps getting wetter.

Finally I went ahead to look for the next station and popped into a little room with a sand bank on one side with the passage making a ninety degree turn to the left. We quickly surveyed into the room and took a rest out of the water to get warm again.

After that room the passage forks. I explored down the left fork since it looked drier and followed it for seventy feet or so, stood up, and all of a sudden realized I was back in the main passage. I came out under some breakdown which I had walked over many times before without thinking much of it. I went back and told the others of the new connection, then we surveyed it, making a loop into the main passage. We then began to survey down the right fork. This connects back into the main passage at several places, mostly along stream crawls. Following the water however, you finally come to where it sumps. Less than a hundred feet away is the surface resurgence that forms the small creek you must cross to get to the entrance of the cave.

That finished the survey of the downstream Spring Passage, and we all decided to call it a day since we were all wet, tired, and hungry. With the completion of the Spring Passage all of the "big" passage was surveyed, with only a few side leads to complete before DePriest Branch Cave could be considered done.

April 2, 1994: Mark Deebel, Steve Lockwood, and James Reyome.

After a few weeks' break to allow our brains and bodies to recover from the veritable orgy of surveying we'd done a few weeks before, Mark and Steve returned to help "finish" the job. As it turned out, there was a lot more work to be done than we thought, and we wound up just shy of actually completing the survey.

We found the route into the US survey a little easier than we had before and quickly arrived at the stream, finding to our pleasant surprise that the water was way down from before. The Phantom Ship looked like it had run aground. We were actually able to stay dry until we came to the big turn to the east, where one has little choice but to get in the water to proceed. The dry lead is across the passage at this point, the floor underwater being for the most part rather slick breakdown, which Mark discovered much to his dismay by slipping on it and receiving a nice soaking.

It was sort of a nice crawl. Dry, airy, and big enough to allow easy survey. It wasn't virgin, of course, but it hadn't seen a heck of a lot of travel either, and that made it especially nice.

The footage racked up quickly in those conditions. A hundred feet, two hundred…the passage lowered, but rewarded our persistence by revealing some rarely viewed formations, some nice soda straws, and a goodly display of off-white flowstone; nice considering its location. The crawl continued to lower, eventually becoming a flat-out belly crawl at about the three-hundred-foot mark before opening into a cross joint room which allowed us to stand up and stretch and have a bite to eat.

Here things looked interesting. The main passage seemed to continue ahead, but very low. Mark was game enough to shove on ahead to have a look, while Steve and I puzzled over the cross joint and what appeared to be a passage diverging from the little chamber we were in.

Mark called back to us that the crawl he was in seemed to continue, so we followed to survey another fifty feet or so in unpleasant conditions. The passage was every bit of ten feet wide and two feet high, but the usable space was actually much less, and a good deal of it required bellying in an aggravating little stream of water. We pushed it and

Figure 17.16. Erica Sughrue by broomstick stalagmites in DePriest Branch Cave. Photo by Bob Biddix, December 16, 2017.

shot to the point where the passage got too low to continue without digging.

Back at the cross joint, Steve and Mark approached the diverging lead, a tall, extremely narrow canyon that seemed to be heading due south, back to the main stream. Mark led with Steve shouting encouragement from just behind. I took notes from behind. I might have fit through the passage if I'd wanted to expend the energy, but with two enthusiastic pushers along, why bother? Mrs. Reyome didn't raise any fools. And judging by the language issuing from the canyon, I made the right decision. Young Mr. Deebel used words I hadn't heard since I left the Marine Corps eleven years ago. As such, I felt the name "Blue Canyon" was more than appropriate. Eventually they connected, as expected, back into the US survey not far from the Bitter End.

October 22, 1994: Mark Deebel, Chris Fielder, Ron Johnston, Ryan Johnston, James Reyome, Josh Roberson, Steve Vaughn, Rene, Kelly, Linda.

With the official "DePriest Issue" of *The Michiana Caver* virtually finished and the map not, the cave itself still called out for one last survey trip. We knew of at least three leads that needed to be looked into, and Ron told us he knew of another he thought we'd missed.

We split up before entering the cave. Steve would lead the ladies out towards the pretties and have a look at the lead at the end of the Sunnyside Up Room, while the rest of us did the mop up. Our group stopped first by Station 9, where Ron said he'd noticed a lead we hadn't shot. It took about three shots and it was finished. This was the easy one though; the next was way upstream.

It had been a long time since Ron had been to the end of the cave. It was fun seeing him react to some of the formation areas along the route. He didn't recall just how nice some of them were, not the least of which was the Boonjam, which apparently neither he, nor Ryan, nor Christ had ever noticed before. We then pushed on to the Terminal Room, where we took one last look at the rise pool, which

Figure 17.17. Jennifer Dento in DePriest Branch Cave. Photo by Kelly Smallwood, 2018.

didn't look any more promising or less frustrating than it had the two times before. No airspace, no hope. Maybe some ridge-walking above the cave this winter will reveal more.

The work began. We hit the cut-around at station US 27 first and it was virtually dry, indicating that the water appears to never get up too far, at least in the back of the cave. Proof of that was the rather large mass of crystals Ron encountered leads the survey through the wide, low passage.

Our only other objective was the pair of leads at station US 15. Like the rest of the leads at this end of the cave that showed any sign of going anywhere, these headed almost due north, indicating they would end eventually at the hillside. These turned out to be more extensive than any of us thought, though. The passage actually opened to walking size briefly and had a couple of connecting offset rooms, one of which led back out to the main passage as the second lead. The main thrust of the passage continued north though, and Mark and Josh pushed ahead a hundred feet or so in pretty grim conditions. With a little over 300 feet in the book we headed for the entrance.

With the exception of possible continuing digs at JC 13 and in W 7, the survey is finished. Satisfied, we retired to the Fish Camp, where Ron joined us a little later to help us put the hurt on some serious table loads of catfish. It was a fine way to put a cap on a finely turned project.[4]

4 Dan McDowell and Jim Reyome, "The Survey of DePriest Branch Cave," The Michiana Caver, v. 21 (1994), no. 7, pp 42-61.

When you look at the finished map, it is obvious that the length of the stream passage is relatively short, especially considering the amount of water that it occasionally carries. If someone could find a way around or over the Bitter End, there must be miles of additional cave just waiting to be explored. The Northern Indiana Grotto did a remarkable survey job in a short amount of time. Usually, surveys like these drag on for years.

My First Visit to DePriest Branch Cave

My first visit to DePriest Branch Cave was on September 30, 1979. Caver Mark Mitckes wrote the following trip report:

> The last day of September, Larry Matthews, Art Bosnak, Frank Bogle, Ron Johnston, Sylvester ?, and I visited DePriest Branch Cave in Lewis County. The cave is owned by Ron Johnston and is located about 10 miles from his home in beautiful Hohenwald.
>
> Barr's description of the cave is typical of those in west Middle-Tennessee: of moderate length with maze-like passages. DePriest has additional features which Barr did not mention, probably because he never got far enough into the cave to see them. There are three fairly small but very beautiful formation areas.
>
> A scenic spring emerges from the cave about 50 feet from the well-gated 5 X 12-foot entrance. The cave is indeed a walking, stooping, and crawling maze to the first formation area. This area of the cave contains fairly large flowstone formations, several of which are blood-red in color. These formations rival formations in Nichol's Blowhole for their color and intensity.
>
> The second formation area is only several hundred feet from the first. This area is a fairly recent discovery and requires ingress through what appears to be a very tight crawlway. Having no desire to reenact birth, I skipped this area. Larry Matthews, who did get through, later stated that this was the best of the three formation areas which would definitely make it pretty spectacular.
>
> The third formation area is fronted by a number of white totem pole type formations which gives the impression of a graveyard. Behind these is a small room about 10 feet in diameter crammed full of white stalagmites, soda straws, and assorted flowstone formations. This has to be one of the most beautiful small rooms I have ever seen in a cave!
>
> I would like to thank Ron Johnston for taking us to the cave – I only wish all cave owners were as friendly as Ron![5]

I took a lot of photos on that trip. Back when photos were taken on color slide film. The quality doesn't compare to the new digital technology, but they were good at the time.

Ron Johnston purchased DePriest Branch Cave and the surrounding 84 acres of land in 1975 and built a secure gate on the cave in 1976. Ron has been a wonderful steward of the property and has shared his cave with many thousands of cavers over the years. Thanks, Ron.

Cave Access

This cave is located on private property and is securely gated. Do not enter this cave without the owner's permission.

Suggested Reading

The entire Fall 1994 issue (Volume 21, Number 7) of The Michiana Caver is titled: "The Survey of DePriest Branch Cave." The Michiana Caver is published by the Northern Indiana Grotto of the National Speleological Society. This issue is numbered pages 41-61 and contains a wealth of information about DePriest Branch Cave, its exploration, and the survey.

---

5 Mark Mitckes, "DePriest Branch Cave," *Speleonews*, v. 24 (1980), no. 2, p. 23.

CHAPTER 18
Godwin Cave

Godwin Cave is located in Maury County, Tennessee. It is well-known locally and heavily visited. It has a mapped length of 3.59 miles.

Barr's Description of the Cave

Godwin Cave is described by Thomas C. Barr, Jr., in his book, *Caves of Tennessee* (1961):

> Godwin Cave and Godwin Community derive the name from Col. Aaron Godwin, who for many years served as agent at "River Station" on the Louisville and Nashville Railroad near the cave. The cave is well known and is frequently visited. The entrance is 5 feet high and 8 feet wide and is in the bottom of a sinkhole, where it receives a wet-weather stream. The cave is constructed along two sets of normal joints which strike N. 20° E. and S. 70° E. The major development is in a northeasterly direction.
>
> The mouth of the cave faces west. Three forks extend out from the entrance room, all leading into the main cave, but the middle fork is a low crawlway. The right and left forks each run about 180 feet before reaching the main cave in a chamber called the "Ballroom," which is 225 feet long, 8 feet high, and 12 feet wide, with a level silt floor. At the northeast end of the cave the main passage drops into a narrow crevice 2 feet wide, 25 feet high, and 100 feet long. At the southwest end the ceiling lowers, and the cave becomes a narrow, wet crawlway. The length of the main passage is 1,050 feet, and the total length of the readily penetrable passages of the cave is easily half a mile. No dripstone formations are developed.[1]

In 1986, Gerald Moni added the following, additional information:

> A second entrance opens in a 10-foot-deep sinkhole. This entrance is 3 feet wide and 1.5 feet high. A 100-foot crawl leads to a stream passage. After another 100-200 feet a high overflow lead goes 1,500 feet, or

Figure 18.1. The entrance to Godwin Cave. Photo by Joseph C. Douglas.

> more. A couple of side leads were noted. One went 300 feet and the other leads to the main cave.
>
> The cave was mined for saltpeter. Some (Civil War years) names found in the cave were:
>
> Treave N. Arnold, Co. E, 39th Inf, July 1862
> F. Sullivan, Co. F, 17th Ind.
> Issac M. Arnold, Co. E, 69th Inf, Jaysville, O.[2]

Based on the unit information with these names, these were Union soldiers. Doug Plemons found two additional names of Union Soldiers:

> William H. Fisher, Co. D, 17th Ind. Vol.
> Oren S. Hadley, Co. H, 175th OVI[3]

There are dozens of other names in the cave that date from the Civil War period, but they either were not soldiers, or did not list their regimental affiliation.

Prehistoric Visitors to Godwin Cave

Cave historian Joseph C. Douglas reports that there are stoke marks preserved in several dry areas of Godwin

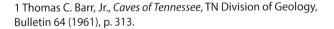

1 Thomas C. Barr, Jr., *Caves of Tennessee*, TN Division of Geology, Bulletin 64 (1961), p. 313.

2 Gerald Moni from the TCS Narrative File for Maury Co., TN, Edited by Thany Mann, February 1993, pp MU-8 – MU-9.

3 Doug Plemons, We Four and No More, Section 5, "The Civil War Years and Other Tales."

Cave, indicating that prehistoric Indians were in the cave with cane torches. He also notes that these are areas where the gypsum has been removed (mined) from the cave.[4]

Saltpeter Mining

According to both Gerald Moni and Joseph C. Douglas, there is ample evidence of saltpeter mining in Godwin Cave in the form of pick marks, stacked rocks, and areas where dirt has been dug out and removed.[5] Doug Plemons provides even more information:

Many Tennessee caves were used by pioneers for vegetable storage, moonshine production, church services, dance halls, music halls, saltpeter mining, and other utilitarian uses. The most obvious use of mostly dry and easily penetrable Godwin Cave was a source of cave saltpeter. Portions of the entire central "historic" section of the cave were mined. An examination of the cave by Speleo-historian Marion Smith and some of his caver associates in 1986 found plenty of evidence of this.

Not far from the entrance going "downstream" toward the Ballroom, at a right-hand bend, one sees two dig faces in the fill with mattock marks and a torch poke hole. Torches were necessary for the miners to see the passage clearly. This dig face was five feet deep, three feet wide, and four feet high. This means that sixty cubic feet of dirt was removed in this one spot alone. The mattock marks are distinct and clear at both faces.

Continuing toward the Ballroom on the left is another small dig face. On a trip in 1997, Larry Matthews, author of *Descriptions of Tennessee Caves*, gently pried out the rotted remains of a torch stub in a poke hole in this spot. This rotten piece of wood was literally the only wooden artifact found in the cave left behind from the saltpeter era. Anything else has been long ago removed or destroyed by vandals. Mattock marks are visible here also.

In Barr's Ballroom itself are a number of niches in the walls which were mined out. On the right wall is a large dig face, where many mattock marks are visible. It appears the floor itself was not lowered, only the side passages which were filled or nearly filled with silt.

Turning left and leaving the Ballroom, one sees the remains of an old rock wall, and following this connection passage into what I named "VMI Hall" because of the large signature depicting that institution on the ceiling. It is easy to see that the floor of this connector has been mined out and rock spoils thrown to the side. In places the rocks have been carefully piled on ledges. VMI Hall itself was heavily mined, with even more fill removal and spoils piles. Old pieces of torches were found in this spot. There are mattock marks and many old names on the walls. It is curious to see that most all the artifact signatures in this passage were placed there following or just at the start of the Civil War. There are a number of Confederate soldier signing in this area, all dated 1861. At the end of VMI Hall near the junction with the Ballroom extension of "parallel #3" is another old rock wall. It seems possible that the mounds of rocks piled in the junction area with the Ballroom Passage are a giant spoils pile.

All told, the central section of the cave shows blatant secondary signs of saltpeter mining. "Primary" evidence, such as artifacts or saltpeter vats, no longer exist in the cave.

We have no idea who mined the cave, the only clue being the signature record during the Civil War and before. Could any of these people, other than the owner, have been involved in the saltpeter mining effort? There is no clue as to exactly when the mining took place, either. We know that it couldn't have lasted through the Civil War due to the repeated enemy encampments nearby but is wasn't just a small dig either—it took time to remove that much dirt. We don't know much, but we can see the results. Piles of rocks in strange places and marks made by hard-working men digging dirt out of a cave to make gunpowder. The stuff of historic mystery.[6]

There is always the possibility that some of the saltpeter mining might date back as far as the War of 1812. However, the oldest date found in the cave by Doug Plemons is 1838.[7] If the cave was mined during the War

4 Joseph C. Douglas, Personal communication, September 17, 2018.
5 Gerald Moni, Personal communication, April 26, 2018.

6 Doug Plemons, We Four and No More, Section 1, "The Cave."
7 Doug Plemons, Personal communication, August 18, 2018.

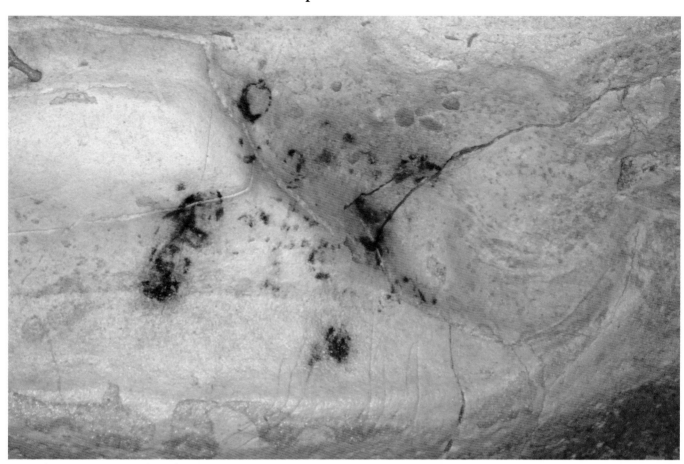

Figure 18.2. Stoke marks left on the wall of Godwin Cave by prehistoric visitors. Photo by Kim Fedrick. November 9, 2014.

Figure 18.3. Signature of Walter Pillow 1861 Aug. Photo by Joseph C. Douglas.

of 1812, one would expect to find some names and dates from that time period.

The Columbia Military Academy Connection

What would become the Columbia Military Academy (CMA) was first known as the United States Military Arsenal at Columbia (1890-1905). Soldiers and cadets were housed and trained there. The Arsenal was both a storehouse for military goods and a small military base as well. The 1900 Census gives the names of thirty-two (32) people living there. The person in charge of the Arsenal was Major James Rockwell, Jr., age 51, who was a native of New York.

On December 18, 1898 eight soldiers from the Arsenal took a trip to Godwin Cave and left their names of the walls. They were:

E. J. Leonard	Co. J, 2nd Miss.
Russell Miller	Co. G, 2nd Miss.
G. O. Montgomery	Yazoo City, Miss.
E. P. Ogden	Co. I, 2nd Miss.
Lonnie S. Shull	Co. D, 2nd Miss.
Joe R. Wells	Co. I, 1st Miss.
S. Woolfson	Co. A, 2nd Miss.
Alfred Paillor	No company/regiment given

In May, 1900 the Chief of Ordnance for the US Army recommended that the Arsenal be "discontinued," and the facility was closed in 1905.

In 1903 the property was deeded over to a self-perpetuating Board of Directors for use as a school. In June, 1904, Company K of the 16th Infantry of the US Army formally abandoned the Arsenal grounds and the 67 acres were turned over to a new, military oriented school, the Columbia Military Academy. The school formally opened on August 28, 1905. Some students were from prominent Maury County families, but advertisements for students were distributed nationwide. Here is a part of one of those ads:

"… A High-Grade School Preparing for Any College or University in the U.S., and for the U.S.A. Cadets at Annapolis and West Point… Small Classes with individual instruction… strict Military Discipline… Building heated by steam and lighted with Acetylene Gas… baseball, football, tennis, gymnasium, Swimming Pool… A Manly School for Manly Boys!"

Military schools are no longer in vogue in the United States at this time, but they were quite popular up through the 1980s. Their place has been taken over by what are now referred to as Private Schools.

At one time it was popular to send children away to boarding schools where they lived on campus and Military Schools filled this need.

Life at Military Academies was strictly controlled, so a chance to do something different and exciting was a rare treat. We know of a trip to Godwin Cave on Wednesday, November 10, 1909 thanks to an article in the *Daily Herald* newspaper. The CMA cadets involved were Herbert H. Maddox, Will A. Shelton, Francis Warfield, Girard Brownlow, and Clarence H. Fry. Apparently two members of the group became lost and had to be rescued. The newspaper account says:

More dead than alive, weak and stiff from cold, tortured with hunger and thirst, in the last throes of despair, Robert Williams and Joe Hoxie were dragged by comrades from the cave at half past twelve o'clock this morning. For more than twelve hours they had wandered through the myriads of paths and chambers that make up this wonderful subterranean curiosity in a vain endeavor to once more behold the light of day---for they had lost all bearings, they seemingly walked in a circle. Finally when found by their devoted comrades, they had huddled close together and were the very picture of despair, and resignation was written upon every feature. When found, Williams and Hoxie were too weak from hunger and fear to walk, and they had to be assisted from the cavern by their rescuers and taken to the station at Godwin, where they boarded the one o'clock (AM) train for the Academy.

Considering that Godwin Cave is a very long and complex maze cave, it was a very easy cave to get lost in for inexperienced cavers.

Godwin Cave continued to be a favorite destination for CMA students. Doug Plemons has documented the names and dates of many students found written in the cave. The school became co-ed in 1969 and soon after became the Columbia Academy, and was no longer a "Military" academy.

One of the most amusing inscriptions that Doug Plemons found on the wall of the cave is the following:

"Don't Tear Down the Wall...IT Will Get Out"

This inscription is located in the northern extension of the cave. At the time of Doug Plemons research he named this area "The Club" for the large number of inscriptions by visitors from the Columbia Military Academy. His theory is that perhaps this cave room was part of a CMA fraternity ritual or hazing wherein the new members were "walled in" to the cave room to see how long it would take them to get out.[8]

Another interesting inscription found on the walls was:

"We Four And No More"

Doug says that this narrative was placed there by four local friends who were off by themselves and separated from the remainder of their much larger group on December 16, 1900. Doug used this inscription as the title for his book on Godwin Cave. His list of names, dates, and associated comments is an invaluable historical resource.[9]

The oldest inscriptions found in the cave were: Gary B. White, 1838, E. W. Morgan, 6/24/1838 and T. E. Mahon with the date 11/6/1838. Next to the Morgan inscription is the note:

Here John (?) eat diner June 24th 1838.

Unfortunately the last name is illegible. Only nine names with dates prior to the Civil War were located by Plemons.

My First Visit to Godwin Cave

Although I have visited this very interesting cave several times over the years, I can find no record of what year I first went there, but most likely in was sometime in the late 1960s or early 1970s.

---

8 Doug Plemons, We Four and No More, Section 4, "The Signature Record Of Godwin Cave."

9 Ibid.

The Survey of Godwin Cave

Godwin Cave was surveyed between June 13, 1998 and November 1, 2015. Twenty (20) different cavers participated in the project and Ken Oeser produced the final map. The cave displays a classic joint-controlled pattern. The surveyed length of the cave is 18,944 feet (3.59 miles) and the total vertical extent is 70 feet. (See Figure 18.9) Ken Oeser shares with us the story of this survey project:

In June 1998 the Cumberland Spelean Association (CSA), a group of middle and east Tennessee cavers, began mapping Godwin Cave in Maury County. Doug Plemons was really interested in the cave because of all the old names and dates in the cave. After three trips mapping a little over 2,000 feet of the cave, they stopped mapping. The CSA disbanded a year or so later and Helen Galloway contacted me to see if I or the Nashville Grotto would want the survey notes in case we wanted to map it in the future. I agreed, and she sent me the notes, which I thought about for a few years on and off.

In early 2015 Dave Wascher asked me about mapping Godwin Cave, saying he would help, and so the project picked back up. I went to the area and found the owner's house. When I knocked on the door, his daughter came and was friendly and said he would likely not mind if we mapped it and said she would call me. Not only did I not hear from them, but they wouldn't answer my phone calls either. Others assured me that access was no problem, so we proceeded with a plan. The CSA had mapped over 2,300 feet in the entrance area and Ballroom section, a mazy area of interconnecting passages. From their notes it seemed like it would be easy to find their points and continue from where they left off.

On May 17, 2015 Dave Wascher, Kim Fedrick, Samantha Richardson, and I started our survey. We easily found the old survey stations and first finished off some loops, then headed southeast and mapped our way to the second entrance, filled in with boulders, and a hose that was apparently used to pump water from the stream passage in that area. I found on this day that the cave has many branches, and although many are stoop or hands-and-knees height, there are some walking passages, and at least

Figure 18.4. Signature of J. Herstein, 1861, written in red on the wall of Godwin Cave. Photo by Joseph C. Douglas.

there are many straight passages, making for long survey shots in fairly easy confines. We were able to map 3,179 feet this day.

Dave, Kim, Samantha, and I returned June 21, joined by Ian Wascher, Zigh Roundtree, and Gerald Moni. We mapped a left side passage shown as a lead on the old map and were able to map the section to completion, adding 1,238 feet. Included were some climbs up and down, plus one main loop.

On July 11 Samantha and I were joined by Brett Schneider. We mapped 825 feet up the main left canyon and a couple of side passages off of it. Of course none of them ended, meaning more leads for later trips. Brett was able to make it up an 11-foot climb in the main passage and find passage continuing at the top.

Dave, Brett, and I continued on August 2. We rigged a handline for the climb-up and started mapping the upper passage. After surveying 200 feet of main passage and a 100-foot side passage we came to a junction with lower passage. We decided to map the lower passage and mapped several hundred feet of lower passage. At first Brett was lead point, but he kept telling us the passage was getting too low. Dave or I would look ahead and find the passage continued, usually opening a little after a low spot. These passages were headed south, somewhat parallel to the main passage. We mapped 1,809 feet this day.

Figure 18.5. Pick marks left in the dirt of Godwin Cave by saltpeter miners. Photo by Joseph C. Douglas.

Samantha and I returned on August 23 and started mapping from a lower passage off the main route before the climb-up. Amongst mostly crawling passages we found two rooms, one we called the Hackberry Room after the hackberries on the floor and the other we called the Tee Room, based on the crawl passage intersecting the 17-foot high room in the middle. We stopped here for the day with 957 feet, with the crawl continuing on the other side.

Dave and I were joined by Brian Buchanan on September 13 and mapped the far-right passages to the southeast. We mapped the main stream passage downstream several hundred feet until it sumped with no airflow. We also mapped several hundred

Figure 18.6. Signature of Miss Mary White, Campbell Station, June 14, 1874, written on the wall of Godwin Cave. Photo by Joseph C. Douglas.

feet in a passage off the main stream passage. This headed northeast, passing to the east of the Tee Room and Hackberry Room. We finally stopped when the passage seemed to lower and end but didn't push to the end. We named this passage the Bone Passage for some rather large bones in the small stream passage here. We were rewarded with 2,370 feet for our efforts this day.

On September 26 Samantha, Brian and Tiffany Buchanan, Josh Young, and I returned for a half day of mapping the middle connecting crawls. We were able to hook the Bone Passage into the Tee Room and then to some gypsum crawls where we had mapped from the main passage. We went to the end of the Bone Passage to push the end where we had stopped on the previous trip here, only to find that it did indeed end just past where we had stopped before. We basically finished the middle section connections on this trip, leaving only a few leads in this part closer to the main passage. Total mapped for the day was 616 feet.

Emily Davis joined me the next day, September 27 and we proceeded to rig the climb-up in the main passage. We mapped the main passage past the climb-down to the lower passage loops and found some of the largest walking passage in the cave. There were only a few side passages and there were roots visible in one room and another spot in the main passage. We were able to map 1,840 feet of large, dry passage this day.

October 17 Samantha and I returned to map some of the right-hand loops from the entrance. I had not been to this section of the cave, so was surprised that it was extensive, yet not surprised that there were several loops involved. We were not able to finish the area, but still mapped 1,493 feet.

The next day, October 18, Kim, Samantha, Dave, and I completed the right-hand passages except for one low lead. Some nice surprises in this area were rooms with flowstone and rimstone dams, and a room we named the Butterscotch Room. We found one old name in this area: John C. Lancaster, August 21, 1869. Total footage for the day was 968 feet.

Samantha and Emily joined me for a final trip on November 1, 2015. We checked the low lead in the right-hand fork and found it didn't go more than a couple of shots. A low lead requiring a squeeze into an empty section of the map was pushed and we were able to map 300 feet before it ended. Although surrounded by other passages there were no side passages heading off for near connections to them. At the junction where this passage starts, smoked on the wall is the name: Archie McLeod, Co. G, 2nd Miss., Dec. 19, 1894. We mapped 1,039 feet, bringing

Figure 18.7. Old names and dates on the wall of Godwin Cave: "W. W. Collins, W. H. N. Co. one, Co. 3 60th, June 6th, 18(??)" and "E. J. Leonard, Co. J, 2nd." Photo by Kim Fedrick, November 9, 2014

Figure 18.8. Looking out the entrance to Godwin Cave. Photo by Joseph C. Douglas.

the total footage to 18,705 feet, just over 3.5 miles long. It was really nice the way some of the farthest passages looped back together, as a larger scale to all the small loops near the entrance to the cave.[10]

Godwin Cave is a very long, interesting cave, but portions of it have been severely vandalized, especially with spray paint. What was the Ballroom in the 1800s is now called the Party Room due to all the spray paint. The final map is shown as Figure 18.9.

Cave Access

This cave is located on private property. Do not enter this cave without the owner's permission.

_____

10 Ken Oeser, Personal communication, September 24, 2018.

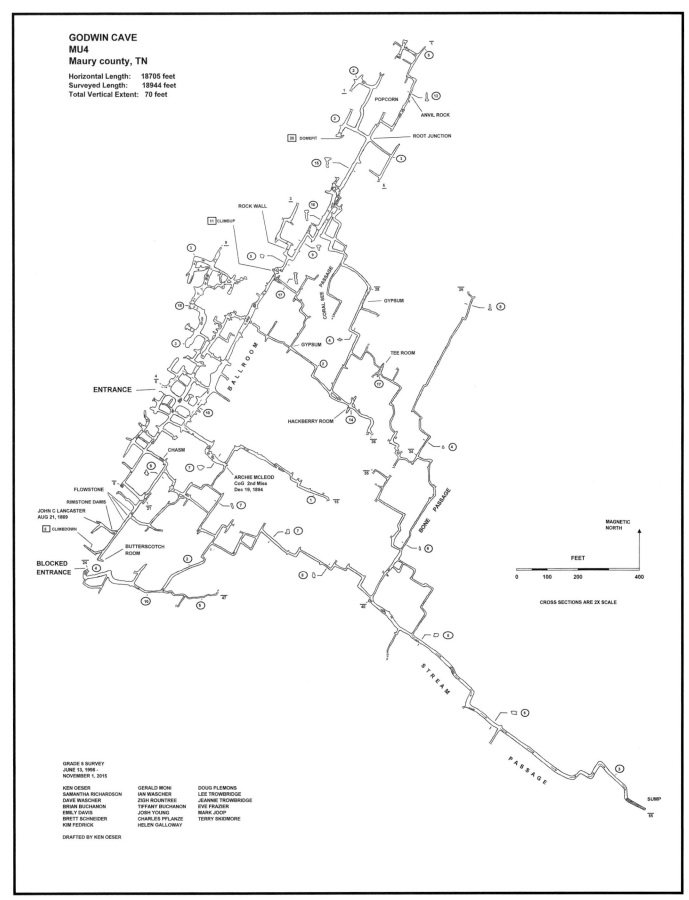

Figure 18.9. Map of Godwin Cave by Ken Oeser, November 1, 2015.

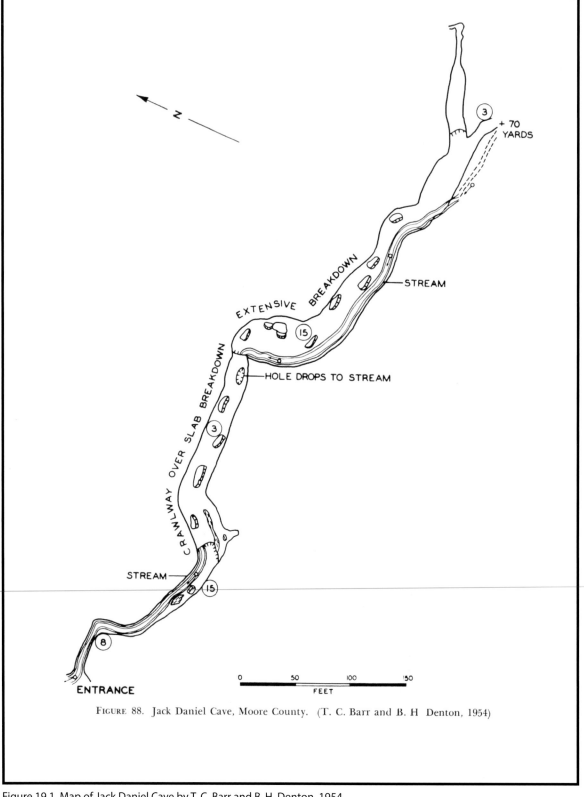

FIGURE 88. Jack Daniel Cave, Moore County. (T. C. Barr and B. H Denton, 1954)

Figure 19.1. Map of Jack Daniel Cave by T. C. Barr and B. H. Denton, 1954.

CHAPTER 19
Jack Daniel Cave

Jack Daniel Cave is located in Moore County, Tennessee. As far as the World is concerned, this is by far the most famous cave in Tennessee. You can't go in the cave, because they use the water to make their "World-Famous Sipping Whiskey," but you can take a wonderful tour of the distillery. For whiskey-lovers it is more than a Road Trip, it is a Pilgrimage.

The Jack Daniel Distillery

Established in the 1830s and registered by Jack Daniel in 1866, the Jack Daniel Distillery is the oldest registered distillery in the United States.

Jack Daniel was born in 1850. His mother and father were both deceased by 1865 and he was taken in by Dan Call, a moonshine distiller in Moore County, TN. Nathan "Nearest" Green, an African-American, was Call's Master Distiller and he taught young Jack Daniel how to make whiskey. Jack Daniel went into business with Call in 1875 and became owner of the business in 1884.

Jack Daniel purchased the land in Moore County, TN where his distillery is located in 1884. The cool, clear spring water flowing from the cave's entrance is perfect for making whiskey. His nephew, Lem Motlow, became the owner in 1907 when Jack was in declining health. Jack Daniel died in 1911.

Tennessee passed a Prohibition Law in 1910, forcing the distillery to close. National Prohibition was not passed until 1920. When National Prohibition was repealed in 1933, the distillery still could not re-open, because the State Prohibition Law was still in effect. Tennessee repealed its Prohibition Law in 1938 which allowed the Jack Daniel Distillery to re-open.

Jack Daniel is the top selling American whiskey in the world. The Distillery has been owned and operated by the Brown-Forman Corporation since 1956.

A Description of the Cave

Jack Daniel Cave is described by Thomas C. Barr, Jr. in his book, Caves of Tennessee (1961):

Figure 19.2. Ashley Schaffner Fletcher by the entrance to Jack Daniel Cave. Photo by Larry E. Matthews, June 26, 2018.

The Jack Daniel Cave has long served as the water supply for the well-known Jack Daniel Distillery in Lynchburg. In 1866 "Little" Jack Daniel purchased the hollow and the cave and established what has become the oldest registered distillery in the United States. His statue stands at the mouth of the cave, 25 feet from the old office building. The cave stream issues from the mouth.

The entrance is 8 feet high and 30 feet wide. The cave extends east-southeast and is 900 feet in length. A considerable amount of crawling over slab breakdown is necessary, and the entire cave is full of breakdown. A number of attractive formations, mostly small are to be seen. Average dimensions of the cave, exclusive of crawlways, are 15 feet high by 25 feet wide. The last 200 feet is a low crawlway over breakdown beside the stream, and a large rockfall finally bars further penetration. This cave is said to connect with Motlow Cave.[1]

Barr includes a map of the cave (Figure 19.1) and a photograph of some attractive flowstone formations. A significant and reliable stream flows from the entrance and it is this "pure limestone spring water" that is used to

1 Thomas C. Barr, Jr., Caves of Tennessee, TN Division of Geology, Bulletin 64 (1961), pp 334-337

Figure 19.3. Kelly Smallwood next to the statue of Jack Daniel. The entrance to Jack Daniel Cave can be seen in the background. Photo by Kelly Smallwood, December 21, 2014.

manufacture their famous "Tennessee Sipping Whiskey." The flow of this stream would indicate a significant recharge area and a much longer stream passage than that surveyed by Barr, which ended at a breakdown.

My First Visit to Jack Daniel Cave

I first visited Jack Daniel Cave in the summer of 1968. Of course, I did not go inside the cave, since it is rarely open for visitation. But I did enjoy the beautiful entrance and the tour of their distillery.

I have returned several times over the years and out-of-state visitors always enjoy the tour. On one tour, a person asked the Guide, "How many people work here?" Without missing a beat, the Guide turned around and answered: "About half of them."

The Survey of Jack Daniel Cave

The original survey of Jack Daniel Cave was done by T. C. Barr and B. H. Denton in 1954. It shows approximately 900 feet of cave.

At some point in time, the management of the Jack Daniel Distillery realized that it would be very nice to know where their water supply originates and to make sure that it was protected. They hired Logan Hickerson and Associates, Inc. of Murfreesboro, TN to survey the cave for them. This survey showed a respectable 6,670 feet of passages (1.26 miles) and even more importantly showed them what area is the watershed that supplies the water for this important cave system.

This map is labeled: "Compiled by Logan Hickerson and Associates, Inc., Murfreesboro, Tennessee." In the

Figure 19.4. Ashley Schaffner Fletcher by Jack Daniel's original Office Building, with the entrance to Jack Daniel Cave in the background. Photo by Larry E. Matthews, June 26, 2018.

bottom left-hand corner is the notation: "Surveyed by Harry White, October, 1980." Harry White was a well-known caver and a member of the Nashville Grotto. (See Figure 19.6)

Motlow Cave

Motlow Cave is located 300 yards northeast of Jack Daniel Cave. Barr (1961) gives the following description of the cave:

> Motlow Cave is the most impressive and the most frequently visited of Moore County caves. It is reputed to connect with Jack Daniel Cave. The mouth is a small hole on the hillside and opens immediately into the first large room of the cave.
>
> The cave consists of two rooms connected by a passage 300 feet long, a narrow extension of this passage, and two side passages 150 feet long. The

Figure 19.5. Joel Diaz at the entrance to Motlow Cave. Photo by Larry E. Matthews, June 26, 2018.

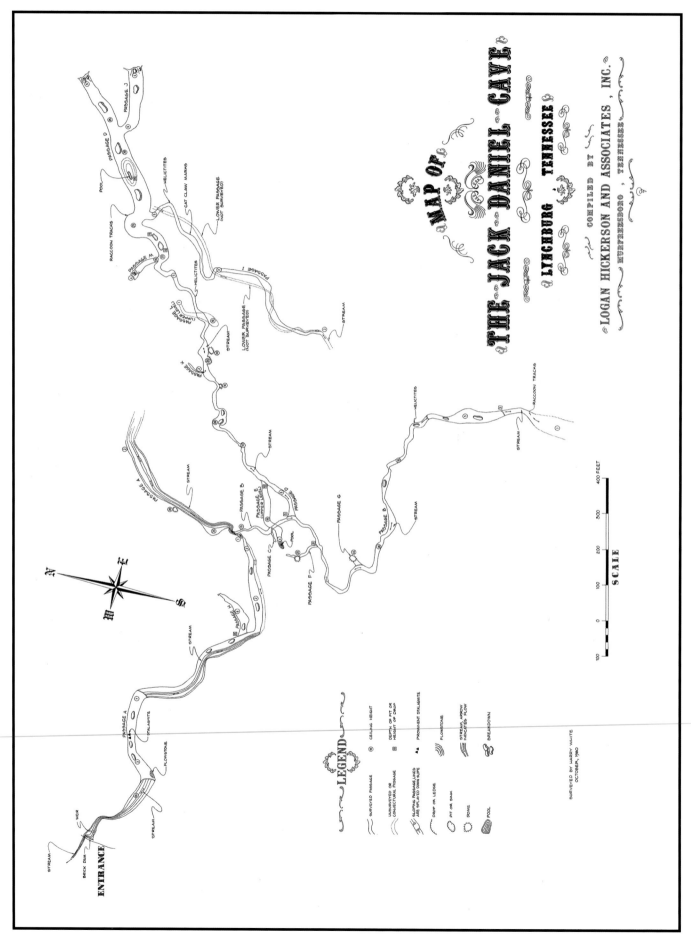

Figure 19.6. Map of Jack Daniel Cave by Logan Hickerson and Associates, Inc., October, 1980.

Figure 19.7. Blaine Grindle looking out the Entrance to Motlow Cave. Photo by Kelly Smallwood, 2016.

Figure 19.8. Main Passage between the entrance and the Big Room in Motlow Cave. Jason Hardy in blue, Nicole Miller in red, and Blaine Grindle in silhouette. Photo by Kelly Smallwood, 2016.

first room is 30 feet in diameter and 30 feet high, and the second room is 75 feet by 40 feet by 40 feet high. The main passage connecting the rooms runs northeast, and the side passages run northwest approximately at right angles to the main passage.

Formations in Motlow Cave are few, but some flowstone and a few gypsum crystals may be seen.[2]

Barr included a map prepared by him and B. H. Denton in 1954. (See Figure 19.10.)

Saltpeter Mining in Motlow Cave

There is a map of Motlow Cave that was provided to me by Kelly Smallwood. It seems well done, but the surveyors are not listed, the draftsman is not listed, and it is undated.

This map shows an area along the southwest wall of the Central Tunnel that is labeled "Evidence of Saltpetre Workings." Since there are names and dates in this cave from this time period, it is certainly possible that the cave was mined for saltpeter, but it must have been a

2 Barr, op. cit., pp 337-338.

small operation. The map by Jason Hardy and Kelly Smallwood dated 2016 also notes "Evidence of Saltpeter Workings" on their map in the same location.

When I visited Motlow Cave on June 26, 2018, I looked at this area very carefully. It has seen recent excavation in an effort to improve the trail for tourists. The marks that I saw in the dirt on the walls that looked like pick marks may have been made during this widening project. They were definitely wider than a normal pick mark and may have been made by excavation machinery. At any rate, there is no way at this point in time to prove or disprove that Motlow Cave was mined for saltpeter from physical evidence in the cave.

Motlow Cave was recently surveyed by Jason Hardy and Kelly Smallwood. Kelly gives the following account of that survey:

In the fall of 2016, Jason Hardy and I were contacted by the Jack Daniel Distillery about surveying a cave on their property, Motlow Cave. We of course jumped on the wonderful opportunity and enlisted a few of our good friends to help out (Ben Miller,

Figure 19.9. Blaine Grindle (upper right) and Nicole Miller (lower left) on the breakdown pile at the northeast end of the big room in Motlow Cave. Photo by Kelly Smallwood, 2016.

Katie Ingram, Brian Ham, Nicole Miller, Hali Steinmann, and Jason Lavender). During September 2016 we surveyed the cave in two trips and made a third to document historical signatures with Marion O. Smith and Joe Douglas and to also take photos. After we finished our survey, another fellow caver who is also a Tennessee Squire nominated both Jason and I to become Tennessee Squires for our work in surveying the cave. The Tennessee Squire Association is a private membership by nomination only and it was created by Jack Daniel, so we were very honored to become Squires.

Motlow Cave is located in the northeast corner of Lynchburg, Tennessee on the east side of Stillhouse Hollow, 300 yards northeast of Jack Daniel Cave. Motlow Cave is the most impressive and most frequently visited of Moore County caves. It was reputed to connect with Jack Daniel Cave, however after the 2016 survey it is noted that no physical connection can be made but it is likely that the water that flows through the passage near the entrance does end up in the famous spring cave. It is also suspected that Motlow Cave is an old paleo trunk passage that was once connected to the spring cave but is now blocked by breakdown in the New Discovery Room.

As noted by Tom Barr in his 1961 book, *Caves of Tennessee*, the cave opening was a small hole on the hillside. During the Brown-Forman renovations in 1982 the distillery made some significant renovations to the cave which included enlarging the entrance to 28 feet wide and 25 feet tall. They installed large western cedar doors that were made by Larry Shockley from Belvidere, TN. Larry also re-used the lock that was on the old gate on the new doors, which is noted to be over 100 years old and

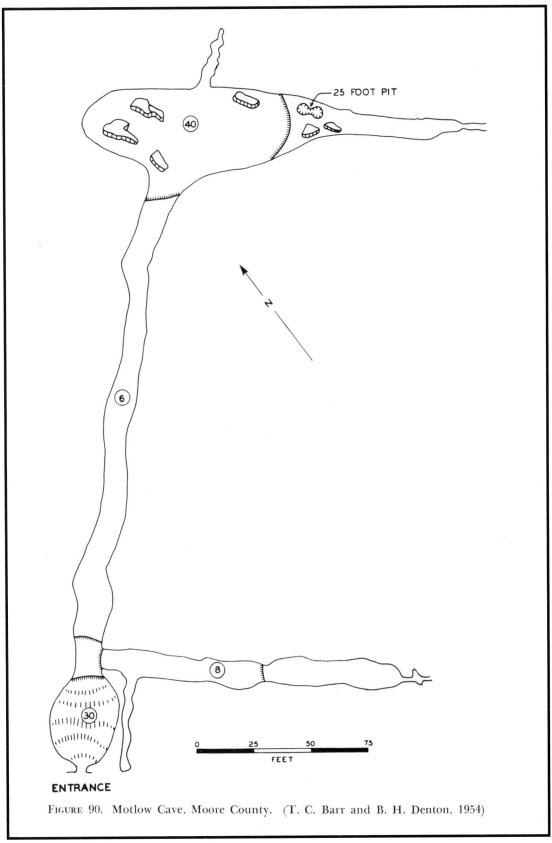

FIGURE 90. Motlow Cave, Moore County. (T. C. Barr and B. H. Denton, 1954)

Figure 19.10. Map of Motlow Cave by T. C. Barr and B. H. Denton, 1954.

Figure 19.11. Nicole Miller by the Formation Gallery in the big room of Motlow Cave. Photo by Kelly Smallwood, 2016.

each door weighs 400 pounds. According to Gary K. Soule, these renovations were done by Roy A. Davis, operator of Cumberland Caverns.[3]

The cave consists of three large rooms. The Entrance Room and the Big Room are connected by a passage 300 feet long, a narrow extension of this passage, and two side passages 150 feet long. The Entrance Room is 30 feet in diameter and 30 feet high, and the Big Room is 75 feet by 40 feet by 40 feet high. The main passage connecting the two rooms runs northeast, and the side passages run northwest approximately at right angles to the main passage. In 1982 the Brown-Forman Corporation spent $97,000 in renovations to commercialize the cave and remapping it. During their renovations a 62-foot pit system in the Big Room was filled in, most likely for tourist safety and a new portion of the cave was discovered and named New Discovery.

The side passage off the entrance of the cave runs in a southeast direction for 150 feet to a very impressive Signature Room and a very tight 20-foot-long crawlway. In the Signature Room there are hundreds of signatures. The most notable are three sets of initials dated January 16, 1863, along with 51st ALA. It is believed these signatures are from Civil War soldiers with the 51st Regiment of Alabama. Also in the Signature Room is the signature of Tom Motlow, who was the younger brother of Lemuel Motlow. The oldest noted signature is also in this area and is scratched in the right wall and dated 1834.

During wet weather a rimstone dam flows in the Signature Room and flows into the tight crawlway. After the tight crawlway there is a 20-foot pit that goes into a mud room. From here there is a 10 foot climb up through breakdown into the New Discovery Room. The New Discovery Room is

3 Gary K. Soule, Personal communication, June 28, 2018.

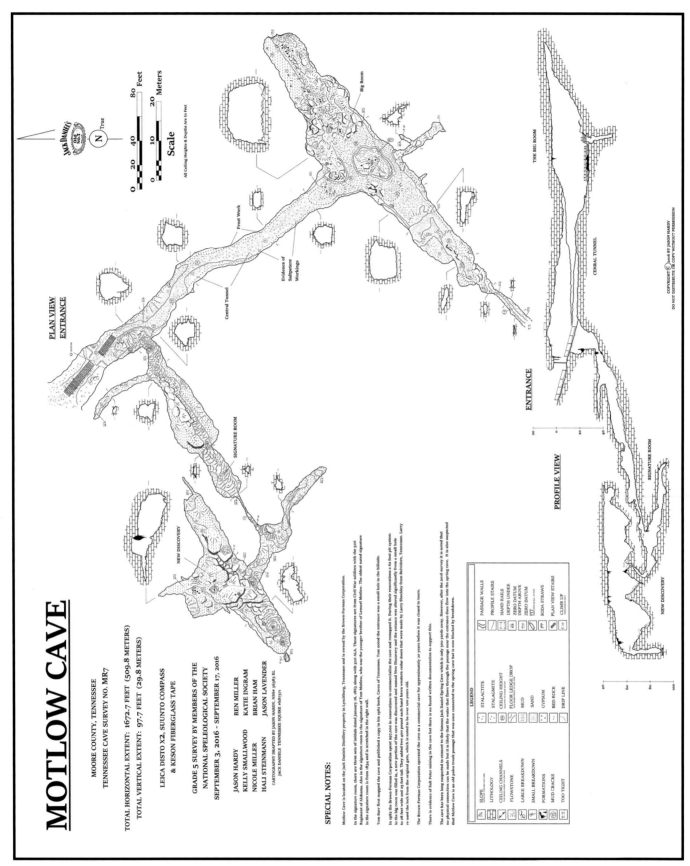

Figure 19.12. Map of Motlow Cave by Jason Hardy, 2016. Used by permission.

Figure 19.13. Marion O. Smith looking at old names and dates candled on the ceiling of Motlow Cave. Photo by Kelly Smallwood, 2016.

Visit Scenic

MOTLOW CAVE
and Nature Trail

FOR TOUR INFORMATION

See Ladies at
Lynchburg Soda Fountain

Figure 19.15. Old sign: "Visit Scenic Motlow Cave and Nature Trail," courtesy of Gary K. Soule. Acquired in 1982.

approximately 240 feet by 100 feet wide and 40 feet tall. There is one large haystack formation and several other nice formations in this area.

There is evidence of saltpeter mining in the cave but there is no found written documentation to support this. It is suspected that the saltpeter mining marks were made by the distillery during their renovations in making it a commercial cave.

The Brown-Forman Corporation operated the cave as a show cave for approximately 20 years before it was closed to tours. In 2016, the Brown-Forman Corporation reached out to Jason Hardy and Kelly Smallwood to re-map the cave. Their plan is to reopen the cave for VIP tours as part of their distillery tours. The total cave length is 1,672.7 feet long and it 97.7 feet deep. (See Figure 19.12)

In the spring of 2017, in exchange for their work in surveying the cave the Jack Daniel Distillery allowed Jason and Kelly to host the Tennessee Cave Survey (TCS) meeting on the distillery property and allow TCS members the opportunity to tour Motlow Cave. The meeting was well attended and there were two bus loads of cavers that were driven up to the cave after the meeting to tour the cave. Jason and I continue to work with the distillery with hopes

Figure 19.14. Jason Hardy by flowstone on an old stone wall in Motlow Cave. Photo by Kelly Smallwood, 2016.

of possibly re-surveying the famous spring cave in the future.[4]

This is a wonderful example of commercial property cave owners working with local cavers for the benefit of both.

Cave Access

Since Jack Daniel Cave is the water supply for the manufacture of their whisky, access to the cave is prohibited. But, it is still worth going to the site to see the entrance and take the guided tour of the facility.

Motlow Cave, however, was made into a show cave with gravel paths and electric lights and is open during certain events. You may wish to call ahead and see if tours will be available.

Suggested Reading

Cave historian Marion O. Smith wrote an article titled "Confederates of Motlow Cave" that describes Confederate soldiers' names and dates located in Motlow Cave. It is located in the 2017 issue of the Tennessee Caver on pages 19-21.

---

4 Kelly Smallwood, "Motlow Cave, Lynchburg, Tennessee," TN Caver, 2017, pp 14-18.

Erica Sughrue observes a very unusual formation in a Highland Rim Cave. Photo by Bob Biddix, January 28, 2017.

Section 4: Conclusions

Figure 20.1. Walker Howell by pick marks left in the dirt by saltpeter miners in Piper Cave, Smith County. Photo by Larry E. Matthews, February 22, 1975.

CHAPTER 20

Saltpeter Mining in the Caves of the Highland Rim

As you have read this book, you will have noticed that several of the caves are described as having been mined for saltpeter. Those caves include: Espey Cave, Cannon County, Godwin Cave, Maury County, Indian Grave Point Cave, DeKalb County, Piper Cave, Smith County, and Robinson Ridge Saltpeter Cave, Cannon County. Saltpeter mining was an important industry in Tennessee during both the War of 1812 and the Civil War. Saltpeter is the main ingredient of gunpowder and during both of those time periods there was a very high demand for gunpowder. Even in times of peace, gunpowder was needed for hunting and self-defense.

The mining of caves for saltpeter dates back to at least the American Revolutionary War. Mining first began in the east in the caves of Virginia and what is now West Virginia, then spread westward. By 1810 caves in Kentucky and Tennessee were perhaps the most important saltpeter mines in the country.

Espey Cave has the remains of saltpeter vats and trails. In all likelihood, it was a major operation, but no one has done a detailed study to document the number of vats and the amount of dirt removed. Mining occurred in the dry Upper Level, which was conveniently located next to the cave stream in the Lower Level.

Godwin Cave has ample evidence of saltpeter mining in the form of pick marks, stacked rocks, and areas where dirt has been dug out and removed. However, there are no remains of leaching vats located in the cave. In all probability, the leaching vats were located outside.

Indian Grave Point Cave has the remains of fourteen (14) very poorly preserved leaching vats located in the passage extending from the entrance to the NAASEA Room. All that is left now of these leaching vats are mounds of dirt with pieces of decaying wood extending out from the bottoms. They are relatively small and may have been V-shaped vats, but they are so deteriorated it is difficult to tell. These vats are located on the 1981 map of the cave. The vats are denoted on the map as small black squares. (See Figure 11.11) Barr (1961) mentions ladders left by the saltpeter miners, but no trace of these were located when the author began visiting the cave is 1962.

Piper Cave was a major operation, involving dozens of leaching vats. Unfortunately, due to the high humidity of the cave, the vast majority of the wood in these vats has rotted away, leaving the dirt casts behind to indicate the location, type, and number of vats. The 1955 map by C. E. L. McCary and Edward Davis shows the location of eighteen (18) saltpeter vats denoted as black squares and black rectangles. I suspect that these are the locations of the better-preserved vats and that many of the poorly preserved casts are not indicated. (See Figure 4.3)

Robinson Ridge Saltpeter Cave has five (5) square-shaped saltpeter vats, with most of the wood rotted away leaving the dirt cast behind. The vats were five (5) feet long, four (4) feet wide and three (3) feet high.

Dozens of other caves along the Highland Rim were also mined for saltpeter, but they are not among the caves covered by this book.

Saltpeter Mining in Tennessee

Saltpeter mining in Tennessee peaked during the War of 1812 and the Civil War. During peacetime there was considerably less demand for gunpowder. Angelo I. George makes the following observation:

> The heyday of domestic saltpeter mining is bracketed between 1804-1815. This time period is significant because all of our saltpeter prior of 1804 was being imported from British controlled India. As war raged in Europe (1804-1807), supplies of this important commodity became uncertain to American manufacturers of gunpowder. Thus began a concerted effort to build up the necessary

Figure 20.2. Larry E. Matthews by round saltpeter vat casts in Piper Cave. Photo by George L. Benedict, III, summer 1968.

infrastructure to produce saltpeter from caves and rock-shelters found in the interior of America.[1]

The states where saltpeter was mined during the War of 1812 are primarily Virginia, West Virginia, Kentucky, and Tennessee, since those are the states where most of the caves are located.

When the Civil War began in 1861, the Confederate States of America found themselves in the same position that the United States of America had been in during the War of 1812. They were blockaded by the United States Navy and, therefore, had no reliable way to import gunpowder from foreign countries. Fortunately for the Confederate States, many of the great limestone caves lay in the South. Saltpeter was mined in the caves of Alabama, Georgia, Tennessee, and Virginia.

Manufacture of Gunpowder

Gunpowder is made by grinding together specific amounts of charcoal, sulfur, and saltpeter. Saltpeter is the name given to a family of nitrogen-containing compounds (nitrates) that are normally found in the

soil. On the surface of the Earth, plants constantly remove these nitrates from the soil and rain water dissolves these highly-soluble compounds, washing them into the streams and rivers, which eventually flush them into the oceans.

Due to these conditions, surface soils are unable to accumulate significant amounts of nitrates except in a few rare desert localities. Caves, on the other hand, sometime provide an environment in which nitrates have a chance to accumulate over long periods of time. There are no plants to use the nitrates in the cave dirt and in some caves there are no dripping waters, running streams, or annual floods to remove these chemicals as fast as they accumulate. The very best saltpeter caves were dry and dusty.

The Earth's atmosphere is rich in nitrogen, 78%. Naturally occurring bacteria in the soil have the ability to remove nitrogen from the air and convert it into nitrogen compounds (nitrates). This process is accelerated by the presence of organic matter. In caves, the frequent accumulations of bat guano, cave rat guano, cave cricket guano, and other organic debris can significantly contribute to the production of saltpeter in the cave dirt.

1 Angelo I. George, Mummies, Catacombs, and Mammoth Cave, 1994, p. 42.

Figure 20.3. Walker Howell by the remains of two V-Shaped saltpeter vats in Piper Cave, Smith County. Photo by Larry E. Matthews, February 22, 1975.

Recent studies also indicate that the oak-hickory forest in the southeastern United States has relatively high levels of nitrates in the soils which tend to migrate through the limestone into the dirt of dry caves.

The mining of saltpeter required the construction of leaching vats near or in the cave. These leaching vats were built from local materials using simple hand tools. For this reason, the details of craftsmanship and construction vary from cave to cave.

Next the miners excavated the saltpeter-bearing dirt and filled the saltpeter vats with it. Normally, the vat was lined with straw to help prevent dirt and water from leaking through the cracks between the planks. Water was poured into the vats until the dirt was saturated.

The water dissolved the highly soluble saltpeter and then slowly drained out of the bottom of the saltpeter vats into wooden collecting troughs. The saltpeter bearing solution (called "liquor") was then taken outside the cave for processing. A lye solution was prepared by leaching water through oak and hickory ashes. Interesting, the leaching vats used to produce lye were almost identical in construction to the saltpeter leaching vats, although usually smaller in size.

Concentrated potash lye liquor was then added to the saltpeter liquor until no further turbidity was produced.

This not only converted the dissolved calcium nitrate ($CaNO_3$) into potassium nitrate (K_2NO_3), which is the type of saltpeter necessary to manufacture gunpowder, but it caused some other unwanted minerals in solution to precipitate out so that they could be easily removed by straining.

The resulting liquid was then strained, and the remaining liquid was poured into a large iron kettle where it was boiled until much of the water evaporated, leaving behind crystals of saltpeter. These crystals were then removed, dried, packed in bags, and shipped to a powder mill where they would be ground with charcoal and sulfur to make gunpowder.

Suggested Reading

The book Descriptions of Tennessee Caves (1971) by Larry E. Matthews devotes a section to saltpeter mining in Tennessee caves and has numerous photographs of saltpeter mining artifacts.

The book Big Bone Cave (2006) by Larry E. Matthews goes into great detail about the history of saltpeter mining in Tennessee. At the present time it is still available from the National Speleological Society's Bookstore which can be accessed at www.caves.org.

Figure 21.1. Tri-colored bat *(Perimyotis subflavus)*. Photo by Bob Biddix, February 7, 2010.

CHAPTER 21
The Biology of the Caves of the Highland Rim

The caves located along the Highland Rim are biologically rich and diverse. Some of these caves carry large amounts of surface water that drains into them. This surface water carries in organic materials that provide food for the animals inside the cave. Other caves contain bats and the excrement (guano) from these bats is another important food source in some of these caves. Cave cricket guano and cave rat guano is also an important food source in other caves.

The animals that live in caves are generally divided into three groups depending upon their degree of specialization to subterranean life. Animals that are so specialized that they can live only in caves are referred to as troglobites. Animals that spend part of their lives underground and part on the surface (such as bats) are referred to as trogloxenes. Animals that can live in caves, but also can live in cool, moist habitats of the Earth's surface are referred to as troglophiles. Animals from all three of these categories live in the Highland Rim caves and are discussed below. Other animals occur in caves either by accident, or do not fall into one of the above categories.

Listed below are some of the various animals that have been reported from the Highland Rim caves. This list is rather short and is not intended to be a comprehensive biological inventory for these caves.

Bats

White Nose Syndrome is a disease that was first identified in Howe Caverns in New York state in February, 2006. Since that time it has spread across much of the eastern United States and Canada. White Nose Syndrome is caused by a fungus, *Pseudogymnoascus destructans*, which was apparently introduced from Europe, most likely by European bats hitch-hiking in containers on ships. European bats have a natural resistance to the fungus, but American bats do not and it has been

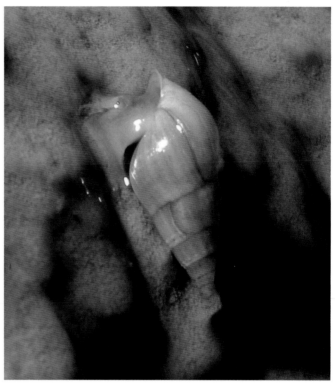

Figure 21.2. Cave snail. Photo by Bob Biddix, May 27, 2007.

deadly to most species of bats in North America. Most species of Tennessee bats have seen dramatic declines in their numbers.

White Nose Syndrome is spread from bat to bat and human beings apparently play no significant part in its spread. Bats are in serious trouble due to the disease known as White Nose Syndrome. Please avoid bat caves while bats are present. Disturbing bat colonies during hibernation can cause bats to wake up and use more of their fat supply than when they are hibernating. This can result in starvation before the end of the hibernation period. Disturbing bat colonies during the summer, especially maternity colonies, can also cause increased mortality.

A large colony of bats, predominantly Gray Bats (*Myotis grisescens*), inhabits Piper Cave during the summer months. However, the owner has recently

Figure 21.3. Bear skull in a Middle Tennessee Cave. Photo by Bob Biddix. June, 23, 2012.

closed off the entrance and the colony may no longer be able to use this cave.

John Fisher Cave also had a large colony of bats before the Upper Entrance was bulldozed shut by the owner. It is unknown if the bats are able to utilize the Lower Entrance at this time.

For some unknown reason, farmers and other land owners who wantonly kill wildlife, even species covered by the Endangered Species Act, are rarely if ever prosecuted.

Bears

At one time, Black Bears (*Ursus americanus*) were quite common in Middle Tennessee. However, hunters exterminated them from most of Tennessee by the early 1900s. Bear claw marks have been found in a number of Highland Rim caves, including Cripps Mill Cave. Other evidence includes skeletons and hibernation wallows.

Now, with controlled hunting, black bears are making a recovery, and a few have been spotted here in Middle Tennessee recently. If so, they may again use caves as dens and hibernation sites.

Cave Beetles

Highland Rim caves contain a number of cave beetles. Some of these beetle species occur in caves over a range of many miles and some are reported from only one cave.

Piper Cave in Smith County is the type locality for the blind cave beetle *Pseudanophthalinus cumberlandus*.

Cave Crayfish

Blind, white crayfish are found in a number of Highland Rim caves.

The cave crayfish, *Orconectes pellucidus*, is reported from Ruskin Cave in Dickson County.[1]

Cave Crickets

Hubbell and Norton (1978) list the cave cricket *Euhadenoecus insolitus* from Cripps Mill Cave and Indian Grave Point Cave in DeKalb County, Neil Fisher

---

1 Jennifer E. Buhay, Thany Mann, and Gerald Moni, "Cave Crayfish in Tennessee: Current Distributions and Locality Records," TN Caver, v. 2 (2005), no. 5, pp 1-9.

Figure 21.4. Erica Sughrue next to bear claw marks on a mud bank. Photo by Bob Biddix, December 3, 2016.

Cave in Smith County, Mason Cave in Sumner County, and Hayes Cave in Wilson County.

Cave Millipedes

Cave millipedes are common in Tennessee, but there is no inventory of them in the caves in the area covered by this book. Any cave with organic debris is likely to have millipedes. Some of these may be common surface millipedes, but deeper in the cave they may be true troglobitic millipedes.

Cave Rats

The Allegheny wood rat (*Neotoma magister*) frequently uses caves as a site to build its nest. For this reason, it is frequently referred to as the "cave rat." This same animal is referred to as the "Pack Rat" out West, due to its habit of bringing all sorts of objects back to its nest. It is a cute little animal that looks somewhat like a hamster.

Fish

Charles E. Mohr and Thomas L. Poulson report a springfish, *Chologaster*, from Jewel Cave, Dickson County. They make the following comment:

> Can these small-eyed fish live permanently in total darkness? Evidently they can. At Jewel Cave, Tennessee, *Chologaster* lives well inside the cave, but it is also seen regularly in sunlit springs near the cave. *Chologaster* is a troglophile, able to come and go. Since it is nocturnal at all times, it can find food in the dark. And it has already overcome the mysterious limitations that prevent most animals from breeding successfully in caves.
>
> Biologists are now studying these transitional troglophiles. By learning more and more about them, they hope to discover the steps by which surface dwellers evolved into the highly adapted troglobites able to live in caves and nowhere else.[2]

2 Charles E. Mohr and Thomas L. Poulson, *The Life of the Cave*, McGraw-Hill Book Company, 1966, p. 125.

Figure 21.5. Cave crayfish with eggs and baby crayfish. Photo by Bob Biddix, November 13, 2016.

Ken Oeser reports blind cave fish from Ruskin Cave. In all likelihood, this is the southern blind cave fish (*Typhlichthys subterraneus*).

Isopods

Isopods are frequently found in Highland Rim caves, but there is no inventory of these animals for the caves in this study area.

Raccoons

The raccoon (*Procyon lotor*) frequently ventures into caves and its footprints can be seen in the mud along cave streams. Barr (1961) states that raccoon feces are an important source of food for collembola, millipedes, and catopid beetles. Somehow, they are able to navigate in total darkness and seem to have no trouble finding their way in and out of caves.

Salamanders

The cave salamander (*Eurycea lucifuga*) is commonly found in Highland Rim caves. It is orange with black spots. Other salamanders are also frequently encountered in damp or wet caves, including the Slimy Salamander (*Plethodon glutinosus*).

Snails

Cave snails are so small that most of us never notice one. They are true troglobites. The cave snail pictured in Figure 21.2 is a beautiful example.

Spiders

Tennessee caves contain a variety of spiders, but no inventory has been conducted to my knowledge. Some of these spiders are true troglobites.

Figure 21.6. Slimy Salamander (*Plethodon glutinosus*). Photo by Bob Biddix, April 9, 2017.

Figure 21.7. Cave salamander (*Eurycea lucifuga*). Photo by Chuck Sutherland. February 10, 2019.

Figure 21.8. Cave cricket. Photo by Bob Biddix, May 12, 2013.

Figure 21.9. A spider guards its egg case in a Middle Tennessee Cave. Photo by Bob Biddix. September 12, 2015

Suggested Reading

Charles E. Mohr and Thomas L. Poulson produced a wonderful book on these animals, titled *The Life of the Cave*. McGraw-Hill Book Company published this book in cooperation with The World Book Encyclopedia in 1966. This book is part of a series of books, called "Our Living World of nature." This book contains exquisite color photographs of cave life accompanied by a text that is easily read by the non-scientist. Although this book is out-of-print, you may be able to find it in your local library. If not, copies are usually available at on-line book and auction sites.

Thomas C. Barr Jr.'s *Caves of Tennessee* (1961) contains a chapter titled "Animal Life in Tennessee Caves" on pages 28-54. It is a very helpful guide to the variety of cave life found in Tennessee caves.

CHAPTER 22
The Geology of the Caves of the Highland Rim

The Basics of Cave Formation

The caves of the Highland Rim (and all major caves in Tennessee for that matter) are formed in limestone. Limestone in Tennessee tends to be a hard, grayish rock that occurs in layers, called "beds." Many of the road cuts in middle Tennessee will show you a cross section of these limestone beds. Limestone is the rock that is quarried locally in middle Tennessee to make gravel, so if you live in middle Tennessee, you see limestone rock outcrops and limestone gravel almost everywhere you go.

Limestone is a sedimentary rock. The term sedimentary rock simply means that these rocks form from material deposited by wind or water. For example, another sedimentary rock known as sandstone forms when wind or water has accumulated beds of sand grains that become buried and cemented together to form a hard rock. When deposits of clay particles become buried and cemented together to form a hard rock, these sedimentary rocks are called shale. Limestone, however, forms in clear, warm tropical seas, such as occur in the Caribbean. If you were to travel to the Bahaman islands today, for example, you could observe limestone forming on the floor of the ocean. The source material for the limestone is the slow accumulation of corals and seashells. Occasionally, the mineral calcite precipitates directly from ocean water and accumulates on the ocean floor. These round pellets are called oolites. If you look carefully at the limestone rocks in middle Tennessee, you will frequently see fossil shells, corals, and other traces of animals that lived in those prehistoric, tropical seas.

Now you are probably asking yourself, "How could there have been a *tropical* sea over middle Tennessee? Middle Tennessee is in the temperate zone, not the tropical zone." The answer to that question is what geologists refer to as "continental drift." The continents are not fixed in place. They "float" on the lower layers of the Earth and can actually move as much as a couple of inches each year. So, over hundreds of millions of years they have moved thousands of miles. When the limestone deposits of middle Tennessee formed during the time periods known as the Cambrian, Ordovician, and Silurian, approximately 541 to 419 million years ago, what is now Tennessee was located very close to the equator. The major bed of limestone in the Highland Rim area in which caves are formed is known to geologists as the Bigby-Cannon Limestone.

What makes limestone so uniquely suitable for the formation of caves is that it is slightly soluble in water. We are all familiar with items that are highly soluble: sugar and salt, for example. If you place a teaspoon of salt in a glass of water and stir for 30 seconds, it disappears. A chemist would say, "The salt went into solution." If you put that same glass of water in a pan on the stove and boiled it until the water all evaporated, the salt would stay behind as a deposit on the bottom of the pan. So the salt doesn't "go away," it just goes from a solid form to a dissolved form and back to a solid form. If you took a drink of water from the glass, you would know instantly that the salt was in the water.

If you tried the same experiment with small pieces of limestone rock, you could stir the glass all day and you wouldn't see any change. It would take months or even years for the same amount of limestone to dissolve, and you would have to use much more water. That is why we say limestone is only *slightly* soluble. However, when you have thousands and thousands of years available, the water naturally moving through the Earth's crust can dissolve and carry off the millions of tons of limestone necessary to create the large caves like those described in this book.

Limestone is barely soluble in pure water, but *pure* water is not present in nature. Rainwater dissolves carbon dioxide from the air, which makes a mild solution of carbonic acid. As the rainwater filters through the soil, the water becomes more acidic by picking up organic acids and more carbon dioxide. Therefore, by the time rainwater becomes groundwater, it is mildly acidic and can more easily dissolve limestone and form caves.

Although the area that is now middle Tennessee was under water for at least 400 million years, it rose above sea level approximately 65 million years ago and has been above sea level ever since. During this time, erosion has worn down the surface to its present shape. But also, slightly acidic water has been dissolving away the limestone to form the many caves that we have now. In middle Tennessee, this water initially moves down the cracks in the limestone (geologists refer to these as "joints"), then moves out horizontally along the spaces between the beds of limestone (geologists refer to these as "bedding planes"). Naturally, the water follows the easiest path and with time the water slowly dissolves the limestone and forms cave passages. Much of this solution to form large caves goes on beneath or close to the water table.

Once cave passages develop to the point that there is significant stream flow underground, physical erosion can also occur and speed the growth of the cave passages. As the surface stream cuts downward, the cave passages eventually become higher than the surface stream level. Then the water drains out of the cave passages leaving behind an air-filled cavity that we call a cave.

What Is the Highland Rim?

Nashville sits is a geographical basin. On all sides it is surrounded by higher land known as the Highland Rim. The Nashville Basin would be a large lake, if not for the fact that the Cumberland River has cut a channel through the Highland Rim on the northwest side and drains into the Tennessee River.

To make matters more interesting, Nashville sits on a structural dome. All the strata dips away from the center of the basin to the outside. This makes the point where the Nashville Basin rises to the Highland Rim more pronounced. This Highland Rim Escarpment has outcroppings of cave-forming limestone and is home to many of the largest caves in Middle Tennessee.

The Highland Rim Escarpment is approximately 300 feet high and exposes various beds of limestone. For millions of years they have been subjected to erosion. This erosion has resulted in one of the most cave-rich areas in Tennessee. It is only surpassed by the Cumberland Plateau Escarpment in cave density.

Geological Sequence for the Highland Rim

The oldest geological formations exposed in the Central Basin are of Ordovician age. Even older formations of Cambrian age are buried beneath them but have not yet been exposed by the erosional processes. The Highland Rim Escarpment exposes Ordovician age formations at the base, then Silurian age, then Devonian age, and then Mississippian age, which are the youngest formations exposed in the sequence.

The Ordovician Period began about 488 million years ago and ended 443 years ago. It was followed by the Silurian period which began about 443 years ago and ended 416 million years ago. This was followed by the Devonian period which began about 416 million years ago and ended 359 million years ago. Then this was followed by the Mississippian period which began 359 million years ago and ended 323 years ago. So the Highland Rim Escarpment exposes rocks that span 165 million years of Earth's history.

The vast majority of the largest caves are developed in the Ordovician limestones, which tend to be thicker and more suited for the development of caves. And, the vast majority of these are formed in the Bigby-Cannon limestone.

A typical sequence of geological formations exposed in the Highland Rim Escarpment is listed below. The Warsaw Limestone is at the very top (geologically the youngest strata) and the Carters Limestone is at the very bottom (geologically the oldest strata). All of these geological formations can contain caves, except for the Chattanooga Shale.

Figure 22.1. A crystal-studded stalactite in Blowhole Cave, Cannon County, TN. Photo by Bob Biddix, January 20, 2014.

Figure 22.2. Calcite in its pure form is white or colorless, but it can be various colors due to impurities. Orange and red, shown here, are caused by the presence of iron. Photo by Bob Biddix, December 25, 2013.

Figure 22.3 Erica Sughrue admires a lacy flowstone drapery in Blowhole Cave, Cannon County, TN. Photo by Bob Biddix. December 2, 2013.

Figure 22.4. Erica Sughrue next to pools of water containing beautiful cave pearls. Photo by Bob Biddix. late summer, 2004.

Geological Sequence for the Highland Rim

Name of Formation	Thickness (feet)	Age
Warsaw Ls.	50+	Mississippian
Fort Payne Fm.	140-220	Mississippian
Chattanooga Sh.	20-35	Devonian
Leipers & Catheys Fm.	150-270	Ordovician
Bigby-Cannon Ls.	100-120	Ordovician
Hermitage Fm.	60-100	Ordovician
Carters Ls.	30-92	Ordovician

The **Carters Limestone** is the oldest formation exposed at the base of the Highland Rim Escarpment. It is a thin-bedded to massive limestone with abundant fossils.

The **Hermitage Formation** is a shaly limestone that sits atop the Carter Limestone. Due to its shaly nature, it does not form large caves.

The **Bigby-Cannon Limestone** is a thick-bedded limestone that sits atop the Hermitage Formation. It is one of the most important cave forming formations in Tennessee and is famous for its many large caves.

The **Leipers and Catheys Formation** is a thin to medium-bedded limestone that sits atop the Bigby-Cannon Limestone.

The **Chattanooga Shale** contains both traces of uranium and petroleum. It is not a cave forming formation.

The **Fort Payne Formation** is a cherty limestone that is erosion resistant. This formation forms the stabilizing cap for the Highland Rim Escarpment. It contains many small to medium-sized caves.

The **Warsaw Limestone** is a thick-bedded limestone that sits atop the Fort Payne Chert. It is well-suited for cave formation and contains many large caves.

Suggested Reading

Without a doubt, the book "Caves and Karst of the USA," Edited by Arthur N. Palmer and Margaret V. Palmer and published by the National Speleological Society in 2009, is the best single guide to caves and karst in the United States. This book should be in every serious caver's library. On pages 101-102 you will find the section on "The Highland Rim and Central Basin" by John Hoffelt. This book is still In-Print and available from the NSS Bookstore at the time this book went to press. The entire book is 445 pages long and is an incredibly useful reference book.

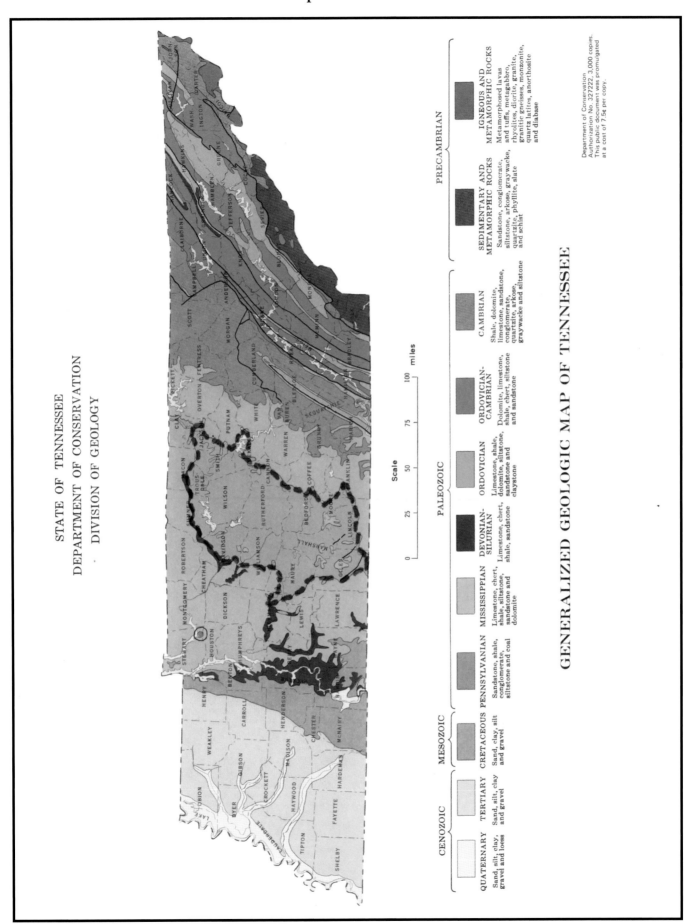

Figure 22.5 Generalized Geologic Map of Tennessee, Tennessee Division of Geology, 1966. The Highland Rim is the contact between the blue-colored central area and the surrounding pink-colored area. It is denoted by a dashed line.

Figure 23.1. Alan Lenk, Standiford R. (Tank) Gorin, and Roy Davis in the parking lot below Alum Cave in the Great Smoky Mountains National Park. Photo by Edward M. Yarbrough. June, 1975.

CHAPTER 23
Epilogue

It has been my ongoing goal since I published *Cumberland Caverns* in 1989 to record and preserve the history of cave exploration in Tennessee. This has resulted in a series of nine (9) books, some focusing on exceptionally large caves (*Big Bone Cave, Blue Spring Cave, Cumberland Caverns, Dunbar Cave: the showplace of the South*, and *Snail Shell Cave*) and others focusing on geographical areas (*Caves of Chattanooga, Caves of Falls Creek Falls, Caves of Grassy Cove*, and *Caves and Knoxville and the Great Smoky Mountains*). This new book will fall in the latter category and focus on a geographical area known for its outstanding caves.

Cave exploration began with the arrival of the first humans in Tennessee. The American Indians were skilled cave explorers, penetrating miles from some cave entrances using cane torches for light. When European settlers arrived in Tennessee, they, too, continued the exploration of the caves. True, some exploration was for material goods: clay, crystals, salts, saltpeter, etc. but without a doubt some of the exploration was due to the insatiable curiosity that drives the human race.

The cave explorers of my generation have been blessed with a seemingly endless number of caves to discover and explore. No doubt, future generations will be jealous of us. Even now, major new finds are still being made. At the Fall 2018 Tennessee Cave Survey Meeting it was announced that Tennessee now has 10,423 known caves and 240 of these are one mile long, or longer.

I hope the next generations of cavers have as much fun as we have had.

The following poem, written by Alan Tenthoff and published in the May 1977 *NSS News* explains some of the magic that we cavers find underground.

Figure 23.2. Ken McLean (left) and Larry E. Matthews (right) after a trip to Indian Grave Point Cave, DeKalb County, TN. Photo by Floretta McDole, September 9, 1978.

WHY
Alan Tenthoff

I was sitting with some caving friends, one sunny afternoon, when a youth came over and looked at me with wide round eyes of scorn and questioned us in a skeptical voice.

"Why?" he asked of me.

How does one tell of the thrill of a cave, of the lure that won't let you rest? How can one speak of the crawls and the falls, and the mud and the slime and the rest? How does one put into words for a boy who has never seen the Night, the mixture of emotions that are yours when the daylight fades from sight?

I did my best. I told him what a cave was like as well as I was able, and stuck to truth not sinking into the realm of fable.

I told him of the gaping hole, no matter large or small, wherein lies the eternal night which hides the way from all: of how a shaft of light from the lamp above my head rolls back the dark from down the halls to which my search has led: of crawlways low, squeezes tight and chimneys steep: of dangers hidden in pits beneath one's feet.

I mentioned the feel of the limestone wall as it scrapes against your hand, and the chirping flight of a lonely bat as it seeks a place to land: the myriad speleothems hidden far beneath our lands: Stalactites, Stalagmites, Bacon Strips with running bands: Helictites, Angel Hair, Gypsum Needles—formations rare: fluted columns, sculptured domes—the calcite gleams where'ere one roams.

I told him, too, of dangers dared: of the fellowship with men who cared enough about a beautiful thing to seek it, scorning Death's dread sting. Comrades all, in work or play, we'd talk and drink the night away, then up at dawn to explore again. Who wouldn't be proud to know such men?

All this, I told him, and more, this youth with his questioning look, but I knew that he could not comprehend even tho I wrote him a book.

One cannot describe the feel of a cave any more than one can the sea. There's a smell to a cave and a sense of age that just won't let you be. And once you have turned off your light in a room, far from the light of day, and sat in the dark to breathe the cave and ease you troubles away, and have thought of the ages that passed away 'ere the rock you're sitting on formed and the peace and quiet in which it lay, while, above, the elements stormed: once you have gazed on a virgin floor, unmarked by print or scrape, where light had never been before, nor a man to mark its shape: once you have gone to see for yourself and to feel the lure from beyond, you will never wonder what draws us on, as tho charmed by a magic wand.

Yet, in spite of all that I could not say, something of my feeling must have gotten through. The youth had lost his scornful way: the light that shone in his eyes was new. He stood up and looked around at the faces of my friends, then turned to me, and seemed to seek a way to make amends. At last he found the key.

"When?" he asked of me.

Reprinted from the May 1977 *NSS News*

APPENDIX A
Do You Want To Be A Caver?

The fact that you are reading this book and are interested in the caves of the Highland Rim is an indication that you may want to become a cave explorer. Exploring caves can be a lot of fun; but, unfortunately, it can also be dangerous if you are not properly trained and equipped. There is a national organization, the National Speleological Society (NSS), that can provide you with information on local chapters in your area, and can put you in contact with local cave explorers. They can be reached easily by email, at:

nss@caves.org

If you are not a computer user, you can contact the NSS by mail or telephone.

**The National Speleological Society
6001 Pulaski Pike NW
Huntsville, AL 95810-1122
256-852-1300**

The NSS has a bookstore that sells books on caving and caving techniques. Several suppliers of caving equipment advertise on the NSS web site, and in NSS publications. The NSS web site is located at:

http://www.caves.org

If you decide to explore caves, please remember the NSS' motto:

**Take nothing but pictures
Leave nothing but footprints
Kill nothing but time**

Tennessee is located in one of the most cave rich areas of the world. The NSS has active chapters (grottos) in Chapel Hill, Chattanooga, Cookeville, Knoxville, Livingston, Nashville, Oak Ridge, Pikeville, Sewanee, and Spencer, that you may wish to join, if you live in this area. The NSS web site can give you up-to-date information on how to contact a grotto in your area. Never go into a cave without proper training and proper equipment. Some commercial caves offer wild cave tours. These tours are an outstanding way to learn safe caving techniques from experts, before you venture out into wild caves on your own.

Have fun and be safe.

Erica Sughrue admires the Buddha's Hand Formation in a Highland Rim Cave. Photo by Bob Biddix, March 12, 2011.

APPENDIX B
Other Books by This Author

Big Bone Cave, 2006, National Speleological Society, Huntsville, Alabama, 220 pages. **ISBN 978-1-879961-24-1.**

The fascinating story of America's largest saltpeter mine, located 50 miles north of Chattanooga. Also the site of the discovery of giant ground sloth skeletons, an Ice-Age jaguar skeleton, and several American Indian mummies. The book includes many photographs and maps.

Blue Spring Cave, 2010. National Speleological Society, Huntsville, Alabama, 346 pages. Co-authored with Bill Walter. **ISBN 978-1-879961-36-4** (Soft Cover). **ISBN 978-1-879961-37-1** (Hard Cover).

Blue Spring Cave is Tennessee's longest mapped cave with over 35 miles of surveyed passages. Although its natural entrance has been known since prehistoric times, only 500 feet of cave had been explored as recently as 1989. In that year a group of cavers pushed a tight, blowing crawlway at the rear of the cave and discovered miles and miles of fantastic, virgin cave passages. This book is the complete story of that exploration. It is lavishly illustrated with photographs and maps.

Caves of Chattanooga, 2007. National Speleological Society, Huntsville, Alabama, 198 pages. **ISBN 978-1-879961-27-2.**

The exploration, use, and commercial development of nine Chattanooga-area caves. Learn how for 8,000 years, the caves were used by the Cherokees until their relocation in 1838; how settlers explored and used these caves; how the caves were mined for saltpeter, the main ingredient of gunpowder, during both the War of 1812 and the Civil War. Read never-before-published stories of fascinating discoveries deep inside Lookout Mountain. Be amazed by the Great Cave Hoax of 1927. Included are the complete stories of Lookout Mountain Cave, Mystery Falls Cave, Ruby Falls Cave, Raccoon Mountain Caverns, Nickajack Cave, Sequoyah Caverns, Mystic Caverns, Russell Cave, and Wonder Cave.

Caves of Fall Creek Falls, 2016. National Speleological Society, Huntsville, Alabama, 322 pages. **ISBN 978-1-68044-007-2.**

The greater Fall Creek Falls area has the largest number of caves of any public land in Tennessee. The many large, interesting caves, combined with the stunning wilderness area makes this a Caver's Paradise. The roughly 15 miles wide by 16 miles long area covered in this book contains 1,184 known caves, 12 of which are over a miles long.

Modern cave explorers have been unraveling the secrets of these caves since the early 1950s. Exploration, mapping, and dye tracing show two huge underground drainage systems: one in the valley of the Caney Fork River and the other in the valley of Cane Creek. This book describes those caves and their hydrological connections.

This book is not only about these caves, but also the cavers who explored them. There are tales of secrecy and mistrust as rival groups of cavers sought to hide their discoveries from others. There is also the story of the development of land adjacent to Fall Creek Falls State Park by greedy and unscrupulous developers who threatened to ruin the groundwater.

Come along for thrill tales of exploration and adventure.

Caves of Grassy Cove, 2014. National Speleological Society, Huntsville, Alabama, 286 pages. **ISBN 978-1-879961-49-4.**

Grassy Cove is the largest sinkhole in North America. It is 3 miles wide and 6 miles long. All of the precipitation falling into Grassy Cove and draining into Grassy Cove flows into Mill Cave and reappears

7 miles to the south to form the headwaters of the Sequatchie River. Dye traces show that water sinking underground in Haley Cove and Bat Town Cove another 4 miles to the north also join into this system.

The erosional processes that formed Grassy Cove have created a vast, underground network of caves that is still being explored today. Cavers are still discovering new caves and new passageways. They all hope to be the one to find a way into the main Mill Cave Trunk, still mostly inaccessible at this time.

Caves of Knoxville and the Great Smoky Mountains, 2008. National Speleological Society, Huntsville, Alabama, 304 pages. **ISBN 978-1-879961-30-2.**

The history of the exploration, use and commercial development of fourteen caves in the Knoxville/Great Smoky Mountains area. Learn how these caves were used by American Indians for 8,000 years, how Daniel Boone explored these caves and opened the first saltpeter mine west of the Appalachian Mountains, how settlers explored and used these caves, how the caves were mined for saltpeter, the main ingredient of gunpowder, during both the War of 1812 and the Civil War. Included are the complete stories of Cherokee Caverns, English Cave, Gap Cave, Indian Cave, Meredith Cave, New Mammoth Cave, Alum Cave, Forbidden Caverns, Gregorys Cave, The Lost Sea, Tuckaleechee Caverns, Appalachian Caverns, Bristol Caverns, and Morrill Cave.

Cumberland Caverns, Third Edition, 2010, Greyhound Press, Bloomington, Indiana, 196 pages. **ISBN 978-0-9663547-5-1** (Soft Cover). **ISBN 978-0-9663547-6-8** (Hard Cover).

The story of how this cave, first discovered by Aaron Higgenbotham in 1810, has grown to become one of the world's largest and most famous caverns, including historical anecdotes from the 1800s and the modern exploration during the 1900s. Features fourteen full-page maps and numerous photographs, including fourteen in full color. The First Edition was published in 1989 by the National Speleological Society. The Second Edition was published in 2005 by Greyhound Press.

Descriptions of Tennessee Caves, 1971. Tennessee Division of Geology, Nashville, Tennessee, 150 pages.

This book provides descriptions of 316 caves, along with numerous maps and photographs. There is a special section on the history of saltpeter mining in Tennessee during both the War of 1812 and the Civil War. Although this book was first published in 1971, it has been reprinted numerous times and is still in print.

Dunbar Cave: The Showplace of the South, Second Edition, 2011. National Speleological Society, Huntsville, Alabama, 240 pages. **ISBN 978-1-879961-41-8.**

This is the fascinating story of how this cave, first explored by Native Americans 8,000 years ago, grew to become one of America's major caves. Includes the complete story, maps, and photographs as modern explorers add miles of passage to this former show cave that had been explored for the last 150 years. Featured are recently discovered Indian Glyphs, the Big Band Era (1931-1947), and the Roy Acuff Era (1948-1966). This cave is currently a Tennessee State Natural Area and is open to the public.

Snail Shell Cave, 2012. National Speleological Society, Huntsville, Alabama, 246 pages. **ISBN 978-1-879961-44-9.**

This book describes the complete history of the exploration of Snail Shell Cave and the other caves that comprise the Snail Shell Cave System. This vast underground drainage system begins near Eagleville and flows northeast for 13 miles to emerge as a huge spring on the bank of the West Fork of the Stones River. Approximately one-fourth of Rutherford County, Tennessee is drained by this complex, three-dimensional system. Serious exploration began in the 1950s by NSS members and continues today, with cave divers making startling new discoveries.

APPENDIX C
Glossary

A

Acetylene – A flammable gas (C_2H_2) formed by combining carbide and water.

Anastamoses – A very wavy, irregular, bedding plane between two beds of limestone.

Anthodite – A cave formation consisting of radiating or branching crystals of calcite or aragonite.

Anticline – An upward, convex fold in sedimentary rocks.

Aragonite – A mineral composed of calcium carbonate ($CaCO_3$), the same as calcite, but forming orthorhombic crystals instead of hexagonal crystals as calcite does.

Archaeologist – A scientist who studies human history and prehistory.

Archaeology – The science that studies the material remains of past human life.

Ascenders – Mechanical clamping devices for ropes with a ratcheting action that allows them to be raised easily, but to lock when weight is applied. They are placed on the rope then attached to the body and feet with slings.

B

Bacon Rind – A thin, banded, flowstone formation that resembles a strip of bacon.

Bat – A nocturnal, flying mammal of many different species. They frequently spend the daylight hours inside caves and some hibernate inside caves during the winter.

Bedding Plane – The contact between two layers of sedimentary rocks.

Belly Crawl – A crawlway so low that it can only be negotiated flat on your stomach.

Biology – The science that studies the living organisms of the Earth.

Blue Hole – A Blue Hole is a sinkhole that extends down beneath the water table. Frequently, cave passages lead off underwater from these features. Their name derives from their appearance when viewed from an airplane.

Bolt – A metal pin, usually about ¼ inch wide and 1 inch long, driven into a hole drilled into rock. Used to provide a point of support where no natural anchor is available.

Bolt Climb – To climb a vertical, or even overhanging, wall, by placing bolts progressively higher and using them to anchor the rope.

Borehole – A very large walking passage.

Breakdown – A pile of rocks in a cave room or passage, formed by the collapse of the cave roof.

Breakdown Block – An individual piece of rock in a pile of breakdown.

Breakdown Slope – A sloping surface inside a cave, composed of or covered by breakdown.

C

Cable Ladder – A flexible ladder consisting of two small steel cables with small, aluminum rungs. These are available commercially in 10-meter sections. They can be rolled into a small bundle for easy transport through a cave. Two, or more, sections can be connected to make longer lengths.

Calcite – A mineral composed of calcium carbonate ($CaCO_3$), which is the main component of limestone. Calcite is also the main component of most cave formations, such as stalactites and stalagmites.

Canyon – A cave passage that is several times as high as it is wide.

Carabiner – A metal snap link used in technical climbing, especially to rig ropes.

Carbide – A man-made chemical, calcium carbide (CaC_2). Reacts with water to form acetylene gas. $CaC_2 + H_2O = C_2H_2 + CaO$.

Carbide Lamp – A lamp, usually manufactured from brass, which combines carbide and water to produce acetylene gas, which burns with a very bright flame.

Cave – A naturally occurring cavity in the Earth's crust, which is large enough to permit human exploration.

Cave Cricket – A species of cricket specifically adapted for life in caves. During mild weather some species of cave crickets leave their cave at night to forage for food on the Earth's surface.

Cave System – A group of caves connected by exploration. Frequently used to describe a large cave with several entrances.

Caver – A person who explores caves. This is the term cave explorers use to describe themselves.

Cavern – A term used to denote a very large or extensive cave.

Chamber – A large, room-like portion of a cave.

Charcoal – A black, organic substance formed by burning wood in an oxygen poor environment, resulting in incomplete combustion. Charcoal is composed primarily of organic carbon.

Chert – A microscopically grained quartz mineral (SiO_2) of various colors that forms beds, lenses, and nodules in limestone. Frequently used by prehistoric peoples to make stone tools.

Chimney – n. A passage narrow enough that you can climb up or down by placing your hands and feet on the opposite walls.

    v. To climb up or down by placing your hands and feet on the opposite walls of a cave passage. The back is also occasionally used as a point of contact.

Clay – A very small, microscopic grain of sediment or dirt, usually composed of hydrated aluminum silicates.

Climb – n. A vertical section of a cave that requires climbing skills to ascend or to descend.

    v. To ascend or descend a vertical section of a cave.

Column – A cave formation that extends from the ceiling to the floor.

Commercial Cave – A cave that has all or part of its passages developed with walkways, steps, and lights and is open to the public for guided tours. A show cave.

Connection – A naturally occurring passage which, when discovered, connects two caves which were previously considered separate caves.

Conservation – The preservation and wise use of our natural resources.

Crawl – n. A horizontal section of cave that requires crawling on your hands and knees or stomach to negotiate, due to a very low ceiling height.

    v. To move on your hands and knees or your stomach.

Crawlway – A cave passage that is so low that cave explorers must crawl on their hands and knees or stomachs.

Crystal – The solid form of a mineral, which displays symmetrically arranged plane surfaces. This external shape is determined by the internal atomic structure.

Curtain – A thin, wide, frequently wavy speleothem hanging from the ceiling or wall and resembling a curtain. Also called a drapery.

D

Dendrochronology – A method for dating wood by comparing the width of the growth rings.

Dome – A vertical passage extending upward from the ceiling of a cave passage or room.

Domepit – A vertical passage extending both upward and downward in a cave passage or room.

Drapery – A thin, wide, frequently wavy speleothem hanging from the ceiling or wall and resembling a drapery. Also called a curtain.

Dripstone – Cave formations composed of calcite or aragonite, formed when dripping water deposits dissolved limestone.

Drop – A pit or a cliff that must be rigged with rope or a ladder to descend.

E

Entrance – A point where a cave opens to the surface and is large enough to permit human passage.

Escarpment – A steep slope, usually with cliffs, that separates two relatively level areas of different elevations.

F

Fill – Secondary deposits of sediment in a cave passage, usually consisting of clay, silt, sand, gravel, or a combination of two or more of these.

Flint – A lustrous, microscopically grained quartz mineral (SiO_2), usually gray of black, which forms beds, lenses, and nodules in limestone.

Flowstone – A cave formation composed of calcite or aragonite, formed when flowing water deposits dissolved limestone.

Formation – A secondary mineral feature in a cave, such as stalactites, stalagmites, columns, helictites, soda straws, shields, bacon rind, and the like.

Fluorescein Dye – Fluorescent, organic dye frequently used in groundwater tracing studies. It is a red powder in the pure state and a bright, yellow-green in the dissolved state.

Fossil – The remains or traces of animals and plants that lived in prehistoric times.

Fossil Trunk – A trunk passage that no longer carries water, even during flood events, and is now high and dry.

G

Geologist – A scientist who specializes in the study of geology.

Geology – The science that studies the structure, history, and origin of the Earth.

Gibbs Ascender – A brand of mechanical ascender. It will slide up the rope but not down, unless all weight is released,

Grotto – A term used to describe a single cave room. Also the term used for a chapter of the National Speleological Society.

Ground Water – Any water below the surface of the ground.

Guano – The accumulated excrement of cave-dwelling animals, especially bats.

Gypsum – A mineral composed of hydrous calcium sulphate ($CaSO_4\text{-}H_2O$), which forms colorless to white crusts and crystals in a variety of forms.

Gypsum Crust – A layer of fibrous or crystalline gypsum that can occur on cave walls and ceilings.

Gypsum Flower – A flower-like group of curved gypsum crystals.

H

Hand Hold – A projection, depression, or other irregularity in the rock that can be used by a climber to support himself with his hand.

Hard Hat – A protective helmet worn by cave explorers to protect their heads from bumping the ceiling in low passages, from falling rock dislodged by cavers climbing above them, and in case of a fall.

Helictite – A cave formation that grows in bizarre, twisting shapes apparently without regard to gravity.

Horror Hole – A cave that is tight, wet, muddy, and with multiple drops that is extremely difficult and dangerous to explore.

Hydrology – The scientific study of water and its distribution and movement.

I

Instant Cave – Explosives used to enlarge a tight spot in a cave so that it is large enough for human passage.

J

Joint – A fracture in sedimentary rocks, usually perpendicular to the bedding planes.

Jumar Ascender – A brand of mechanical ascender. It will slide up the rope, but not down, unless the release button is pushed.

K

Karst – A type of topography found in areas of limestone bedrock, characterized by caves, sinking streams, sinkholes, and other features.

Karst Window – A relatively large sinkhole, sometimes with vertical sides, that opens all the way down to the water table in an area of karst

L

Lapiez – A surface composed of weathered limestone.

Leach – To remove minerals by dissolving them in water.

Lead – An unexplored passage in a cave.

Ledge – A horizontal projection along the side of a wall.

Limestone – A sedimentary rock composed primarily of calcite.

Limestone Pavement – A relatively flat area where limestone is exposed at the surface.

Lower Level – A series of cave passages developed at a lower elevation than the rest of the cave.

M

Map – n. A two-dimensional representation of a cave, showing its horizontal extent that may include cross-sectional representation to also show the vertical extent.

v. To gather the data necessary to draw a map.

Moni-sized – A restriction in a cave passage that has been enlarged enough that even Gerald Moni can fit through.

N

National Speleological Society – An organization of cave explorers and speleologists, founded in 1941, to promote the exploration, preservation, and scientific study of caves. NSS.

Native Americans – This is the "politically correct" term for the people who lived in North America before the arrival of Europeans in 1492. These people prefer to be known as American Indians.

Nitrates – Chemical compounds that contain the NO_3^- ion. Nitrate minerals are highly soluble in water.

Nitrogen – A colorless, odorless gas that makes up 78% of the Earth's atmosphere.

NSS – The National Speleological Society.

O

Onyx – A term use to describe lustrous, sometimes layered, flowstone.

P

Paleontologist – A scientist who studies fossils to learn about the history of life on Earth.

Paleontology – The science that studies the history of life on Earth.

Palette – A disk-shaped flowstone formation, usually growing from the wall of a cave. Also referred to as a shield.

Passage – A horizontal section of cave.

Phreatic – Refers to water below the water table. Also, cave passages that form beneath the water table.

Pit – A vertical passage extending downward from the surface, the floor of a cave passage, or the floor of a cave room.

Pitch – A vertical section of cave that requires difficult climbing or rope to negotiate.

Piton – A metal spike, pointed on one end and with a ring or opening on the other end. It is driven into a crack in the rock with a hammer and a carabiner is attached to the end to provide a point of attachment for a climbing rope.

Polje – A very large, flat-bottomed, closed depression in a karst landscape.

Popcorn – An irregular flowstone or gypsum formation with many rounded knob-like surfaces.

Prussik – To ascend a rope by any of a variety of methods.

Prussik Knot – A knot that will slide easily when there is no weight on it, but that will hold securely when weight is placed on it. By using two or three Prussik knots, a climber can ascend a standing rope.

R

Rappel – To descend a rope by any of a variety of methods.

Rhodamine WT Dye – An organic red dye used for tracing ground water flow.

Rig – To secure ropes or cable ladders so that a drop can be safely descended and ascended.

Rimstone – A raised flowstone edge surrounding a pool of water.

Rimstone Dam – A naturally formed flowstone dam occurring at the downstream edge of a cave pool.

Rimstone Pool – A pool of water surrounded by a raised edge of flowstone.

Rock – The solid material that forms the Earth's crust.

Rock Shelter – A rock overhang that resembles a cave entrance but does not open into an actual cave.

Room – A room-shaped opening in a cave.

S

Saltpeter – A naturally occurring mineral, calcium nitrate $Ca(NO_3)_2$, used in the manufacture of gunpowder.

Saltpeter Cave – A cave with enough saltpeter in the dirt to have been mined commercially.

Saltpetre – A spelling of saltpeter that was widely used in the 1800s.

Sandstone – A sedimentary rock composed primarily of cemented sand grains.

Scallops – Shallow, rounded pockets in a cave wall, formed when water was flowing in the cave passage.

Sedimentary Rock – A rock formed by the deposit of water-borne and/or wind-borne particles or by the accumulation of chemically or organically precipitated materials.

Selenite – A clear, colorless variety of gypsum, occurring in distinct, transparent, monoclinic crystals.

Shale – A sedimentary rock composed primarily of cemented clay particles.

Shield – A disk-shaped flowstone formation, usually growing from the wall of a cave. Also referred to as a palette.

Show Cave – A commercial cave.

Side Passage – A cave passage that leads off of another cave passage.

Silt – A small grain of sediment or dirt, approximately the size of a particle of flour. Larger than clay particles, but smaller than sand grains.

Sink – n. An abbreviated form of the term sinkhole. v. For a surface stream to disappear underground.

Sinkhole – A surface depression in an area of limestone rock formed either by solution as water drains underground or by the collapse of a cave passage or room.

Sinkhole Plain – An area of relatively flat topography with numerous sinkholes.

Sinking Stream – A surface stream that abruptly disappears and goes underground into a cave.

Siphon – A section of water-filled cave passage connecting two section of cave passage with air is frequently referred to as a siphon. However, true siphons rarely, if ever, occur in caves. The more proper name for these water-filled sections of cave passage is a sump.

Skylight – A natural opening to the surface in the ceiling of a cave passage or room.

Soda Straw – A thin, hollow stalactite, similar in size and shape to a drinking straw.

Soluble – Capable of being dissolved, usually referring to water.

Speleogenesis – The origin and development of caves.

Speleologist – A scientist who studies some aspect of caves, such as their biology, geology, meteorology, and the like.

Speleology – The scientific study of caves, their origins, and their features.

Speleothem – A secondary mineral deposit in a cave.

Spelunker – A person who explores caves. Cave explorers rarely use this term to describe themselves, preferring instead to call themselves cavers.

Spring – A place where water naturally flows out from underground onto the Earth's surface.

Squeeze – n. A section of cave passage so small that it is just barely possible to fit through.

> v. To move through a very small section of cave passage.

Squeezeway – A passage so small and tight that the explorers must squeeze to get through it.

Stalactite – An icicle-shaped cave formation that hangs down from the ceiling.

Stalagmite – A conical-shaped cave formation that grows upward from the floor.

Stoopway – A cave passage that is too low to stand up completely, but not as low as a crawlway.

Suck – If air flows into the entrance of a cave, that cave is said to suck.

Suckhole – A cave that is miserable to explore and has few, if any, redeeming features.

Sump – A section of cave passage that is completely filled with water.

Survey – n. A map prepared by using an accurate compass, a measuring tape, a clinometer, and sketches.

> v. To prepare an accurate survey or map.

Survey Station – A point in the cave from which compass direction, inclination, and distance are measured to the next point.

Surveyed – A cave or cave passages that have been accurately mapped.

Swallet – An opening in a karst area where a surface stream disappears underground. Also known as a swallow hole.

T

Terminal Breakdown – A breakdown that completely blocks a cave passage.

Topographic Map – A map that represents the surface of the Earth by using lines to indicate points of equal elevation at selected intervals. These lines are referred to as contour lines.

Totem Pole – A tall, cylindrical stalagmite.

Trunk – A large, main passage in a cave that extends for a long distance compared to other passages.

Traverse – n. A difficult ledge or section of wall that must be crossed to continue exploring a cave.

> v. To move across a difficult ledge or to move laterally across a wall.

U

Unsurveyed – A cave or cave passages that have not been accurately mapped.

Upper Level – A series of cave passages developed at a higher level than the rest of the cave.

V

Vadose – Refers to cave passages that form above the water table.

Vandal – A person who vandalizes a cave.

Vandalism – Altering a cave, either accidentally or intentionally, by breaking formations, leaving trash, writing on walls, or otherwise changing the original appearance of the cave.

Vat – A container built to hold cave dirt to allow water to percolate through the dirt and remove the nitrate minerals.

Virgin Passage – Cave passage that has not been entered previously.

W

Walking Passage – A cave passage large enough to walk without stooping.

Water Table – The horizontal plane beneath which all open spaces in the Earth are filled with water.

Wild Cave – A cave that has not been developed for guided tours. Also, any portion of a commercial cave that has not been developed for guided tours.

Index